Robert Adam

Edinburgh Records

The Burgh Accounts: Vol. II

Robert Adam

Edinburgh Records
The Burgh Accounts: Vol. II

ISBN/EAN: 9783744717014

Printed in Europe, USA, Canada, Australia, Japan

Cover: Foto ©ninafisch / pixelio.de

EDINBURGH RECORDS:

BURGH ACCOUNTS

EDINBURGH RECORDS.

THE BURGH ACCOUNTS: VOLUME TWO.

Dean of Guild's Accounts, 1552-1567.

EDITED BY

ROBERT ADAM, F.S.A.SCOT.

LATE CITY ACCOUNTANT AND CHAMBERLAIN, EDINBURGH.

With Preface

BY

THOMAS HUNTER, W.S., F.S.A.SCOT.

TOWN CLERK OF EDINBURGH.

EDINBURGH:

PRINTED FOR THE LORD PROVOST, MAGISTRATES AND COUNCIL.

MDCCCXCIX.

PREFACE TO VOLUME II.

THE present is the second volume of the Old Accounts of the City of Edinburgh, and contains the Dean of Guild Accounts from Michaelmas 1552 to Michaelmas 1567, with the exception of the period from October 1558 to May 1560. As explained in the Preface to the first volume, these have been transcribed and edited by Mr Adam at the request of the Town Council.

The Dean of Guild was the Chairman or Chief Officer of the Guildry, the merchant class of the Burgesses, who till near the end of the sixteenth century had the control of the Town's affairs. The "Gilda Mercatoria," or Merchant Guild of Edinburgh, was in existence at a very early period, but the first reference to it in the existing records is in a Minute of 3rd October 1403, which gives the names of the Officers of the Guild then elected, and among others the Dean, who was also the custodier of the Church fabric (Decanus Gilde et Custoditor operis ecclesiae). In 1518 the Guildry was reorganised by a Charter from the Town Council. The "Merchants Fraternity and Gild * Brethren" were granted an

* *Note.—Gild.* The common spelling of the word has for a long time been "Guild," but it is now maintained by many competent authorities that the proper form is "Gild," without the "u." Etymologically, this view has much to be said for it; the ancient usage seems to support it; and in the Accounts here presented the word is invariably spelt "gild" in the text.

aisle in the Church of Sanct Geill, and held extensive mercantile jurisdiction and privileges.

In Edinburgh, as in some Continental cities, there was a long struggle between the merchants and the craftsmen or members of the incorporated trades, who were practically excluded from the administration of the Town's affairs. At length, under a Decreet Arbitral of King James VI. in 1583, the craftsmen were admitted to substantial representation in the Town Council.

The Merchant Guild of Edinburgh must not be identified with the Merchant Company of Edinburgh, established in 1681, and which is so well known at the present day, although each member of the latter requires to be a Burgess and Guild Brother of the City.

The payments in the Accounts relate mainly to the Kirk of Saint Giles, the secular affairs of which were under the special care of the Dean of Guild.

Saint Giles (Saint Egidius)—or, as he was popularly called, "Sanct Geill"—was the patron saint of the City; and the Church named after him was the first parochial one in Edinburgh. The Saint, who had been an Abbot in France, died on 1st September 721, and the anniversary of that date was held as his Festival. According to tradition, he at one period of his life owed his preservation to a hind, the figure of which appears on the City Arms to this day. The religious life of the Town's people was bound up with the City Church. The Merchants' Guild, as already mentioned, had an aisle and altar; and each of the incorporated crafts or trades had its patron saint with an altar in the Church, and contributed to the up-keep of the services. The Church, which had previously been subject to the Abbot of Dunfermline, and at an earlier period to the Bishop of

Lindisfarne, was in the fifteenth and sixteenth centuries a collegiate charge under the patronage and care of the Lord Provost, Magistrates and Council. The Accounts now presented show the Dean of Guild's intromissions during the period from 1552 to 1567, with the exception already mentioned.

The Reformation or change of the National Religion took place in the middle of the period embraced in the Accounts. The old faith and system of worship, with which the whole social order and civic organisation seemed to be inseparably bound up, is seen in full operation in the earlier part of the period. Then comes an upheaval and a brief time of confusion, followed in the later years of the period by the firm establishment of the new or reformed religious regime. The prosaic details of these Accounts may throw light on not a few points in the history of the time which must remain of profound interest to all Scotsmen.

The Accounts in the volume begin with the intromissions of James Carmichael, Dean of Guild from 4th October 1552 to 8th October 1553. On the charge side, there are entered the sums collected on the "piece silver" in the Kirk each Sunday; the dues received in respect of the freighting of ships in the port of Leith; the entry money of Burgesses and Guild Brethren; the rents for the shops surrounding the Kirk and in the Kirkyard; charges for burial lairs and tombstones; fees for the use of the Seal; penalties for the attempted evasion of shipping dues; charges for the use of the four great golden candlesticks, when required by individuals at funerals or special services; similar charges for the use of the silver candlesticks; and the sums drawn for the exhibition of Saint Giles' arm on Relic Sunday and Saint Giles' Day.

On the Discharge side, there is given the expenditure relating to the up-keep of the fabric and furnishings of the Church; the purchase of candles; sums paid for cleaning; and fees to Officers. Dean of Guild Carmichael also enters the balance on his Accounts for the previous year, details of which are not preserved.

The Accounts continue, placidly enough, with similar entries for the next five years. John Symsoun was Dean of Guild in 1553-4; James Carmichael again in 1554-5; James Barroun in 1555-6; and James Carmichael again in the two succeeding years, 1556-7 and 1557-8. Each year there is an entry of the payment of ten shillings or six shillings for the "painting of Sanct Geill."

At the close of Mr Carmichael's Accounts in October 1558, there is a hiatus. John Charteris was Dean of Guild in 1558-9, but his Accounts for that year are wanting, although the balance due by him upon them appears as received by his successor. When the Accounts are resumed in May 1560, James Barroun is again Dean of Guild, and a marked change is at once seen to have meanwhile taken place. To fill up the interval of about eighteen months, when the Accounts preserved to us are silent, and to explain the complete change that interval had produced, it is necessary to recall briefly the circumstances of the time.

Though Dean of Guild Carmichael carried his Accounts to the close of his period of office in the beginning of October 1558, and gave no sign of the impending change, the winds were rising ominously and the waves were beating around the walls of the old regime. The storm outside was growing louder; the signs of social earthquake and religious upheaval were becoming daily more visible. The Magistrates were beginning to realise that a crisis was at hand, and were looking into the future with foreboding.

On Saint Giles' Day, 1st September 1558, when the populace

seized the image which was being carried in an imposing ecclesiastical procession—" young Sanct Geill," as they called it—and broke it in pieces and scattered the procession, this was an indication that their reverence for the symbols which had been regarded with such veneration by their fathers had ceased, and the time of overthrow was nigh. No doubt we find that, in November 1558, the vacant niche in Saint Giles was filled by a new image of Sanct Geill supplied by the Town Treasurer, at the cost of thirteen pounds, but that only shows that the Magistrates and Council had not as yet advanced so far on the wave of change as the populace. This is farther shown by the steps taken by the Council to protect the Kirk jewels and valuables, which they with good reason felt to be in danger.

Foremost among the treasures of the Kirk was the relic known as the arm-bone of Sanct Geill In 1454, Sir William Prestoun of Gourton had bequeathed to the community of Edinburgh the arm-bone of Saint Giles, which he had got from Charles VII., King of France. The Magistrates and Council were delighted to get such a precious relic, and promised to build an aisle forth from Our Lady Aisle (where the testator was buried), with a suitable inscription in brass and stone, and assigned a chaplain to sing at the altar there. This relic was annually borne in procession through the streets of the City on 1st September, and was held in great veneration. It was exhibited for a small charge on Relic Sunday and Saint Giles' Day, and the sums received are duly entered in the Accounts.

On 16th December 1558, the Magistrates and Council caused James Mossman, Goldsmith, in their presence, to weigh particularly the whole Kirk jewels and valuables. On 17th January 1559, they took these over from Sir Henry Bonche, sacristan of the Church, evidently feeling that the Church was no longer a safe place for them to be kept in. The jewels were then handed to the Dean of Guild, John Charteris, with strict injunctions to keep them safely and deliver them up to his successor on the termination of his year of office. It had evidently come to this already, that the valuables could not be left in use in the Kirk as before;—the utmost that could be sought was to keep them safe in a place of concealment.

On 8th March 1559, such of the jewels as were still left in the Church were weighed in the presence of the Council assembled in the "ravestre" of the Kirk.

On 14th May, the Queen Regent wrote to the Council referring to the popular tumult which had just taken place in Perth, when the religious houses and images were injured or destroyed, warning them to take precautions against a similar outbreak in Edinburgh. The Council on this placed artillery in position throughout the Town.

In the month of June, the Lords of the Congregation, as the leaders of the Reformed party were called, were advancing to the Town, the Dean of Guild protested that he could not be responsible for the safe-keeping of the Kirk valuables, and the Council "before the coming of the Congregation" distributed the jewels and vestments among the leading citizens for safe-keeping. They then sent a deputation to meet the Lords, and "commune with them for upholding the roofs of the religious places and kirks, and for saving the stalls and other timber works within the kirks." At the same time, they hired sixty men of war at 2s. 6d. per day to protect the Kirk and stalls. In the following month, the

"Congregation"* had taken possession of the Kirk and established the new or reformed system in it. In September, the Council ordered the Dean of Guild to put away the writs of the Town in a place of safety, and he seems to have done this so faithfully, in so far as his own Accounts were concerned, that, as sometimes happens with buried treasure, they cannot now be found. In October, the Congregation had so far the upper hand that they were able to get a stent imposed upon the inhabitants for two thousand merks to raise men of war. Saint Giles' arm was in the keeping of Thomas Makcalzeane, and the Council sent to get it from him that it might be given in pledge of the extent, or else to ask him to lend the money himself on security of the relic.

In November, the Council became doubtful of the wisdom of having the valuables scattered all over the Town, and issued orders that they were to be brought back to them. Evidently, they meant to try and keep them safe in the City Chambers until the clouds rolled by. But the new men who were coming into power found another way of dealing with the articles which relieved the Town Council for ever from all anxiety on their account.

James Barroun again became Dean of Guild in 1559-60. In April 1560, at the "request, desire and will" of the Lords of the Congregation, the Town Council imposed a tax or stent of £1600 to pay a month's wages of four hundred men of war to aid in expelling from Leith the French troops which had come to the aid of the Queen Regent and the adherents of the old faith.

* *Note.*—The word "congregation," used in the text, was applied to the members of the new or reformed party, as distinguished from the adherents of the old faith and Church system.

In the same month, the Dean of Guild received instructions to repair and whitewash the Kirk, mend the glass windows, and make the seats convenient. In the following month, he was instructed to take down the bell known as the Marie Bell, and the brazen pillars of the Kirk, and make them into artillery.

In May 1560, the sum of £80 having been hastily borrowed from Michael Gilbert, Goldsmith, the silver candlesticks which he had in keeping were impledged to him in security. In June, the Dean of Guild was instructed to make seats, forms, and stools for the people to sit upon during service in the Kirk, and to do all other things to fit it for their use.

When the Kirk Bell and brazen pillars were made into artillery, and the sacred relic of Saint Giles' arm and the silver candlesticks of the Kirk were pledged for debt, it does not surprise us to learn that the next step was to sell off and turn into money all the gold and silver articles which had been devoted to sacred uses for ages. This final step which marked the passing away of the old order was soon taken.

When the Accounts are resumed by James Barroun, Dean of Guild, in 1560, he calmly enters in the beginning of his Account the sums realised for the sale of the "Jowellis of the Kirk" as follows:—A Eucharist, with four little bells of gold, blue bell of gold, two little hearts, and two little crosses hanging at it; the arm of Sanct Geill, with the ring on the finger of it; a silver cross with pedestal; four silver candlesticks; two censers; a ship for incense; a cresum stick; a round Eucharist; a chalice; a plate; a spoon; and two cruets. All these, he states, were "of clean silver, two stones, fifteen pounds and eight ounce," and of gold, five and a half ounce. The silver realised 21s. per ounce, and the gold £10,

5s. per ounce. These produced a total of £854, 7s. 6d. Nothing extra is entered for the relic of the Saint's arm, which, thenceforward, disappears, but the diamond stone which was in the ring "on the fingar of the foresaid arme of S. Geill" was sold to Michael Gilbert for £9, 6s. 8d. These two sums, with the entry money from Burgesses and Gild Brethren, the freighting of ships, and the shop rents, form the charge in the Accounts of the year. The "pece silver," the charges for the exhibition of relics, and the dues of gold and silver candlesticks, are found no more. On the Discharge side, there is a long array of entries giving the details of the payments in renovating the Kirk and adapting it to the ideas of its new masters. At the end of the year, Dean of Guild Barroun had "super-expendit" his charge by the sum of £147, 15s. 5d., and the proceeds of the Kirk jewels were thus exhausted.

James Watsoun was Dean of Guild in 1560-61. His Account begins with the price realised on the sale of three bellows of the Organ, a silver cross, a chalice of the Holy Blood, and another of St Anthony, at 23s. per ounce, and also brazen pillars and lectern, sold for 18s. per stone. There is a large increase in the amount received on the entry of Burgesses and Guild Brethren, and for the freighting of ships going out of Leith. On the Discharge side, he continues the payments for tradesmen working upon and within the Kirk, including a mud wall and a lock to John Knox's study (page 145).

Alexander Guthrie, the Town Clerk, was Dean of Guild for 1561-62. He gives entries of payments for the study of deals made for John Knox (page 153), and for the expenses of a Mission in which he accompanied John Knox to Angus for the choosing of a Superintendent there (page 157). He was again Dean of Guild in the following year, 1562-3, and once more in 1563-4. Alexander Park was Dean of Guild in 1564-5, and his successor was John Prestoun, whose Accounts for the two succeeding years, 1565-6 and 1566-7, close the volume now presented. These later Accounts give numerous entries in detail which the older Deans of Guild used to summarise, and it may be that in the details many useful incidental references will be found.

These Accounts are now made accessible to the public, and this completes the task undertaken by Mr Adam, at the request of the Town Council.

THOMAS HUNTER.

City Chambers,
Edinburgh, *26th July* 1899.

TABLE OF CONTENTS.

LIST OF THE SEVERAL ACCOUNTS OF THE DEANS OF GILD OF EDINBURGH, BOUND UP IN THIS VOLUME, VIZT.:—

						Pages in Print
1.	James Carmichael, from Michaelmass 1552 to Michs. 1553 from page 1 to p. 20					1-17
2.	John Sympson	1553	1554	21	40	17-30
3.	James Carmichael	1554	1555	41	62	30-46
4.	James Barroun	1555	1556	63	79	46-60
5.	James Carmichael	1556	1557	81	106	60-78
6.	Ditto	1557	1558	107	118	78-91
7.	John Charters	1558	1559	wanting.		
	Thos. Uddert having refused the office, James Barroun entered to it in May A°. 1660 [1560]			143		
8.	James Barroun	1560	1560	121	144	91-117
9.	Mr James Watson	1560	1561	145	169	117-145
10.	Mr Alexr. Guthrie, Common Toun Clerk	1561	1562	171	191	146-166
11.	Ditto	1562	1563	193	216	166-182
12.	Ditto	1563	1564	217	237	183-197
13.	Alex. Park, from Michaelmass 1564 to Michs. 1565 from page 241 to p. 252					197-211
14.	Mr John Preston	1565	1566	254	268	212-227
15.	Ditto	1566	1567	270	281	228-240

NOTE.—The Church Plate of St Geils, Silver, Gold, Jewels, etc., are sold by the D Gilds, page 121, 145.
The Silver at 21sh. the oz.
The Gold at £10. 5. 0 the oz.

NOTE.—After the Reformation it appears that the Sacrament of the Lord's Supper was celebrated in Edinburgh quarterly in March, June, Septr. and Decemr., and that at the first Communion given by John Knox in March 1561 there was used, vizt. :—

8¼ gallons Wine at 12 pennies each pint, as per page 158 is, Scots, £3, 8s.
60 Bread, at 6 pennies per piece, at 2nd Communion, page 162, is ,, 1, 10s.

ILLUSTRATIONS.

PHOTO-LITHO FACSIMILES OF PAGES OF THE OLD ACCOUNTS:—

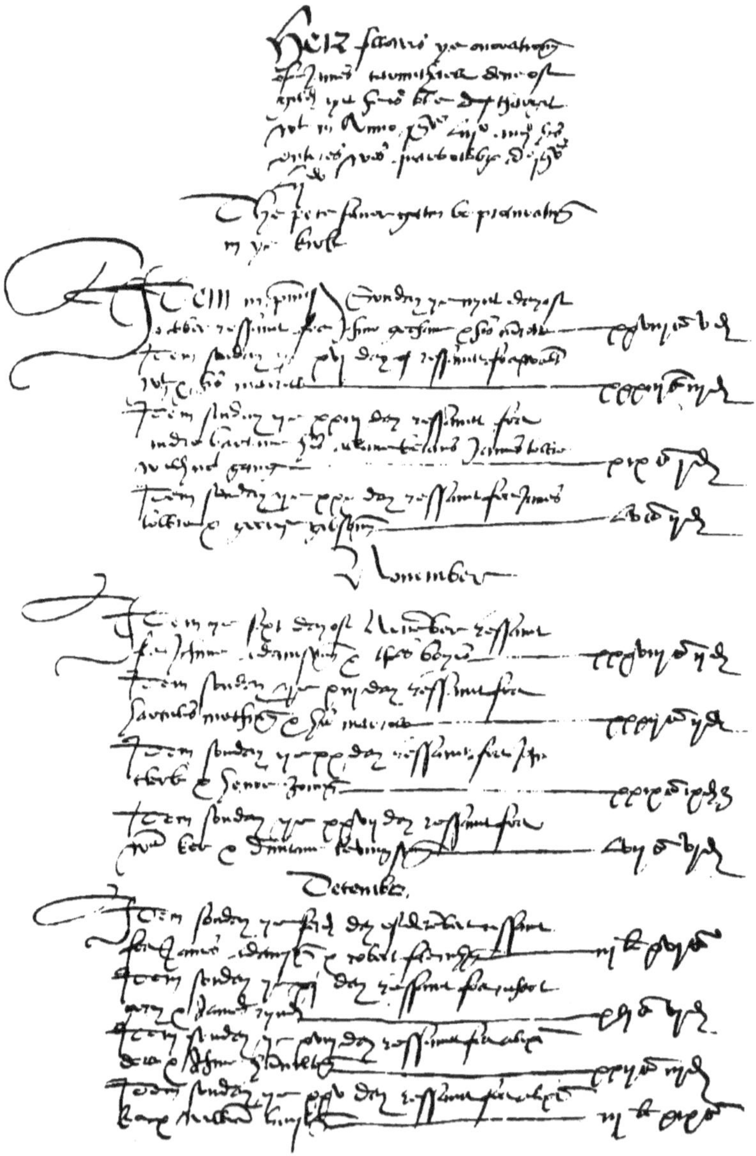

EDINBURGH ACCOUNTS:—Page 1 of old Accounts of Deans of Guild.

EDINBURGH RECORDS.

THE BURGH ACCOUNTS.

III.—ACCOUNTS OF DEANS OF GUILD.

[1] HEIR followis the ONERATIOUN of JAMES CARMICHAELL, Dene of Gild, that he is to be chargit with in anno J^{m} v^{c} liij^{o}, and his enteres wes quarto Octobris, anno J^{m} v^{c} lij^{do}:— JAMES CARMICHAEL Dean of Guild. 1552-53.

The Pece Silver gottin be procuratioun in the Kirk:—

Item, in primis, Sonday, the nynt day of October, ressavit fra Johne Grahame and his marrow, ... xxviij^{s} v^{d}

Item, Sonday, the xvj day, ressavit fra Walter Wycht and his marrow, xxxiij^{s} iij^{d}

Item, Sonday, the xxiij day, ressavit fra Andro Bartane his allane, because James Lowrie wald nocht gang, ... xix^{s} j^{d}

Item, Sonday, the xxx day, ressavit fra James Lowrie and George Gibsoun, lv^{s} ij^{d}

November.

Item, the saxt day of November, ressavit fra Johne Adamsoun and Thomas Boyis, ... xxxviij^{s} ij^{d}

Item, Sonday, the xiij day, ressavit fra Harculis Methven and his marrow, xxxij^{s} ij^{d}

Item, Sonday, the xx day, ressavit fra John Clerk and Henre Young, xxix^{s} ix$\frac{1}{2}$^{d}

Item, Sonday, the xxvij day, ressavit fra William Ker and Duncane Levingstoun, ... lvij^{s} vj^{d}

JAMES CARMICHAEL, Dean of Guild, 1552-53.

December.

Item, Sonday, the ferd day of December, ressavit fra James Adamsoun and Robert Flemyng, ... iij^{li} xvj^{s}

Item, Sonday, the xj day, ressavit fra Richert Gray and James Rynd, . xlj^{s} vj^{d}

Item, Sonday, the xviij day, ressavit fra Alexander Dein and John Hammiltoun, ... xxij^{s} iij^{d}

Item, Sonday, the xxv day, ressavit fra Alexander Ka and William Lausoun, iij^{li} xix^{s}

Januar.

[2] Item, Sonday, the first day of Januar, ressavit fra Johne Uchiltre and John Levingstoun, ... xxx^{s} v^{d}

Item, Sonday, the viij day, ressavit fra Eduerd Thomsoun and his marrow, xxj^{s}

Item, the fiftene day, ressavit fra Johne Frog and William Makcay, xxvij^{s} ij$\frac{1}{2}^{d}$

Item, Sonday, the xxij day, ressavit fra Mongo Hunter and Johne Hopper, xxv^{s} ij$\frac{1}{2}^{d}$

Item, Sonday, the xxix day, ressavit fra Williame Scott and his marrow, xxiij^{s} iij$\frac{1}{2}^{d}$

Februar.

Item, Sonday, the fift day of Februar, ressavit fra Johne Clerksoun and James Scharp, ... xxvij^{s} iiij$\frac{1}{2}^{d}$

Item, Sonday, the xij day, ressavit fra William Aikman and Thomas Todinar, ... xlvj^{s} j$\frac{1}{2}^{d}$

Item, Sonday, the xix day, ressavit fra James Sym and James Stewinsoun, iij^{li} vj^{s} ix$\frac{1}{2}^{d}$

Item, Sonday, the xx [vj] day, ressavit fra William Newtoun and Alexander Robesoun, . . xxxv^{s} iiij^{d}

Marche.

Item, Sonday, the fift day of Marche, ressavit fra Patrick Wilsoun and Archibald Edyer, ... xxxvij^{s} iiij^{d}

Item, Sonday, the xij day, ressavit fra James Gray and Alexander Chaip, xlix^{s} j$\frac{1}{2}^{d}$

Item, Sonday, the xix day, ressavit fra Johne Kyle and James Young, . xl^{s} j^{d}

Item, Sonday the xxvj day, ressavit fra Maister Johne Moscrop and Alexander Bannatyne, ... liij^{s} iij^{d}

Aprile.

Item, the secund day of Aprile, ressavit fra Johne Mosman and Michael Rynd . . . . l^{s} vij^{d}

JAMES CARMICHAEL, Dean of Guild. 1552-53.

[3] Item, Sonday, the nynt day, ressavit fra Michael Gilbert and Mongo Naper, ... lvj^s ix^d

Item, Sonday, the xvj day, ressavit fra Alexander Gilbert and Archibald Grayth, ... xxvj^s iij^d

Item, Sounday, the xxiij day, ressavit fra Thomas Ewene and Johne Westoun, ... lj^s j$\frac{1}{2}^d$

Item, Sonday, the last day of Aprile, ressavit fra Alexander King and Allane Dikkesoun, . iiij^{li} xvj^s $\frac{1}{2}^d$

Maij.

Item, Sonday, the vij day of Maij, ressavit fra Johne Rechisoun and William Rechisoun, ... xxvj^s ix$\frac{1}{2}^d$

Item, Sonday, the xiiij day, ressavit fra Adam Cauldwell and Andro Wigholm, ... xl^s vij^d

Item, the xxj day, ressavit fra James Marjoribanks and David Corsbe, . l^s

Item, Sonday, the xxviij day, ressavit fra Adam Allane and George Johnstoun, xliij^s j$\frac{1}{2}^d$

Junij.

Item, Sonday, the ferd day of Junij, ressavit fra Johne Cunynghame and his marrow, ... xx^s v$\frac{1}{2}^d$

Item, Sonday, the xj day, ressavit fra John Dougall and Johne Cathkyn, xxxij^s j$\frac{1}{2}^d$

Item, on Sonday, the xviij day, ressavit fra James Forrat and William Trumbill, ... xlvij^s v^d

Item, Sonday, the xxv day, ressavit fra David Towris and Thomas Reidpeth, . . xxxviij^s vj$\frac{1}{2}^d$

Julij.

Item, Sonday, the secund day of Julij, ressavit fra William Scott and Johne Banks, ... xxxj^s v^d

Item, Sonday, the nynt day, ressavit fra Alexander Purves and Alexander Lyell, ... xlj^s vj^d

Item, Sonday, the xvj day, ressavit fra William Thomsoun and Johne Purdy, ... xxxij^s iiij^d

[4] Item, Sonday, the xxiij day, ressavit fra Johne Wat and his marrow, xxviij^s v^d

Item, on Sonday, the xxx day, ressavit fra Johne Wilke and his marrow, . . . xvij^s vj$\frac{1}{2}^d$

August.

Item, Sonday, the vj day of August, ressavit fra Francis Ur and his marrow, ... xxv^{s}

Item, Sonday, the xiij day, ressavit fra Johne Herhisoun and Thomas Galbrayth, ... xxx^{s} v^{d}

Item, Sonday, the xx day, ressavit fra Thomas Trowp and his marrow, xxviij^{s} iiij$\frac{1}{2}^{d}$

Item, Sonday, the xxvij day, ressavit fra William Robertsoun and his marrow, . . xxij^{s} vj^{d}

September.

Item, on Sanct Gelis day, the first day, ressavit fra Eduard Hop and James Bassinden, ... iij^{li} ij^{s} iiij$\frac{1}{2}^{d}$

Item, Sonday, the thrid day, ressavit fra Robert Cunynghame and William M'Calwy, ... xl^{s} vij^{d}

Item, Sonday, the tent day, ressavit fra Francis Bell and his marrow, . xxij^{s} vj^{d}

Item, Sonday, the xvij day, ressavit fra Thomas Pettigrefe and his marrow, ... xxiij^{s} iij^{d}

Item, Sonday, the xxiiij day, ressavit fra James Cranstoun and William Andersoun, . . xxx^{s} v^{d}

October.

Item, Sonday, the first day of October, ressavit fra Eduard Litle and James Nycoll, ... xxxix^{s} ij^{d}

Summa of the hale charge of the pece, this instant yeir, extends to . . . . . . j$^{c\,li}$ xiiij^{s} viij$\frac{1}{2}^{d}$

[5] Item, I am to be chargit with the nowmber of the schippis of this instant yeir, quhilk extendis, as the buke beris, to iij^{xx} xvj schippis :—

Summa of the schippis, ... liij^{li} iiij^{s}

Heir followis my charge of the Burgesses and Gilds, bayth togidder becaus thai are in the lokkit buik :—

Item, in primis, Patrik Crag, x^{li}

Item, Johnne Aikman, . . v^{li}

Item, Johnne Tod, xxxiij^{s} iiij^{d}

Item Johnne Small, . xiij^{s} iiij^{d}

Johnne Purdy, . . xiij^{s} iiij^{d}

Item, Michaell Windeyettis,	v^{li}
Item Andrew Makkilwych,	v^{li}
Item, Alexander Wardlaw,	v^{li}
Item, John Young, .	xiij^{s} iiij^{d}
Item, William Aikman,	v^{li}
Item, John Dalzell,	v^{li}
Item, Allane Purves, .	xiij^{s} iiij^{d}
Item, William Darling, .	vj^{s} viij^{d}
Item, Alexander Pentland,	v^{li}
Item, Johnne Gibsoun, .	v^{li}
Johnne Thane, . .	v^{li}
James Terbat, . .	xxxiij^{s} iiij^{d}
Item, Robert Cunynghame,	xxxiij^{s} iiij^{d}
Item, Johnne Blakburn, . .	xx^{s}
Item, Alexander Naper, . .	xxxiij^{s} iiij^{d}
Item, Maister Archibald Grahame,	xxxiij^{s} iiij^{d}
Item, Alexander Achisoun,	xv^{li}
Item, Alexander Tennend,	v^{li}
Item, Michaell Mailvill, .	xiij^{s} iiij^{d}
Item, James Spottiswod, .	v^{li}
[6] Item, Johnne Watsoun,	v^{li}
Item, Adam Cauldwell,	v^{li}
Niniane Bruce,	xxxiij^{s} iiij^{d}
Thomas Rannald, . .	xv^{li}
Maister Henre Foulis,	xxxiij^{s} iiij^{d}
Maister James Watsoun, .	xv^{li}
Item, Neill Layng, ...	xv^{li}
Summa of the burgessis and gildis, bayth togidder, this yeir extends to	ij^{c}lj^{li} vj^{s} viij^{d}

Item, I am to be chargit with the Choppis of the Kirk and the fute of the Kirk-yard this instant yeir :—

Item, John Gilbert, . . .	xxx^{s}
Item, Uxor Rynd, . .	xxx^{s}
Item, Thomas Mereles, .	xxvj^{s} viij^{d}

JAMES CARMICHAEL, Dean of Guild. 1552-53.

Item, David Bane,	xxvj^s viij^d
Item, Johne Broderstanis,	xxvj^s viij^d
Item, Johne Bane,	xx^s
Item, George Marschell,	xx^s
Item, Johne Forrest,	xx^s
Item, William Forsyth,	xx^s
Item, Marioun Scott,	xx^s
Item, Nicoll Haisty,	xx^s
Item, Alexander Diksoun,	xx^s
Item, George Elwand,	xx^s
Item, Johne Cunynghame,	xx^s
Item, Margrete Rutherfurd,	xx^s
Item, William Harperfeild,	xx^s
Item, George Cowane,	xx^s
Item, Michaell Windeyettis,	xx^s
Summa of the hale choppis, this instant yeir, extends to	xx^{li}

[7] Item, I am to be chargit with the Throuchtis of the Kirk this instant yeir :—

Item, in primis, Richart Wrycht,	vj^s viij^d
Item, Elizabeth Duncane,	vj^s viij^d
Item, Andro Patersoun,	vj^s viij^d
Item, Elizabeth Aikenheid,	vj^s viij^d
Item, twa servands of the lard of Kynfawns,	xiij^s iiij^d
Item, Johne Cunynghame,	vj^s viij^d
Item, Williame Davidsounis wif,	vj^s viij^d
Item, Patrik Edyearis barn,	ij^s
Item, Thomas Mudeis wif,	vj^s viij^d
Item, Maister William Wytman,	vj^s viij^d
Item, Maister Robert Wedderburn,	vj^s viij^d
Item, Alexander Achisounis barn,	ij^s
Summa of the throuchis, this instant yeir, is	iij^{li} xvj^s iiij^d
Item, for the making of ane throuche of Williame Craikis, and the rowme thairof,	xx^s

JAMES CARMICHAEL, Dean of Guild. 1552-53.

Item, I am to be chargit with the Grete Sele of this instant yeir :—

Item, ressavit fra Alexander Hereot for the sele to his few of Ravilstoun,	xl^{s}
Item, ressavit ane unicorn fra my Lord Provest, at Michaelmes, to the work,	xxiiij^{s}

Item, I am to be chargit with ane Eschete of William Brone, of ane compositioun for certane hydis put in ane schip unfrauchtit :—

Item, ressavit for the compositioun of the foirsaid hydis, modifeit be the counsale, the sowme of ten punds ; summa, . .	x^{li}

[8] Item, I am to be chargit with the foure Grete Goldin Candilstikks in this instant yeir :—

Item, in primis, Leonard Stevinsoun,	ix^{s} vj^{d}
Item, Thomas Broun,	ix^{s} vj^{d}
Item, Dame Chepman, .	ix^{s} vj^{d}
Item, the lard of Kynfawnis,	ix^{s} vj^{d}
Item, Johne Craik, .	ix^{s} vj^{d}
Item, Maister Thomas Fischear, . . .	ix^{s} vj^{d}
Item, Alexander Adamsoun and William Adamsoun,	iiij^{s}
Item, Nicoll Carncross,	ij^{s}
Item, Eduard Litill,	ij^{s}
Item, Mongo Tennend,	ij^{s}
Item, George Leche,	ij^{s}
Item, Issobell Hopper,	ij^{s}
Maister James Foulis,	ij^{s}
Item, Henre Ramsay,	ij^{s}
Item, Patrik Fleming,	ij^{s}
Item, William Rynd, . .	ij^{s}
Item, Maister Robert Widderburn,	ix^{s} vj^{d}
Item, to Michaell Lochmyln,	ix^{s} vj^{d}
Item, Andro Makclen, .	ix^{s} vj^{d}
Item, William Carncorss, .	ix^{s} vj^{d}
Item, Jonett Purves, .	ij^{s}
Item, Thomas Terbat, .	ij^{s}
Item, David Taittis wif, . .	ij^{s}
Item, Maister Adam Otterburn, .	ij^{s}

JAMES CARMICHAEL. Dean of Guild. 1552-53.

Item, Gilbert Lauder,	ij^s
Item, George Henrisoun, .	ij^s
Item, William Henrisoun, .	ij^s
James Gray, . . .	ij^s
Item, James Barronis wif, .	ij^s
Item, the laird of Balcleuche, ...	ij^s
Summa of the hale grete candilstikks, . .	[vj^{li} xvij^s]

[9] Item, I am to be chargit of the Silver Candilstikkis, of the money for thame, this instant yeir :—

Item, James Purves,	viij^d
Item, Thomas Terbat, . .	viij^d
Item, for Maister William Wychtman,	viij^d
Item, David Taittis wif, .	viij^d
Item, Margrete Fynlausoun,	iiij^d
Item, Johne Hekke,	viij^d
Item, Johne Adamsoun, .	viij^d
Item, Maister Adam Otterburn, . .	viij^d
Item, for Maister Robert Wedderburn, .	xvj^d
Item, for Michaell Lochmyln, .	viij^d
Item, for the Fraternite of Sanct Ann,	iiij^d
Item, Sir Johne Kerss,	iiij^d
Item, Patrik Cukis wife, . . .	viij^d
Item, for the Fraternite of Sanct Cristell,	iiij^d
Item, Patrik Wilsonis wif, .	viij^d
Item, for Gilbert Lauder, .	viij^d
Item, Andro McClen,	viij^d
Item, Patrik Rechisoun, .	iiij^d
Item, Thomas Broun, .	viij^d
Item, Alexander Achisonis barn, .	viij^d
Item, William Brounis wif,	viij^d
Item, William Carncorss, .	xvj^d
Item, James Barronis wif,	viij^d
Item, the lard of Balcleuche,	xvj^d
Item, Sir Robert Hopper, .	iiij^d

JAMES CARMICHAEL, Dean of Guild. 1552-53.

Item, William Adamsoun and Alexander Adamsoun, xvj^{d}
Item, Eduard Litill, . viij^{d}
Item, Nicoll Carncorss, . . . viij^{d}
Item, the Confrere of Crispe and Crispenene, . iiij^{d}
Item, Maister William Foular and Johne Foular, viij^{d}
Item, Michaell Makquhen, iiij^{d}
[10] Item, Maister John Chepman, iiij^{d}
Item, Mongo Tennend, viij^{d}
Item, George Leche, . . viij^{d}
Item, the Fraternite of Sanct Bla, iiij^{d}
Item, William Lokhart, . iiij^{d}
Item, Maister Henre Quhyte, iiij^{d}
Item, Issobell Hopper, . viij^{d}
Item, Maister James Foulis, viij^{d}
Item, Walter Chepman, . iiij^{d}
Item, Johne Reiddis barn, viij^{d}
Item, Maister Johne Murray, viij^{d}
Item, Henre Ramsay, viij^{d}
Item, Dame Chepman, . viij^{d}
Item, Sir Thomas Maxwell, iiij^{d}
Item, the lard of Kynfawns, xvj^{d}
Item, John Craik, viij^{d}
Item, Dame Weche, . viij^{d}
Item, William Davidsoun, viij^{d}
Item, Maister Johne Spittell, xvj^{d}
Item, the Dene of Dunbar, xvj^{d}
Item, Andro Law, viij^{d}
Item, Patrik Flemyng, . . viij^{d}
Item, Johne Bruce, ... iiij^{d}

Summa of the silver chandlers for this instant yeir, [j^{li} xv^{s} viij^{d}]

Item, I am to be chargit with Sanct Gelis arme on Relik Sonday and Sanct Gelis day, ... iij^{s} vij^{d}

Summa of the hale charge, is, . $\text{iij}^{c}\text{lj}^{li}$ xiij^{s} xj^{d} ^{obs}

JAMES CARMICHAEL, Dean of Guild. 1552-53.

Heir efter followis the EXONERATIOUN and DISCHARGE of the Dene of Gild, of the compt of befoir writtin, of the yeir of God J^m v^c lii yeris :—

[11]

In the first, begynnis the expenses of the Wrychtis sen the secund day of October 1552 :—

In primis, said day, the viij day of October, to Andro Mansioun and his thre servandis for their ulkis wage, . . . iiij^li xix^s
Item, to Robert Finder, . . xxx^s
Item, for candill that oulk, ... xiij^s iiij^d
Item, for xviij pund of glew, price of the stane xxiiij^s; summa, . . xxvij^s
Item, for sawing of xv draucht of buirds and xxvij quarter dalis; summa of the hale, . . xiij^s
Item, for sounds, ... vj^s
Item, said day, the xv day of October, to Andro Mansioun and his thre servands, . . . iiij^li xix^s
Item, to Robert Fynder, . xxx^s
Item, for candill this oulk, ... xij^s
Item, for ane croce band of irne and ane lok and ane pype to the watter stop, ... viij^s vj^d
Item, to the glassinwrycht for vj fute of new glas in ane pannell in Sanct Thomas ile, and four fute of auld gles, payit for the fute of new gles xx^d and for the fute of auld gles vj^d; summa, ... xij^s
Item, to ane workman to mend the kapis and the blew welvet stands, and for ribbonis to thame, ... xij^s vj^d
Item, for peonar fie of ane grete standart ledder furth of the Abbay of Halyrudhous to the kirk, and lifting about to the woundokkis mending round about the kirk, ... iiij^s iiij^d
[12] Item, for vj laid lyme to poynt the windois, . . vij^s
Item, for ane dousone sand coft, . . . v^s
Item, for watter drawing, and riddeling, ... iij^s viij^d
Item, on said day, the xxij day of October, to Andrew Mansioun and his thre servands, ... iiij^li xix^s
Item, to Robert Finder, ... xxx^s

JAMES CARMICHAEL, Dean of Guild. 1552-53.

Item, for peonar fee of iij^{xx} xiiij buirds to be kitters furth of the luge to the kirk, and fra the kirk to the Abbot of Dunfermelingis lugeing, for glewing and for bering of thame to the kirk agane, . . . x^{s} viij^{d}

Item, for iij lame piggis, . . . xij^{d}

Item, for ane eln of canves, . . ij^{s}

Item, for sawing of xv dosone buirds, ... vij^{s} vj^{d}

Item, for iij pannells of gless to Sanct Anthonis windowis, contenand of new gles xij fute, and xviij fute auld gles, xxiiij^{s} vj^{d}

Item, for candill, . . . xij^{s}

Item, for sounds to the mixt glew, ... vij^{s}

Item, said day, the xxix day of October, to Andrew Mansioun and his thre servands, . . . iiij^{li} xix^{s}

Item, to Robert Finder, ... xxx^{s}

Item, for the lane of blakks to hing the queir of the south side, at the making of the contract with Andro Mansioun, for keping of thame twa dayis, v^{s} viij^{d}

Item, in Our Lady ile, new gles four fute, and in Sanct Gabryell's ile vj fute new gles, price of the fute xx^{d}; summa, xviij^{s} viij^{d}

Item, thre fute auld gles, . . xviij^{d}

Item, for ane stane candill, ... xij^{s}

Item, to Lane and Hainsle to beir the ketteris to the hous above the kirk duir, and uthir tymmer, togidder, . iiij^{s} v^{d}

Item, for drinksilver to the glassinwrycht, . v^{s}

Item, for rynging of the bellis all nycht on Salmes evin, . . . ij^{s}

[13] Item, that samin day to Broun for xxvj doson burds and uthir grete tymmer, xvij^{s} iiij^{d}

Item, said day, the fift day of November, to Andro Mantioun and his thre servands, ... iiij^{li} xix^{s}

Item, to Robert Fynder, ... xxx^{s}

Item, to Johne Ahannay, for twa new gles bands, and ane band to the nether queir duir, and ane cleik, . . . vij^{s} viij^{d}

Item, the vij day of November, for candill, . . xij^{s}

Item, for ane stane of glew, the price thairof, . . xxiiij^{s}

Item, the xvj day of November, for candill, ... xiij^{s} iiij^{d}

Item, to Broun for sawing of buirds and geists to the bak of workbands, xiiij^{s} viij^{d}

Item, the third day of December, for candill, ... xj^{s} vj^{d}

JAMES CARMICHAEL, Dean of Guild. 1552-53.

Item, for four fute of new gles in Sanct Johnis ile, and ten fute auld gles,	vj^s x^d
Item, for peonar fee of the ledder fra the kirk to the abbay,	viij^d
Item, the nynt day of December, for candill,	xij^s
Item, for irne werk, nalis, and ilikis to Andro Mansioun turnying stulis,	x^s iiij^d
Item, the xvij day of December, for candill,	xij^s
Item, for ane stane and ane half glew, price of the stane xxiiij^s; summa,	xxxvj^s
Item, for sawing of five dosone buirds, xj quarter drauchtis,	v^s iij^d
Item, the xxiiij day of December, for candill,	xiij^s iiij^d
Item, to mending the sensars, five grotts, the pece xviij^d; summa,	vij^s vj^d
Item, for clengeing of the kirke about the lectrin, the xxiij day of December,	v^s
Item, to James Lauder, that day,	xxiiij^s
Item, the viij day of Januar, for candill,	viij^s vj^d
Item, for sounds to the glew,	viij^s
Item, for peonar fee of the lintellis fra the werkhous to the North Loch, and fra the loch hame to the werkhous,	iiij^s vj^d
Item, the xvij day of Januar, for candill,	x^s
[14] Item, for bukrem to mend the westments and frintell, and for ribbonis and silk,	x^s vj^d
Item, to Home and Hainslie to await upoun Andro Mansioun, and to carry his tymmer to him at his command,	v^s
Item, the xxiiij day of Januar, for candill,	x^s
Item, the last day of Januar, to Andro Mansioun for his quarter payment, conform to his contract mad betwixt him and me, as his contract mad thairupon bers, at the provost, baillies, and counsalis command, gevin to him the sowme of,	l^{li}
Item, the first day of Februar, for candill,	x^s
Item, for v pund glew,	ix^s
Item, for lossing of William Broneis hydis furth of ane schip unfrauchtit, and for bering of thame to the Kingis Werk,	v^s
Item, coft fra Johne Wedderburn, the thrid day of Februar, iij geistis,	xlviij^s
Item, for nalis to mend the grete candilstik,	xij^d
Item, the viij day of Februar, for candill,	xij^s
Item, far cart hyre of the geistis,	iiij^s vj^d
Item, for peonar fee in Leyth, and inlaying in the kirkyard,	ij^s

JAMES CARMICHAEL, Dean of Guild. 1552-53.

Item, for sawing of thame and xvij burds, to Broun and his marrow,	ix^s iij^d
Item, the xv day of Februar, coft ane stane of glew, cost,	xxiiij^s
Item, coft the xx day of Februar, fra Alexander Park, vj geistis, price of the pece xvij^s,	v^{li} ij^s
Item, for cart hyre of thame,	vij^s viij^d
Item, for peonar fee in Leyth,	xij^d
Item, for inbering in the kirkyard,	xij^d
Item, for sawing of thame,	v^s
[15] Item, the xxiiij day of Februar, for ane stane of candill,	xij^s
Item, the last day of Februar, to the sawars,	viij^s ix^d
Item, for weching of the glassin windois the x of Marche, round about the north syde of the kirk, to Patrick Home and Hannislie,	xiiij^s
Item, the xij day of Marche, for candill,	xij^s
Item, for dichting of the kirk round about, at Pasche,	v^s
Item, for keiping of the sepulture,	viij^s
Item, for skowring of the lectrone,	iij^s
Item, for oley to the knok all yeir,	viij^s
Item, for candill to the pann all the yeir in winter,	xxvij^s
Item, for sawing of the wanescot,	ij^s ix^d
Item, for ix punds glew,	xiij^s vj^d
Item, upon the Inventioun of the Haly Croce evin, to Andro Mansioun for his quarter fe, conform to his contract maid betuix him and me, at the counsalis command,	l^{li}
Item, the samyn day deliverit to the prior and convent of the Blackfreris, conforme to ane obligatioun maid to thame be the provest, baillies, and counsale, and the dene of gild for the tyme oblisit thairfor,	x^{li}
Item, for three piggs to melt glew in,	xij^d
Item, coft to glew the grete black standarts ij^c grete nalis, price of j^c, vj^s viij^d; summa,	xiij^s iiij^d
Item, coft fra David Forester j dosone burds, cost,	iij^{li} xij^s
Item, for pynour fe of thame,	viij^d
Item, for sawing of thame,	v^s
Item, for pynour fe of thame fra the Kirk of Feild kirkyard to the kirk,	xij^d
[16] Item, for dichting of the kirk about at Corpus Christpinis day,	v^s

JAMES CARMICHAEL, Dean of Guild. 1552-53.

Item, skowring of the lettrone, ... iiij^{s}

Item, coft fra Johne Aslowane xviij burds, price of the dosone iij^{li} xij^{s}; summa, ... v^{li} viij^{s}

Item, for pynour fe of thame, . xij^{d}

Item, for sawing of thame, ... vij^{s} vj^{d}

Item, for mending of twa ledders borrowit to wesche the kirk windois, . iij^{s}

Item, for ane dow and watter, xviij^{d}

Item, coft $\frac{1}{2}$^{c} wanescot, xv^{li}

Item, for kert hyre, . xij^{s} vj^{d}

Item, for pynour fe of thame, ij^{s} vj^{d}

Item, for sawing of xvij burds, ... vij^{s}

Item, the xvij of July, for sawing of xviij quarter drauchts, iiij^{s} vj^{d}

Item, the xxiiij day, for sawing of twa geists and nyne burds, . . v^{s} iiij^{d}

Item, for dichting of the kirk within, ilk xv days fra Corpus Christpis day to Sanct Gelis day; summa, ... xiij^{s}

Item, the first day of August, to Andro Mansioun for his quarteris payment, conform to his contract, at the command of the counsale, . l^{li}

Item, to John Dalmahoy, in Leyth, for his service awatand on the schippis that past unenterit in the buks and unfrauchtit, x quarters fustiane, price of the eln v^{s}; summa, ... xv^{s}

Item, the v day of August, for xviij punds glew, price of the stane xxiiij^{s}; summa, ... xxvij^{s}

Item, coft ane hundreth grete nalis, cost, ... vj^{s} viij^{d}

Item, for sawing of cuttis of grete tymmer, and xxiiij wanescot, the xij of August, ... xij^{s} viij^{d}

[17] Item, the xx day of August, to sawaris for sawing of burds, . . v^{s} iij^{d}

Item, the samyn day, coft twa dosane dalis, price of the dosane xxxv^{s}; summa, ... iij^{li} x^{s}

Item, thair is xiiij of thame for fluring of thame, and viij put upon the werkhous wall.

Item, for cart hyre of thame, . v^{s}

Item, for pynour fe, ... xv^{d}

Item, the last day of August, to the sawars for sawing of wanescot, . vij^{s} iiij^{d}

Item, for graithing of the kirk on Sanct Gelis day, . . . iij^{s}

JAMES CARMICHAEL, Dean of Guild. 1552-53.

Item, the tent day of September, to the sawaris, . iiij^s j^d
Item, the samyn day, for candill, . vj^s viij^d
Item, the xvj day of September, to the sawaris, . ix^s ij^d
Item, the samyn day, coft ½^c stanis of (*blank*), cost, xv^s
Item, for ane hundreth, . vj^s viij^d
Item, coft ane dosane and ane half lyme, price of the dosane xiiij^s; summa, xxj^s
Item, the samyn day, coft thre dosane sand, price of the dosane v^s; summa, . xv^s
Item, coft half ane dosone firrin sparrs to be spaks to hald up the work, cost, . v^s vj^d
Item, the xxj day of September, for candill, . xij^s
Item, for vj dosane watter, price of the dosane x^d; summa, . v^s
Item, to Gilbert Cleuch, mason, and Johne Anderson, for ane ulkis laubor in the fluring of the soill of the stall, . xlij^s
Item, for xj^{li} glew, . xvj^s vj^d
Item, gevin to Neill Laiying for wryttings and the signet at diverss tymes, at the provest, baillies, and counsale command, in money, . xv^{li}
[18] Item, gevin to Maister James McGill for his procuratioun in the townis effeiris, at the command of the provest, baillies, and counsale, in money, xv^{li}
Item, to ane boy for his drinksilver, . ij^s
Item, Mounonday, the xxij of September, to thre workmen, . iij^s
Item, Twisday, Wednisday, Thurisday, Friday, and Saturday, ilk day to twa workmen, ij^s; summa, . xij^s
Item, the xxiij of September, for inbringing of red to fill up the hollis, xviij^d
Item, for sawing of burds, . iiij^s v^d
Item, for inbringing of the work to the work of the queir, and furth brynging agane, and for inbringing of the haill work, thre dayis, . vij^s vj^d
Item, the xxix of September, for candill, . viij^s
Item, to George Johnestoun, for xj^{li} ½ walx candill to the grete candilstikks all the yeir, price of the lib. iiij^s; summa, . xlvj^s
Item, to Pate for walx to powpet, . vj^s
Item, to Thomas Watsoun, glassinwrycht, for his yeris fe, . iiij^{li}
Item, to Andro Mansioun for half ane ulk's wage deiduceit in the last compts of the Yule ulk, and siclik of the ulk of Witsonday, gevin to

JAMES CARMICHAEL, Dean of Guild. 1552-53.

him and his servands, conform to that yeris ulklie wage, at the provestis and counsalis command, . . . vij^{li} xj^{s}

Item, siclik gevin to Robert Finder for his wage, . . . xxx^{s}

The officaris feis.

In primis, Richard Trowop,	v^{li}
[19] Item, Patrik Baldrany, .	xl^{s}
Item, Thomas Todrik,	xl^{s}
Item, William Cowttis,	xl^{s}
Item, James Henrison,	xl^{s}
Item, James Anderson,	xl^{s}
Item, Johne Wauchlot,	xl^{s}
Item, Johne Richardson, .	xl^{s}
Item, Patrik Wychtman, .	xl^{s}
Item, Richard Plummar, .	xl^{s}
Item, to Thomas Hall, ...	xl^{s}
Item, to Patrik, gevin als for his yeris fe for the dichting of the gutteris,	xxx^{s}
Item, to Home for his yeris fe for keiping of the kirk, . . .	xl^{s}
Item, to Doctor Smyth for his yeris fe, ...	xx^{s}
Item, for mending of twa of the choppis occupyt be Johne Marschell and Michael Windeyeitts at the fute of the kirk yard, . . .	x^{s}
Item, gevin to Andro Aldoth, principall wrycht under the maister of work, for his yeris laubors at the work, drinksilver to him, ane pair of hois of stemmying millane, the price thairof, .	xxx^{s}
Item, for my yeris fe and my chaplanis, ...	x^{li} xiij^{s} iiij^{d}
Item, the compter is to be dischargit of the sowme of foure scoir thre ^{li} xiij^{s} vj½^{d}, quhilk wes restand awing to the compter in his last yeris compt precedand, as ane act maid in the townis bukis, the ix of November 1552 yers purports; summa, .	lxxxiij^{li} xiij^{s} vj½^{d}

[20] Apud Edinburgh, Secundo Martij, Anno Domini J^{m} v^{c} liij^{tio}.

The quhilk day the comptis foirsaid, of the twa yers precedand the dait of Michaelmess last bypast, maid be James Carmichael, dene of gild, hard, sene, and thairwith ryplie avisit, the charge and discharge considerit, finds that the said

James is superexpendit by his charge, quhilk the towne is restand awing to him, the sowme of ane hundreth j pund xv^{s} viij^{d}, de claro, be thir presents, subscrvit be jugis and auditoris of comptis underwritin :— JAMES CARMICHAEL, Dean of Guild. 1552-53.

Mr Johne Prestoun, baillie.	William Hammyltoun, provest.
William Lawson, balze.	Wilzem Craik.
William Murheid, baillie.	Mr James Lyndesay.
Duncane Levingstoun, baillie.	Johne Sym, with my hand.

Primo Februarij J^{m} v^{c} lxj^{mo}. In presence of Maister James Lindesay, James Adamsoun, Thomas Uddert, James Nychole, James Curle, Jhonne Spottiswod, Mychaell Gilbert, David Kinloch, and Thomas Ewyne, the said James Carmychell grantts him satisfeit and payit of the rest above writtin. In witnes quhairof he subscrivis this present in thair presence, being auditors electit to heir the comptis of the toun.

JAMES CARMYCHILL.

[21] HEIR EFTIR followis the COMPT of JOHNE SYMSOUN, Dene of Gild, of his Charge in the yeir of God J^{m} v^{c} fifty foure yers; his entres beand the viij of October the yeir of God J^{m} v^{c} and liij yers precedand :— JOHN SYMSOUN, Dean of Guild. 1553-54.

CHARGE.

In primis, I am to be chargit with the Silver of the Pece of procuratoun :- -

Item, the viij day of October, ressavit fra Johne Purves and Johne Abirnethy,	xxviij^{s} ij^{d}
Item, ressavit the xv day, fra Andro Stewensoun and Alexander Pery,	xl^{s} vj^{d}
Item, ressavit the xxij day, fra Johne Huchesoun and Johne Walker,	xvij^{s} vj^{d}
Item, ressavit the xxix day, fra Maister Archibald Straug and Johne Cowttis,	xliiij^{s} iiij^{d}

November.

Item, ressavit the v day, fra Eduard Home and Patrik Irland,	xliiij^{s} iij^{d}
Item, ressavit the xij day, fra Patrik Edgar and Johne Wicht,	xxx^{s} $\frac{1}{2}^{d}$
Item, ressavit the xix day, fra Alexander Masoun and Robert Dalgles,	xxxiij^{s} ij^{d}
Item, ressavit the xxvj day, fra Robert Lun and Johne Bell,	xxv^{s} $\frac{1}{2}^{d}$
Summa lateris,	xiij^{li} xiij^{s}

JOHN SYMSOUN, Dean of Guild. 1553-54.

December.

Item, ressavit the thrid day, fra Robert Crag and Johne Hammiltoun, . xxxviij^{s}

Item, the x day, ressavit fra Johne Marioribanks and Thomas Gammill, xxix^{s} j^{d}

[22] Item, the xvij day, ressavit fra Alexander Home and Johne Henrisoun, . xlj^{s} iij^{d}

Item, the xxiiij day, ressavit fra Michael Rynd and Andro Henrisoun, . xxxj^{s} ij^{d}

Item, on Yule day, the xxv day, ressavit fra Maister James Lyndesay and Alexander King, ... iiij^{li} viij^{s} iiij^{d}

Item, the last day, ressavit fra Alexander Achesoun and Niniane Bruce, iij^{li} ij^{d}

Januar.

Item, the vij day, ressavit fra James Heot and Johne Robertsoun, . l^{s} viij$\frac{1}{2}$^{d}

Item, the xiiij day, ressavit fra James Broun and Walter Patersoun, xlviij^{s} vij^{d}

Item, the xxj day, ressavit fra Archebald Leche and Robert Finder, . xxx^{s}

Item, the xxviij day, ressavit fra James Aikman and Maister Patrik Bissat, xxxix^{s} ij^{d}

Februar.

Item, the ferd day, ressavit fra Adam Fulartoun and Christpofer Eistoun, ... xxxvij^{s} ij^{d}

Item, the xj day, ressavit fra William Ury and James Josse, . . xxxv^{s} j^{d}

Item, the xviij day, ressavit fra Michael Rynd and William Harlaw, xxix^{s} viij^{d}

Item, the xxv day, ressavit fra Johne Dugall. . . xxvj^{s} viij^{d}

Summa [lateris], . xxix^{li} v^{s} $\frac{1}{2}$^{d}

[23] Marche.

Item, the ferd day, ressavit fra Alexander Bruce and Patrik Gibsoun, xxxviij^{s} ij^{d}

Item, the xj day, ressavit fra Thomas Thomsoun and William Aitkin, xxxvij^{s} viij^{d}

Item, the xviij day, ressavit fra Alexander Park and Johne Charteris, . lv^{s}

Item, the xxv day, ressavit fra Johne Young and Johne Adamsoun, . v^{li} v^{d}

Aprile.

Item, the ferd day, ressavit fra Johne Andersoun and Johne Makdowall, xlvij^{s}

Item, the viij day, ressavit fra David Corsbe and Andro Sclater, . liij^{s}

Item, the xv day, ressavit fra Peter Douglas and James Mure, . iij^{li} v^{s} viij^{d}

Item, the xxij day, ressavit fra Nicolace Ramsy and Johne Hairat, . xl^{s} vj^{d}

Item, the xxix day, ressavit fra David Kinloch and Robert Henrysoun, . lv^{s} iiij^{d}

JOHN SYMSOUN, Dean of Guild, 1553-54.

May.

Item, the vj day, ressavit fra Alexander Moress and James Norwell, . xxx^{s} iij^{d}

Item, on Witsonday, the xiij day, ressavit fra Johne Litil and Luke Wilsoun, ... li^{s} j^{d}

Item, the xx day, ressavit fra Maister Thomas Weddell and Adam Scot, xlvij^{s}

Item, the xxvij day, ressavit fra Maister Robert Glen and William Holdane, . . . xlviij^{d}

Summa lateris, . xxxiij^{li} ix^{s} j^{d}

[24] Junij.

Item, the thrid day, ressavit fra James Hoppringill and Peter Martyne, xxxij^{s} vj^{d}

Item, the x day, ressavit fra David Symmer and Nicoll Purves, . . xl^{s} vij^{d}

Item, the xvij day, ressavit fra Patrik Schang and Thomas Mow, . xlj^{s} iij^{d}

Item, the xxiiij day, ressavit fra Alexander Sydsef and Alexander Hagy, xxv^{s} j^{d}

Julij.

Item, the first day, ressavit fra James Young and Johne Rynd, . xlj^{s} ij^{d}

Item, the viij day, na body, ... (*blank*)

Item, the xv day, ressavit fra William Huchesoun and Walter Dennestoun, xlij^{s} viij^{d}

Item, the xxij day, ressavit fra Thomas Scot and Alexander Johnestoun, xxix^{s} j$\frac{1}{2}^{d}$

Item, the xxix day, ressavit fra Johne Spoetty and Alexander Furd, xxvj^{s} vij^{d}

August.

Item, the v day, ressavit fra Johne Forrest, ... xvij^{s} vij^{d}

Item, the xij day, ressavit fra Johne Watsoun and Johne Maxwell, . xvij^{s} x^{d}

Item, the xix day, ressavit fra Thomas Purves and William Gryntoun, xxx^{s} j^{d}

Item, the xxvj day, ressavit fra James Kincaid and James Broune, xxxiij^{s} ix^{d}

Summa lateris, . . xvij^{li} xviij^{s} 1$\frac{1}{2}^{d}$

[25] September.

Item, the first day, ressavit fra William Murcheid and Duncane Levingstoun, ... v^{li} ij^{d} $\frac{1}{2}^{d}$

Item, the secund day, ressavit fra Andro Bartane and George Todrik, . xxxij^{s} $\frac{1}{2}^{d}$

Item, the ix day, ressavit fra Walter Wicht and Andro Gibsoun, . xxix^{s} xj^{d}

Item, the xvj day, ressavit fra Andro Elphinstoun and Herculis Methven, xviij^{s} iij^{d}

Item, the xxiii day, ressavit fra William Arnot and Gilbert Clewch, xxviij^{s} x^{d}

JOHN SYMSOUN, Dean of Guild, 1553-54.

Item, the last day, ressavit fra Johne Aslowane and Alexander Hoip, xxviij^{s} xj^{d}

Summa particule, . . xj^{li} xviij^{s} ij^{d}

Summa of the haill charge of the pece, of this yeir, . j^{c} vj^{li} iij^{s} v^{d}

Item, I am to be chargit this instant yeir with the nowmer of the Schippis quhilk the buke bers, iiij^{xx} xij schippis at xiiij^{s} the pece.

Summa, lxiiij^{li} viij^{s}

Item, I am to be chargit with the Burgessis and Gildis this instant yeir as the buke bers :—

[26] In primis, Johne Logy, v^{li}

George Scot, v^{li}

Hew Nesbet, v^{li}

Andro Dawling, . . v^{li}

Johne Charteris, youngar, xxxiij^{s} iiij^{d}

Robert Gibsoun, v^{li}

George Lausoun, . vj^{s} viij^{d}

Adam Carnbe, v^{li}

Johne Blak, v^{li}

Johne Aitkin, v^{li}

Andro Wighom, x^{li}

Charles Geddas, v^{li}

Johne Grahame, v^{li}

Johne Patersoun, ... x^{li}

Summa of the burgessis and gildis, . iij^{xx} xij^{li}

Item, I am to be chargit with the Cordiners' Choppis of the kirkyard :—

In primis, thre of the eistmost of thame yeirlie, giffand ilk chop ij merks, and xv of thame ilk pece giffand yeirlie xx^{s} ; and the westmost, quhilk is callit Johne Mitchellis chope, giffand x^{s} yeir, becaus it is at the erd and nocht bet, quhilk extends in the haill to, xix^{li} x^{s}

[27] Item, I am to be chargit with the Choppis of the kirk :—

In primis, Johne Gilbertis chope yeirlie, . xxx^{s}

Item, George Turnouris chope, . xxx^{s}

Summa, . iij^{li}

I am to be chargit with the Layeris of the kirk for this yeir as Patrik Govynnis compt bers :—

In primis, Jonet Kincaid, .	vj^s viij^d
William Tempennis wief, .	vj^s viij^d
Andro Herrises, .	vj^s viij^d
James Johneston, .	vj^s viij^d
Robert Hammiltóun,	vj^s viij^d
Margaret Galbrayth,	vj^s viij^d
Adam Small,	vj^s viij^d
Johne Cok,	vj^s viij^d
Adam Eistoun, .	vj^s viij^d
Adam Hannislie wif,	vj^s viij^d
Henry Williamsoun,	vj^s viij^d
Dame Aitkin,	vj^s viij^d
Aignes Cowane,	vj^s viij^d
Marion Wilsoun, .	vj^s viij^d
James Tennand, .	vj^s viij^d
[28] Item, for ane barnis layer,	ij^s
Item, for Robert Lumis barnis layer,	ij^s
Item, for Johne Howyis barnis layer, . .	ij^s
Item, for Maister Archibald Grahamis barnis layer,	ij^s
Summa of the layres, . .	v^{li} viij^s

I am to be chargit with the foure Grete Candilsticks in this instant yeir :—

In primis, for Andro Lyndesay,	ix^s vj^d
James Rynd,	ix^s vj^d
Margaret Harvy, .	ix^s vj^d
Jonat Reid, .	ix^s vj^d
Nicolace Skewgall,	ix^s vj^d
Dame Margaret Scot,	ix^s vj^d
Margaret Davidsoun,	ix^s vj^d
William Henrisoun,	ix^s vj^d
For the lard of Rosling,	ix^s vj^d
Archibald Grahamis wif, .	ix^s vj^d

JOHN SYMSOUN, Dean of Guild. 1553-54.

Hew Douglas,	ix^s vj^d
Dame Nicoll, ...	ix^s vj^d
Nicoll Carncorss for the twa candilstiks, .	ij^s
George Leche, .	ij^s
Margaret Prestoun,	ij^s
David Carr, .	ij^s
The Lard of Kynfawnis,	ij^s
Patrik Flemyng,	ij^s
Lazarus Coquele, .	ij^s
Niniane Bruce, . . .	ij^s
Maister Thomas Marioribankis wif,	ij^s
[29] Item, George Henrisoun, .	ij^s
William Henrisoun,	ij^s
William Adamsoun,	ij^s
Alexander Adamsoun, . .	ij^s
Summa of the grete candilstiks, .	vij^{li}

I am to be chargit with the foure Silver Candilstiks and the Croce :—

In primis, I haif ressavit fra Patrik Guvane, for the foirsaids candilstiks and the silver croce, the sowme of, ... xlviij^s iiij^d

Item, gottin on Sanct Gelis day, and Relict Sunday for Sanct Gelis day, in fre money, ... vij^d

The haill sowme of my charge this instant yeir extends to, . . . ij^{c}iij^{xx}xix^{li} xviij^s iiij^d

[30] Heir followis the DISCHARGE of the Dene of Gildis compt above writtin, the yeir foirsaid, 1554 :—

In primis, I am to be dischargit at the hands of Andro Mansion, wrycht, for the rest of the completing of the sowme of the stallis of the queir, the sowme of, ... viij^{xx} x^{li}

Item, to James Nicoll, for vj dozone and ½ eistland burd, price of the pece vj^s viij^d : summa, ... xxvj^{li}

Item, to Richard Trowp, with the vij serjands, and Thomas Hall, for thair feyis pertenyng to the dene of gild, . . . xxiij^{li}

Item, for ane dosone of knaphald, . . xxvj^s

JOHN SYMSOUN, Dean of Guild. 1553-54.

Item, for the carying of thame fra Leyth, . xij^{d}
For the out taking of all the stallis furthe of the queir, . . . iij^{s}
Item, the expenssis maid of the calffotting of Sanct Johnis ile, Sanct Anthonis ile, with pik, tar, coffing hards, olie, collis, and warkmanschip thairof, ... xxxj^{s} viij^{d}
Item, for xiiij faldome of corde to hing the pan in the meids of the kirk, iiij^{s} iiij^{d}
Item, ane greit loke to the wolt dure of Sanct Thomas ile, . . v^{s} vj^{d}
Item, bocht the xij day of October, foure laids of Cousland lyme, . v^{s} iiij^{d}
Item, vij laids sand, ... xxx^{d}
Item, Johne Broune and his marrowis, sawars, for foure drauclit of geistis, ilk draucht x^{d}, ... xl^{d}
Item, for xxiiij quarter drauchtis of Eistland burds, ilk draucht ij^{d}; summa of the saids drauchtis, ... vij^{s} iiij^{d}
Item, for ane geist, to Johne Westoun, and carying of it, . . xix^{s}
Summa lateris, ... ij^{li} xxiiij^{li} viij^{s} ij^{d}

[31] Heir followis the viij dayis expensis, precedand the xviij day of November, of the raising of the Throuchis and Payment of the Queir, of this instant yeir:—

In primis, Gilbert Cleuth, Nicoll Andersoun, maissonis, ane oulks waigeis, xl^{s}
Item, ane barroman with thame, this oulk, ... viij^{s}
Item, thre uther barromen redand and beirand eird to the queir, waigeis ilk man on the day xvj^{d}; summa, . . . xx^{s}
Item, for ane riddill and ane schoule with ane irne to it, . xxviij^{d}
Item, for candill to the barromen and maissonis this oulk, . xxxviij^{d}
Item, for naillis to the wrichtis, ... xxxij^{d}
Item, to Maister Johne Prestoun for ane hundreith tylde, . . xv^{s}
Item, to young Johne Auchmowtie for twa hundreith and ane half tylde, xxxij^{s} iiij^{d}
Item, for carying of thame fra Leith, ... ij^{s}
Item, to Johne Broun, sawar, and his marrow, sawars, for twa dayis wark, xij^{s}
Item, for drinksilver to the warkmen this oulk, . . iij^{s}
Summa of this oulk, . . vij^{li} x^{d}

[32] Item, this viij dayis expenseis, precedand the xxv day of the said moneith of November:—

JOHN SYMSOUN, Dean of Guild. 1553-54.

Item, for viij laids Cousland lyme,	x^{s}
Item, for twa dosone sand,	viij^{s}
Item, for ane aickin spair,	xxx^{d}
Item, to Gilbert Cleuch and Nicoll Andersoun, maisonis, thre dayis waigeis,	xx^{s}
Item, ane barroman with thame and with the wrichtis this oulk,	viij^{s}
Item, thre uther barromen feit to plane the throuchis and payment of the queir this oulk,	vj^{s} viij^{d}
Item, for candill to the maisonis this oulk,	xiiij^{d}
Item, for xij elnis of new payment to the queir, and carying of thame,	xxxij^{s}
Item, for ane hundreith planscheor naillis and ane hundreith dur naillis,	iiij^{s}
Item, for carying of the greit ledder to the glassin-wricht to the windok of the eist gavill,	viij^{d}
Item, for drinksilver this oulk,	iij^{s}
Summa of this oulk,	iiij^{li} xvj^{s}

Item, this viij dayis precedand the second day of December of this instant yeir:—

Item, to Gilbert Cleuch and Nicoll Andersoun, maisonis, thre dayis waigeis,	xx^{s}
Item, to ane barroman with them thre dayis,	iiij^{s}
Item, for candill to thame,	xiiij^{d}
Item, for sawing of thre quarter drauchtis of eistland burd,	ix^{d}
Item, for ane hundreith planchoure naillis and ane hundreith dur naillis,	iiij^{s}
Summa of this oulk,	xxix^{s} xj^{d}
Summa lateris,	vj^{li} v^{s} xj^{d}

[33] Item, this viij dayis expensis precedand the ix day of December:—

Item, to Johne Banks, smyth, for twa quhit plait lokks, with thair bands, ryngs, roissis, and quhit nellis to the buke almoreis of the queir,	xij^{s}
Item, to him for xij irne boltis to the stallis,	iiij^{s}
Item, for half ane hundreith planscheour naillis,	iiij^{s} viij^{d}
Item, to Johne Ahannay, smyth, for xij irne boltis to the stallis, ij^{c} greit planscheor naillis, with mending of the loke to Sanct Thomas isle,	xiij^{s}
Item, to Nicoll Andersoun, twa dayis waigeis,	v^{s} iiij^{d}
Item, to ane borroman with him twa dayis,	xxxij^{d}
Item, for viij faddome of corde to the ledderis,	ij^{s} iiij^{d}

JOHN SYMSOUN, Dean of Guild 1553-54.

Item, for ane pund of glew, . xviij^{d}

Item, for caring of the greit standart, vj^{d}

Summa of this viij dayis, ... xlvj^{s}

Item, this viij dayis precedand the xvij day of December, as ut supra :—

In primis, to Peter Baxter, sklater, for poynting of the haill kirk with the illis, afoir Youle, ... xxviij^{s}

Item, for foure laids of lyme, viij laids sand, with watter, . . vij^{s} viij^{d}

Item, to Mungo Hunter, smyth, for ane bar loke with thre keyis to the south dure of the queir, and mending of the lok of the organe loft, xij^{s}

Item, to him for xxvj stobbis of irne for the transs of the queir, . . iiij^{s}

Item, for skowring of the braissin wark afoir Youle, and clainging of the gutteris laith about the kirk and redding of the queir, and drinksilver to the glassinwrichtis cheilder, ... v^{s} iiij^{d}

Item, for foure quarter drauchtis of daillis and naillis to the wrichtis, iij^{s}

Summa of this oulk, . lvj^{s}

Summa lateris, ... v^{li} ij^{s}

[34] Item, this viij dayis precedand the xxiiij day of December :—

Item, to Thomas Watsoun, glassinwricht, for ane pannell of ane glassin windoke aboun the queir, contenane of new glass xij futtis and ane half, price of the fute xviij^{d}; and to him for ane pannell of glass to the Haly-blude ile contenand vij fute of new glass, and in Sanct Gabriellis ile ane pannell contenand vj futtis and ane half of new glass, price of ilk fute of new glass xviij^{d}; item for viij futtis of auld glass new set in leid, price of ilk fut setting vj^{d}; summa of all this glass, xliij^{s}

Item, for xviij laids of Cousland lyme, . xix^{s} iiij^{d}

Item, for fyve dosone sand, . xx^{s}

Item, for iiij dosone watter to this lyme, ... xxxij^{d}

Item, to James Reidheid, sawar, and his marro, for xiiij brond draucht of Eistland burd, price of ilk draucht vj^{d}; and to him and his marro for xviij quarter draucht of eistland burds, ilk draucht iij^{d}; and twa draucht of aikin tymmer xij^{d}; summa of this tymmer, . . . xij^{s} vj^{d}

Item, for xv punds of glew, ... xvj^{s} vj^{d}

Item, for mending of the wrichtis watter tube, . vj^{d}

JOHN SYMSOUN, Dean of Guild. 1553-54.

Item, to Andro Mansionis childer at Fantronis even in drinksilver, . vj^s
Item, for thekin of Johne Michellis choip in the kirkyaird, and betting of the samyn, . . . vj^s
Item, for twa Eistland burds, ... xiij^s iiij^d
Item, to Johne Ahannay, smyth, for iij^c small brind naillis, price of ilk hundreith xvj^d; and ane hundreith dur naill, price of the hundreith xvj^d, and twa hundreith of dure naill schank, price of the hundreith xviij^d; and for ane hundreith plauscheor naillis xxx^d; item, for xl greit naillis to the wreichtis and vj greit irne stappillis iiij^s iiij^d; item, for iij dosone of small naillis xxxij^d; summa of the smyth, . xviij^s x^d
Summa lateris, ... vij^{li} xvij^s viij^d

[35] Item, the beitment of the Hospitall of Sanct Mary Wynd, for iij laids lyme, viij laids sand, ane dosone of watter, . . vij^s iiij^d
Item, to ane sklater for his laboris of the saids chaippell, xiij^s
Item, for ane hundreith sklaittis, . . x^s
Summa, . . xxx^s iiij^d

Item, this viij dayis precedand the xiiij day of Marche :—

Item, to Walter Bynnyng, paynter, for paynting of xviij pannallis of the queir, and the twa greit pannallis of the north gavill of the queir, with osure, and furnesing of all uther stufe to thame, . xxviij^s
Item, for mending of the ledder and runging of it, . . xij^d
Item, to thre Preistis for singing of the Passioun on Palme Sonday, . xxx^d
Item, to Thomas Watsoun, glassinwricht, for ane pannell in Our Ladey ile, contenand vj futts of new glass, price of ilk fute xviij^d; ane uther pannell of new glass in Sanct Gabriellis ile, contenand ij futtis, price of the fute xviij^d; and vj futtis of auld glas new sett in leid in the samyn ile, price of ilk fute setting vj^d; item, twa pannellis in Sanct Thomas ile, callit Prestonis ile, with vj futtis and ane half of new glass, price of ilk fut xviij^d; and in that samyn ile viij futtis auld glass new set in leid, price of ilk fut setting vj^d; and drinksilver till his servand for poynting of the glassin windokis on the haill south syde of the kirk afoir Pasche, ij^s; summa of this glass, . . . xxx^s ix^d
Summa lateris, . . iiij^{li} xij^s vij^d

JOHN SYMSOUN, Dean of Guild. 1553-54.

[36] Item, to Johne Broun, sawar, and his marro, for ten braid drauchtis of Eistland burd, price of ilk draucht v^d; and to him for xxxij quarter drauchtis of eistland burd, price of ilk draucht ij^d; summa of the sawars, ix^s vj^d

Item, to Johne Ahannay, smyth, for vj^c dur naillis, price of ilk hundreith xvj^d; summa, ... viij^s

Item, to Patrik Bikkartoun, maisoun, and his servands, for laying of the stane greifs in Sanct Thomas ile, ... vj^s

Item, for beirring of leid in the said ile, and the reding of tymmer furth of the samyn, and clenging of the samyn, . xxx^d

Item, to Patrik Govane and Doctor Smyth at Pasche, . . ij^s

Item, for beiring of xxxj barrois of erd in Prestonis ile, and filling of the hollis of the samyn, ... xx^d

Item, to Thomas Home for dichting of the gutteris at Pasche, ij^s

Item, for vj laids of Cousland lyme and ane dosone sand, . xj^s viij^d

Item, to Peter Baxter, sklater, for poynting of the haill bodey of the queir, quhilk contenis viij ruds of wark, price of ilk rude poynting work ij^s iiij^d; item, Sanct Johnis ile, quhilk contenis ane rude thre elnis, price of the rude poynting wark ij^s iiij^d; item, the bodey of the kirk betwix the stepil and the west gavill thairof, quhilk contenis nyne rude of wark, price of ilk rude poynting ij^s iiij^d; item, in the myde ile betwix Sanct Katharenis and Sanct Stevinis ile, contenis vij rude worke, price of ilk rude poynting ij^s iiij^d; item, Sanct Ninianis to Sanct James ile, quhilk contenis foure rude and twenty aucht elnis, price of ilk rude poynting wark ij^s iiij^d; item, betwix Sanct Thomas ile and Sanct Gabriellis ile, quhilk contenis twa rudis of wark, price of ilk rude poynting wark ij^s iiij^d; item, Prestounis ile, contenis fyve rude of poynting wark, price of ilk rude xxviij^d; summa totalis of poynting wark, . . iiij^li vj^s iiij^d

Summa lateris, ... vj^li ix^s viij^d

[37] Item, the expenssis maid on the Cordineris Choippis in the kirk yaird :–

Item, for viij laids of Cousland lyme, ane dosone sand, and watter furnist to it, xij^s x^d

Item, to Peter Baxter, sklater, for poynting of the haill saids cordineris choippis, ... ix^s

Item, drinksilver to the sklataris childer, ... ij^s

Item, for scowring of the braissin wark of the queir at Pasche, . xij^d

JOHN SYMSOUN, Dean of Guild, 1553-54.

Item, for viij dosone watter furnisit to the sklatars and to the poynting of the haill kirk, price of ilk dosone viij^{d}; summa, . . . v^{s} iiij^{d}

Item, for beirring of foure scoir xij sklaitts fra the porter luge to the choippis of the kirk yaird, ... vj^{d}

Item, to the said Peter Baxter, for the poynting of the haill ilering of the aislars of the haill kirk, ... vj^{s}

Item, to Thomas Home for scowring and wattering of the haill kirk the tyme of the Parliament, ... ij^{s}

Item, to Mungo Hunter for ane quhit bar loke, with ane pair of quhit bands with ane ring and rois to the southmest queir dur, with ane stoke loke to the west queir dur, and sex pinnis of irne, . . xiiij^{s}

Item, for runging of the kirk ledder, ... xxx^{d}

Item, for vij laids of Cousland lyme and xviij laids of sand, with twa dosone watter to the poynting and alaring of the aislars of the kirk, . xj^{s} viij^{d}

Item, for half ane Eistland burd for making of ane lettroun to the queir, iiij^{s} viij^{d}

Item, for beirring of the aislar stanis of the Walkaris alter to the maisoun luge, ... vj^{d}

Item, to Thomas Home for wattering and deichting of the kirk on the Sacrament day, ... ij^{s}

Item, to Walter Bynnyng for paynting of the foure greit armis, with the twa small armis of the queir, with oly coloris and gold, . v^{li}

Summa lateris, . viij^{s} xiiij^{d}

[38] Item, for ane mess buke to the hie alter, ... xxxiij^{s} iiij^{d}

Item, to Johne Rynd for ane tyne stoip for the watter to the mess, . xxiij^{s}

Item, for scouring of the brassin wark on Sanct Geillis day, and wattering and soupping of the kirk, ... iij^{s}

Item, the expenssis maid on the west queir dur, to sawars and pyoneris :—

Item, thre eistland burds xxxj^{s} : iiij irne botts iij^{s}; to Mungo Hunter for thre pair (*blank*) bands of quhit wark with thair nallis xxx^{s}; to ane maisoun vj^{s}; to the wricht for making of the samyn dur xl^{s}; summa of the expenssis of the dur, . . v^{li} vj^{s} vij^{d}

Item, for twa laids of Cousland lyme, ... iij^{s}

Item, to Thomas Watsoun, glassinwricht, for beitment of ane pannell of glass to Sanct Salvatoris ile, quhilk contenis of new glass v fute and ½ ;

JOHN SYMSOUN, Dean of Guild. 1553-54.

price of ilk fute new glass xviij[d], and in the samyn pannell iiij futts auld glass new set in leid, price of ilk fut new set vj[d]; item, to him for ane pannell in the heich windo in the queir in the south side, quhilk contenis vj fute new glass, price of ilk fute xviij[d], and vij fut and ane half auld glass new sett in leid, price of ilk fut of setting vj[d]; summa of the glass, ... xxiij[s] j[d]

Item, to the said Thomas Watsoun for his fie, ... iiij[li]

Item, to Johne Young, candilmakar, for viij stanis of candill to the wark-men of the kirk, ... iiij[li] v[s] iiij[d]

Item, to Alexander Robesoun for mending of the kaippis of the kirk, . v[s]

Item, to Andro Auld, male wricht, quha beand at the begynnyng of the stallis to the ending, ... v[li]

Summa lateris, ... xxiij[li] ij[s] iiij[d]

[39] Item, gevin to Alexander Ahannay for ryngin of the bellis on Salmes evin, ij[s]

Item, to Thomas Home for his yeiris fie, . xl[s]

Item, to Doctor Smyth for his yeiris fie, ... xx[s]

Item, for bussomis to dicht the kirk with at Youle, Candilmess, Pasche, Witsonday, and Sanct Geillis day, with the laif of the Sundayis of symmer, . . v[s] vj[d]

Item, for oley to the knok, . . . viij[s]

Item, for dichting of the gutteris and spowtis above the kirk, . xxx[s]

Item, to George Johnestoun for walx furnissing to the foure grete candil-stiks this yeir, ... xxxj[s]

Item, to Patrick Tod, for his fe for keiping of the croce and silver candil-stiks, ... x[s]

Item, for twa stanis of candill to the pann in the mydds of the kirk, and keiping of it, ... xxv[s] iiij[d]

Item, to Mungo Huntar for ane patill to patil the kirk with, . vj[s]

Item, for the keping of the sepulture at Pasche, viij dayis, day and nycht, viij[s]

Item, for mending of the lok of the revestry dure, . . xvj[d]

Item, for girs, watter, fyre, and ane dow at Witsonday, . . xviij[d]

Item, for keiping of the funt at Witsonday, . . ij[s]

Item, for the paynting of Sanct Geil, . . x[s]

Item, for my fe and my chaplainis fe, x[li] xiij[s] iiij[d]

JOHN SYMSOUN, Dean of Guild. 1553-54.

Summa lateris, ... xx^{li} xiiij^{s}
Summa of my haill discharge of this instant yeir extends to, ... iij^{c} xiiij^{li} viij^{s} ij^{d}
Sua am I superexpendit this instant yeir above my charge, xxxiiij^{li} viij^{s} x^{d}

[40] The ferd day of Januar, the yeir of God J^{m} v^{c} liiij yers, the compt of Johne Symsoun, dene of gild, in the yeir bygane, hard, sene, red, and ryplie avisit on be the auditors of comptis undirwrittin, in presence of the provest and baillies in the tolbuith thairof, the charge thairof beand laid extendit to ij^{c} lxxx^{li} xviij^{s} iij^{d}, and the discharge to iij^{c} xiiij^{li} viij^{s} ij^{d}, and sua finds that the gude towne restis awing to the said Johne, comptar, the sowme of xxxiiij^{li} viij^{s} ix^{d}. In witnes heirof all the saids auditors and jugis hes subscrivit thir presents.

Mr James Lindesay, bailie.	Kynspindye, prowest of Edr.
Edward Hoipe, baillie.	James Barron.
	William Car.

JAMES CARMICHAEL, Dean of Guild. 1554-55.

HEIR followis the ONORATIOUN of the Dene of Gyldis Comptis, that he is to be chargit with in anno 1554, and his entres in (*blank*) Octobris 1554 to October 1555:—

The Pece Silver gottin by procuratioun in the kirk.

[41] In primis, Sonday, the vij day of October, ressavit fra Andro Lumisdane and James Fasyth, ... xxiij^{s} vj^{d}
Item, Sonday, the xiiij of October, ressavit fra Maister Johne Spenss and William Ker, younger, ... xl^{s} ij^{d}
Item, Sonday, the xxj day, ressavit fra Johne Jaksoun and Hary Young, xxiij^{s} j^{d}
Item, the xxviij day, ressavit fra Patrik Durahane and Johne Uchiltre, xviij^{s} vij^{d}

Nouember.

Item, Sonday, the ferd day of Nouember, ressavit fra Johne Smyth and Adame Levingtoun, ... xxj^{s} vj^{d}
Item, the xj day, ressavit fra Rechard Gray and James Rynd, . xxxiij^{s} iij^{d}
Item, the xviij day, ressavit fra Alexander Dira and Alexander Blak, . xvj^{s} viij^{d}
Item, the xxv day, ressavit fra William Lawsoun and Robert Flemyng, xlviij^{s} j½^{d}

December.

Item, Sonday, the secound day, ressavit fra William Patersoun and Alexander Heriot, baxteris, ... xiij^s ij^d

[42] Item, the ix day, ressavit fra Eduard Thomsoun and his marrow, . xx^s iiij^d

Item, the xvj day, fra Johne Wechtoun and Johne Hammiltoun, xxv^s

Item, the xxiij day, ressavit fra Johne Freg, his allane, . . xij^s vj^d

Item, upon Yule day, ressavit fra James Adamsoun and Johne Sym, . vj^li vij^s

Item, on Sonday, the last day, ressavit fra Mungo Hunter and Johne Hopper, . . . xxij^s j$\frac{1}{2}^d$

Januar.

Item, Sonday the vj, ressavit fra Wirgell Calder and Johne Henrisoun, litstar, ... xxj^s

Item, the xiij day, ressavit fra William Newtoun and James Roger, . xx^s v^d

Item, the xx day, ressavit fra Thomas Toddonar and William Aikman, xxxvj^s vij^d

Item, the xxvij day, ressavit fra James Schairp and Patrik Cuke, xxiiij^s v$\frac{1}{2}^d$

Februar.

Item, Sonday, the thrid day, ressavit fra William Bauchop because Johne Cunnynghame was put in waird for wyne the samyn day, . xvij^s ij^d

Item, the x day, ressavit fra Allexander Rynd and Johne Duncane, xxiiij^s j$\frac{1}{2}^d$

Item, the xvij day, ressavit fra Johne Nynmill and Patrik Wilsoun, xxix^s iiij^d

Item, the xxiiij day, ressavit fra Johne Kyle and Patrik Crag, . . xxv^s vj^d

Marche.

[43] Item, Sonday, the thrid day of Marche, ressavit fra Roger Blak and Michaell Rynd, ... xx^s ix$\frac{1}{2}^d$

Item, the x day, ressavit fra Robert Gray and Adam Henslie, . . xxv^s

Item, the xvij day, ressavit fra William Henrisoun, maltman, and his marrow, ... xiiij^s ij$\frac{1}{2}^d$

Item, the xxiiij day, ressavit fra David Lyle and Michaell Gilbert, . xxxj^s ij^d

Item, the last day, ressavit fra Rechard Carmichaell and Maister James Watsoun, ... xl^s viij^d

Aprile: Pasche Day.

Item, the vij day of Aprile, ressavit fra Johne Mosman and James Ewart, xxxiij^s j^d

Item, the xiiij day, ressavit fra Johne Rechardsoun and his marrow, . xvij^s iij^d

JAMES CARMICHAEL, Dean of Guild. 1554-55.

Item, the xxj day, ressavit fra Allexander King and Maister Johne Prestoun, ... iij^{li} ix½^{d}

Item, the xxviij day, ressavit fra Johne Binnyng and his marrow, . xvj^{s} j^{d}

Maij.

Item, Sonday, the fyft of Maij, ressavit fra Johne Cunnynghame and William Redsoun, ... xxj^{s} iij^{d}

Item, the xij of Maij, ressavit fra Thomas Ewin and his marrow, . xxxv^{s} j^{d}

Item, the xix day, ressavit fra Johne Dougill, maltman, and his marrow, xxij^{s} ij½^{d}

Item, the xxvj day, ressavit fra Johne Blackburn and Leonard Robesoun, xxv^{s} iiij^{d}

[44] Junij.

Item, Sonday, the secund day, ressavit fra Alane Dikkesoun and Maister Archibald Grahame, ... iij^{li} ij^{s} iij^{d}

Item, the ix day, ressavit fra Alexander Naper and Adam Alane, . xlv^{s} iiij½^{d}

Item, the xvj day, ressavit fra Johne Harrat and David Towris, . . xxxj^{s} j^{d}

Item, the xxiij day, ressavit fra James Forret and Thomas Reidpeth, xxxiiij^{s} vj^{d}

Item, the last day, ressavit fra Alexander Purves and his marrow, xxvj^{s}

Julij.

Item, Sonday, the vij day, ressavit fra Johne Davidsoun and his marrow, xxij^{s} ix½^{d}

Item, the xiiij day, ressavit fra Alexander Lyell and his marrow, xxv^{s} j^{d}

Item, the xxj day, ressavit fra Johne Alhannay and his marrow, . . xxvj^{s} ½^{d}

Item, the xxviij day, ressavit fra Thomas Crag and Johne Hammiltoun, xvj^{s} vj½^{d}

August.

Item, the feird day, ressavit fra Alexander Scot and William McMoran, xv^{s} ij^{d}

Item, the xj day, ressavit fra Johne Wat and David Michell, litstar, . xxj^{s}

Item, the xviij day, ressavit fra Francis Le and James Bassenden, . xxvj^{s}

Item, the xxv day, ressavit fra Andro Hammiltoun and his marrow, . xxv^{s} ij½^{d}

[45] September.

Item, Sonday, the first day, quhilk wes Sanct Geillis day, ressavit fra William Murcheid and Alexander Barroun, ... iij^{li} vij^{s}

Item, the viij day, ressavit fra William Galbrayth and Alexander Frude, xxv^{s} iij^{d}

Item, the xv day, ressavit fra James Dalzell and his marrow, . xxvij^{s} xj^{d}

Item, the xxij day, ressavit fra Johne Bell and his marrow, . xxj^{s} ij^{d}

JAMES CARMICHAEL, Dean of Guild. 1554-55.

Item, the penult day, ressavit fra Alexander Bannatyne and Alexander Gray, ... xxij^s

Summa of the haill charge of the pece of this instant yeir extends to, . lxxvj^li xvij^s

Item, I am to be chairgit with the nomer of the Schippis of this instant yeir, quhilk extendis, as the buke beiris, to the nomer of foure scoir fyve schippis.

Summa of the money of the haill schippis, extends to, lix^li x^s

Heir efter followis my charge of the Burgessis and Gyldis, bayth togidder becaus thai are in the lokkit buke.

In primis, William Harlaw,	vj^s viij^d
[46] Item, James Cowper,	xxxiij^s iiij^d
Item, Johne Brown,	v^li
Item, Johne Howesoun,	v^li
Item, Alexander Bruce,	v^li
Item, Walter Maxwell,	v^li
Item, Thomas Creichtoun,	v^li
Item, Patrik Cranstoun,	v^li
Item, Robert Gray,	xx^s
Item, Stevin Cousland,	v^li
Item, James Rowat,	vj^s viij^d
Item, Stevin Boyis,	v^li
Item, Johne Boyis,	xiij^s iiij^d
Item, Maister Rechard Hopper,	xx^s
Item, Johne Stute,	v^li
Item, Thomas Mertine,	v^li
Item, Adam Farnle,	v^li
Item, Johne Ostiane,	v^li
Item, Thomas Matho,	v^li
Item, James Hammiltoun,	v^li
Item, Patrik Fischer,	v^li
Item, William Twedy,	v^li
Item, Alexander Gray,	xxxiij^s iiij^d

Item, Alexander Frude,	xxxiij^s iiij^d
Item, Eduard Jhonestoun,	xiij^s iiij^d
Item, Johne Schoirt,	v^{li}
Item, Johne Kennedey,	v^{li}
Item, William Wilsoun,	v^{li}
Item, James Broun,	xxxiij^s iiij^d
Item, William Eistoun,	xiij^s iiij^d
Item, Robert Meill,	v^{li}
Item, David Mure,	v^{li}
Item, Johne Gilry,	vj^s viij^d
Item, Johne Weddell,	vj^s viij^d
Item, Thomas Rorisoun,	v^{li}
Item, William Lange,	v^{li}
[47] Item, Thomas Wycht,	xiij^s iiij^d
Item, Alexander Heleiss,	xiij^s iiij^d
Item, Alexander Moriss,	x^{li}
Item, Adam Dalgleiss,	xiij^s iiij^d
Item, George Rannald,	xiij^s iiij^d
Summa of the burgessis and gyldis bayth togidder extendis to, this instant yeir,	j^c xl^{li} vj^s viij^d

I am to be chargit with the Choippis of the kirk, and at the futc of the kirkyard, of this instant yeir.

Item, Johne Gilbert,	xxx^s
Item, Uxor Rynd,	xxx^s
Item, Andrew Heleiss,	xx^s
Item, George Turnour,	xx^s
Item, Thomas Mercleiss,	xxvj^s viij^d
Item, David Bane,	xxvj^s viij^d
Item, Johne Broderstanis,	xxvj^s viij^d
Item, George Merchell,	xx^s
Item, Johne Forrest,	xx^s
Item, William Forsyth,	xx^s
Item, Marioun Scot,	xx^s
Item, Nicoll Hasty,	xx^s

Item, Alexander Dikkesoun,	xx^{s}
Item, George Rewand, .	xx^{s}
Item, Johne Cunnynghame,	xx^{s}
Item, Margaret Ruthirfurd,	xx^{s}
Item, Alexander Andersoun,	xx^{s}
[48] Item, William Harpfeild, .	xx^{s}
Item, Gorge Cowane,	xx^{s}
Item, Johne Binnyng,	xx^{s}
Item, Johne Neilsoun, .	xx^{s}
Item, Michaell Windiyetts, .	xx^{s}
[Summa of the Choippis, .	xxiiij^{li}]

I am to be chargit with the Lairs of the kirk this instant yeir.

Item, Maister James McGillis barne,	ij^{s}
Item, Elizabeth Brand, .	vj^{s} viij^{d}
Item, Elizabeth Thomsoun,	ij^{s}
Item, James Henrisonis barne,	ij^{s}
Item, Issobell Gourlay,	vj^{s} viij^{d}
Item, Adam Wilsoun,	vj^{s} viij^{d}
Summa, .	xxvj^{s}

I am to be chargit with the foure greit Candilsteiks of this instant yeir.

Item, James Tarbot, .	ix^{s} vj^{d}
Item, Katharene Alane, . .	ix^{s} vj^{d}
Item, Maister Jhone Spenss wyfe,	ix^{s} vj^{d}
Item, Nicoll Carncoriss,	ij^{s}
Item, Gorge Leche, .	ij^{s}
Item, Maister David Scot,	ij^{s}
Item, Dame King, .	ij^{s}
Item, Thomas Ewin,	ij^{s}
Item, Sir Johne Jurdane, .	ij^{s}
Item, James Aikman, .	ix^{s} vj^{d}
Item, Patrik Barronis wyfe,	ix^{s} vj^{d}
Item, Begis Harwy, .	ix^{s} viij^{d}
Item, Johne Fawsyde,	ix^{s} vj^{d}

JAMES CARMICHAEL, Dean of Guild. 1554-55.

Item, Maister Thomas Marrioribankis wyfe,	ij^s
Item, Sir Patrik Creichtoun,	ij^s
Item, Thomas Mudy,	ij^s
[49] Item, Adam Henslie wyfe,	ij^s
Item, Gilbert Lawder,	ij^s
Item, Gorge Henrisoun,	ij^s
Item, William Henrisoun,	ij^s
Item, William Adamsoun,	ij^s
Item, Alexander Adamsoun,	ij^s

I am to be chargit with the Silver Chandilsteiks this instant yeir.

In primis, Jonet Boldane,	viij^d
Item, Dame Margaret Scot,	viij^d
Item, Patrik Flemyng,	viij^d
Item, Alexander Scot,	viij^d
Item, Nicoll Carncorss,	viij^d
Item, William Meldrum,	viij^d
Item, James Barroun,	iiij^d
Item, Margaret Finlasoun,	iiij^d
Item, Gorge Todis wyfe,	viij^d
Item, Johne Bruce,	iiij^d
Item, The fraternite of Sanctt Chowbart,	iiij^d
Item, Gorge Gibsoun,	viij^d
Item, James Aikman,	viij^d
Item, Dame Beg,	viij^d
Item, The fraternite of Sanctt Johne,	iiij^d
Item, Maitho Kenno,	viij^d
Item, Katharene Cunnynghame,	viij^d
Item, Jonet Harrot,	viij^d
Item, George Russall,	viij^d
Item, Patrik Irland,	xij^d
Item, Elizabeth Steill,	viij^d
Item, Margaret Fawsyde,	viij^d
[50] Item, Adam Wilsoun,	viij^d
Item, Sir Thomas Maxwell,	viij^d

JAMES CARMICHAEL, Dean of Guild. 1554-55.

Item, Maister Adam Otterburn, . viij^{d}
Item, Thomas Broun, . . iiij^{d}
Item, Alane Windiyettis, . . . iiij^{d}
Item, The fraternite of Sanctt Crispiniani, iiij^{d}
Item, Adam Strauthauchin, . . iiij^{d}
Item, Johne McDowgall, . viij^{d}
Item, William Forret, . viij^{d}
Item, Alexander Robesonis wyfe, ... iiij^{d}

I am to be chargit with Sanct Geillis arme this instant yeir.
Item, upoun Relict Sonday and Sanct Geillis day, . . vij½^{d}
Summa of the haill charge, . . . iij^{c} vij^{li} xvj^{s} v½^{d}

THE EXONORATIOUN of the Dene of Gyld of this instant yeir, x^{o} Octobris 1554 to the x of October 1555.

In primis, the xj day of October, upon the north syde of the quier, put up ane pannall of new glass, contenand xviij fut, price of the fute xviij^{d}; summa, ... xxvij^{s}
Item, the xij day, to Mungo Hunter, for ane loke and ane pair of bands, and mending of ane uther loke and ane new key to it, to the sang scole dur, xj^{s} vj^{d}
[51] Item, the xxviij day of October, put up upoun the south syde of the queir ane pannell of new glass, contenand xvj fute, price of the fute xviij^{d}; summa, ... xxiiij^{s}
Item, that samyn day, to the dur at the nether end of the queir, ane loke with ane ourelyar and foure keyis till it, and als vj cleiks and ane sloit under the dur; summa of all togidder, . . xviij^{s} iiij^{d}
Item, to ane wrycht for putting on of the said loke, ij^{s}
Item, for clengging of the kirk about at Alhallomess, . . . iij^{s}
Item, for clengging of the Eirle of Irgyllis clois, that my lord of Irgyle mycht haif entres thairto, ... viij^{s}
Item, to Robert Finder, for mending of the greit trene chandelars, x^{s}
Item, for naillis to thame, . . xviij^{d}
Item, for Dochter Smithis Martimes fie, ... x^{s}
Item, to Thomas Home for his Martimes fie for keipping of the kirk, xx^{s}

JAMES CARMICHAEL, Dean of Guild. 1551-55.

Item, to Sir Eduard Henrisoun, as ane act and his discharge beirris, xj^li xxiij^d

Item, to Alexander Stewinsoun, at the command of the counsale, be ane act and his discharge thairupon, ... v^li

Item, to Andro Mansioun for his Martimes pentioun, conforme to his act and his discharge thairupon, ... v markis

Item, for paymenting of the south kirk dur, quhair the bairnis ar babtist, to Gilbert Cleuth and Johne Andersoun, masonis, iij^li vj^s viij^d

Item, for lyme and sand and watter thairto, ... xviij^s vj^d

Item, to ane warkman fyve dayis to serve, upon ilk day xvj^d; summa, vj^s viij^d

Item, to thair servands for drinksilver, ... ij^s

Item, coft and laid in to the luge, to poynt the kirk windois and uther neces-

[52] sars thairto, xviij laid lyme, the dosone cost xvj^s; summa, xxiiij^s

Item, coft iij dosone ½ sand, the dosone v^s; summa, . xvij^s vj^d

Item, for iij dosone watter, ... xxx^d

Item, for reiddeling and drauking of it, to ane warkman, . iiij^s

Item, to Thomas Henslie for ringing of the bellis on Salmes evin, . ij^s

Item, for ane pair of greit bands to the nether dur of the kirkyaird, and naillis to it, ... vj^s viij^d

Item, for mending of ane lok to the west kirk dur, . . . ij^s iiij^d

Item, for the making of ane geirth to the funt, and making of ane prike of irne, with thre flowris to beir the candillis about the funt, . . vij^s vj^d

Item, the xxviij day of November, for ane pannell of new glass in Sanct Thomas ile, contenand xij fute, the price of the fute xviij^d; summa, . xviij^s

Item, the samyn day, in Walter Cheipmannis ile, ane pannell of glass of vj futt of new glass and xij fute of auld glass, sett in new leid, price of the fute of the new glass xviij^d, and the fute of the auld glass vj^d; summa, bayth, xv^s

Item, for clenging of the kirk about, at Yule, and within, . . v^s

Item, coft twa Eistland burds to be crownall and mullars to the nether queir dur, cost, ... xiij^s iiij^d

Item, to Andro Mansioun, for his warkmanschip thairof, . . xxx^s

Item, to Walter Binnyng for the payntting of the mannikin and the beirrar of the townis armes, ... v^s

Item, for hewing of thre thak stanis to the rufe aboun the revestre dur, to Gilbert Cleuth and Johne Andersoun, . xxx^s

JAMES CARMICHAEL, Dean of Guild. 1554-55.

[53] Item, delyverit to Johne Symsoun, auld dene of gyld, the first day of Februar anno [J^m v^c] liiij^to, as ane act proportts maid thairupoun, the sowme of, ... xxxiiij^li viij^s x^d

Item, the xxj day of Februar, put up ane greit windo on the north syde of the croce kirk, aboun the heid of Sanct Johnis ile, contenand of new glass xxxij fute, price of the fute xviij^d; and of auld glass xxj fute, price of the fute vj^d; summa, ... lviij^s vj^d

Item, for thre lokketts and xxj small bands to it, . . . xij^s viij^d

Item, to the pryor of the Blakfreirs for the rest of the compleit payment of the commoun bell, as ane act and his discharge beirris, . . . xx^li

Item, in Walter Cheipmannis ile, ane pannell of new glass, contenand xij fute, price of the fute xviij^d; summa, ... xviij^s

Item, ane uther pannell of auld glass in new leid, contenand xvj fute, at vj^d the fute; summa, ... viij^s

Item, to Mongo Hunter, for mending of the loke to the loft dure in the revestre, ... ij^s

Item, to ane warkman to put away the rede of the kirkyard bray, and making of it levall, ... ij^s

Item, coft ane sand glass to sett besyde the freir in the polpet, cost, . iiij^s

Item, gevin to mend the silver candilsteiks vij grotts, at xviij^d the pece; summa, ... x^s vj^d

Item, gevin to glassinwrycht's servands, in drinksilver, for poynting of the windois, ... v^s

Item, xxj Marche [J^m V^c] liiij^to [1554-55], for mending of the curfor bell, warkmanschip, irnewark, pynoris feis, and utheris expensis, as followis:—

Item, to David Rowane, ... xl^s

Item, Gilbert Bannawis and Clouss, his servandis, ... xviij^s

[54] Item, to Johne Ahannay, for irnewark, viz., scheirs, bands, wageis, keyis, and nallis, ... xiij^s vj^d

Item, to Robert Findar, and ane servand with him, thre dayis and ane half, ... xviij^s viij^d

Item, to xxij warkmen to draw up the bell and down, for thair waigis, . xxij^s

Item, for fecheing of ane bloke furth of the castell, and ane uther furth of the abbay, and haifing hame of thame agane, . . . xvj^d

James Carmichael, Dean of Guild. 1554-55.

Item, in David Rowanis hous and efter the upputting of the bell, Robert Finder, Gilbert Banawis, Clouss, and utheris, thair servandis disjione, vj^{s} viij^{d}

Item, for twa pair of bands to the durs to the heid of the stepill, . vij^{s}

Item, for nallis to lay part of the fluring of the stepill, . . . xxviij^{d}

Item, coft to poynt the haill kirk with, iiij dosone of lyme, price of the dosone xviij^{s}; summa, ... iij^{li} xij^{s}

Item, vj dosone of sand, cost tho dosone v^{s}; summa, xxx^{s}

Item, v dosone of watter, the dosone x^{d}; summa, . . . iiij^{s} ij^{d}

Item, to Peter Baxter, sklater, for poyntting of the haill kirk, contenand xiiij housis; summa, . . . iij^{li}

Item, for drinksilver to his servands, ... iij^{s}

Item, coft to the south kirk dur ane hingand loke and ane cleke of irne, cost, vj^{s} viij^{d}

Item, in the Passioun oulk, at Sanct Nicolus alter, vj pannellis glass, and twa greit heid pannellis in ane lang windo, quhilk wes all brokin, contenand of new glass xxvij fute, ½, the fute at xviij^{d}; summa, . xlj^{s} iij^{d}

Item, xxxij futt of auld glass set in new leid, at vj^{d} the fute; summa, . xvj^{s}

Item, for ix small bands to it, . vj^{s} iij^{d}

Item, for ane loket, ... ij^{s}

[55] Item, the samyn day, in Lawsonis ile, ane pannell of glass contenand vj fute of new glass and vj fute of auld glass; summa, ... xij^{s}

Item, in the Consistorie ile, quhair the thevis com in and brak the kirk, for twa pannell of glass, contenand xvij fute, at xviij^{d} the fute; summa, ... xxv^{s} vj^{d}

Item, for vj small bands to thame, ... iiij^{s}

Item, in Prestonis ile, for ane pannell contenand iij fute and ane half of new glass and iij fute ½ of auld glass; summa, ... vj^{s} xj^{d}

Item, aboun the heid of the queir, ane heid pannell contenand iiij fute ½ of new glass; summa, ... vj^{s} ix^{d}

Item, the xxviij day of Marche, anno [J^{m} v^{c}] lv^{to}, coft vj laids of lyme, cost, vij^{s}

Item, ane dosone of sand, cost, ... v^{s}

Item, ane dosone watter, ... x^{d}

Item, coft ane boist fra James Symnis wyfe to keip the lettres that wes producit befoir the lords, cost, ... xij^{d}

Item, coft, the xxij day of Aprile, fra Maister Johne Prestoun, thesurar, to

be serking to ane new rufe upon the north syde of the kirk, aboun the Consistorie ile, two dosone ½ of dallis, price of the dosone xxxij^{s}; summa, iiij^{li}
Item, for beirring of thame fra the Brigend of Leyth to the Kingis Wark, ... xviij^{d}
Item, for furth beirring and carying of thame, viij^{d}
Item, for cart hyre, . . vj^{s} iij^{d}
Item, for inbeirring in the kirk-yaird, xij^{d}
Item, for ane key to the Revestre dur, . xviij^{d}
[56] Item, for xviij faddome of ane tow to the pann, . . xxviij^{d}
Item, for tauch candill to the pann in the myds of the kirk all the winter, xxxiij^{s}
Item, the xxviij day of Aprile, coft to theik the hous aboun the Consistorie ile ij^{m} sklait, cost the j^{m}, xj crownis; summa, . xj^{li}
Item, for lossing of thame and walking ij nychts, . vj^{s}
Item, for carying of thame furth of Leyth to the kirkyaird, xxiiij^{s}
Item, for inlaying of thame in the luge, . . ij^{s}
Item, for ane key to the box of the commoun seill, . . . ij^{s}
Item, the xij day of Aprile, anno ut supra, iij pannellis of glass in Prestonis ile, contenand of new glass xj fute and ½, and of auld glass v fute ½; summa, ... xix^{s}
Item, borrowit twa lang leddars, ane of the College and ane uther of the Abbay, to twa warkmen that awatit about the lifting of thame the tyme of the wourking of the windois, . vj^{s}
Item, to the Doctor for his Wotsonday fie, . . . x^{s}
Item, to Thomas Home for his Wotsonday fie for keipping of the kirk, . xx^{s}
Item, to the sawars for sawing of xxx daillis, the dosone at x^{s}; summa, . xxv^{s}
Item, for clenging of the kirk without and in, and skowering of the freir and letteroun, ... v^{s}
Item, the vj day of Julij, coft fra Sir William M'Dowgall, to be pairte of the rufe in the Consistorie ile, x geistis, price of the pece x^{s}; summa, . v^{li}
Item, for cart hyre and pynor fe in Leyth, . vj^{s}
Item, for laying in of thame in the kirkyaird, ... xij^{d}
Item, for the raissing of ane syre in the Cowgait aboun the soutaris choppis, and for thre flaggis stanis, laying and calsaying efter the flagis, and clenging of the syars, all togidder, ... x^{s} viij^{d} [57]

JAMES CARMICHAEL, Dean of Guild. 1554-55.

Item, for clenging of the styllis at the eist end and west end of the kirk-yaird under the irne flailks, ...	x^{s}
Item, coft fra ane Duscheman xij greit geistis to be ane pairte of the rufe of the Consistorie ile, price of the pece xij^{s}; summa, .	vij^{li} iiij^{s}
Item, for pynor fie in Leyth,	ij^{s}
Item, for cart hyre, ...	x^{s}
Item, for beirring of thame to the kirkyaird fra the croce, .	ij^{s}
Item, for ij^{c} greit garroun naillis dowbill, cost the hundreth x^{s}; summa,	xx^{s}
Item, for iij^{c} ½ planscheor naillis, cost the j^{c}, xxx^{d}; summa, .	viij^{s} ix^{d}
Item, coft v^{c} dur naillis, price of the j^{c}, xvj^{d}; summa, . . .	vj^{s} viij^{d}
Item, for thre warkmen to beir the rufe, and to draw it up in the kirk rigging, thre dayis, ilk day iiij^{s}; summa, ...	xij^{s}
Item, to Robert Findar and twa servands with him, viij dayis, for thair laubors, . .	l^{s}
Item, for drinksilver to thame, ...	iij^{s}
Item, to ane masoun for fitting of the rufe to the kippillis, iiij dayis,	xij^{s}
Item, coft fra Maister Johne Prestoun ane tre to compleit the wark, .	xj^{s} vij^{d}
Item, the xxj day of Julij, ij dosone lyme, cost the dosone xvj^{s}; summa,	xxxij^{s}
Item, coft iiij dosone sand, the dosone v^{s}; summa, .	xx^{s}
Item, for watter to it, ...	xxx^{d}
Item, coft ane hundreth and ½ plancheor nallis, cost the j^{c}, xxx^{d}; summa,	iij^{c} ix^{d}
Item, ij^{c} ½ dur naillis, the j^{c}, xvj^{d}; summa, ...	iij^{s} iiij^{d}
[58] Item, gevin to the sklater, Peter Baxter, for his warkmanschip, contenand ane rude iij quarteris and ½, the rude xl^{s}; summa, .	iij^{li} xv^{s}
Item, for the clenging of the waist behind Sanct Johnis ile, . .	ij^{s}
Item, for the clenging of the kirk about quhen my Lord Sanct Androis wesyit, ...	v^{s}
Item, coft to mend the best goldin caip, ane greit hank of gold, cost,	xxviij^{s}
Item, for ane unce of yallow silk, .	vj^{s} viij^{d}
Item, for ane fyne breist to it, ...	vj^{s}
Item, to the broudstar for his laubors in mending of the faltis of the said best caip, ...	xxxvj^{s}
Item, to lyne it with, x quarteris of blak serge, the eln x^{s}; summa,	xxv^{s}
Item, to Alexander Robesoun, tailyeor, for lynnyng of it,	viij^{s}

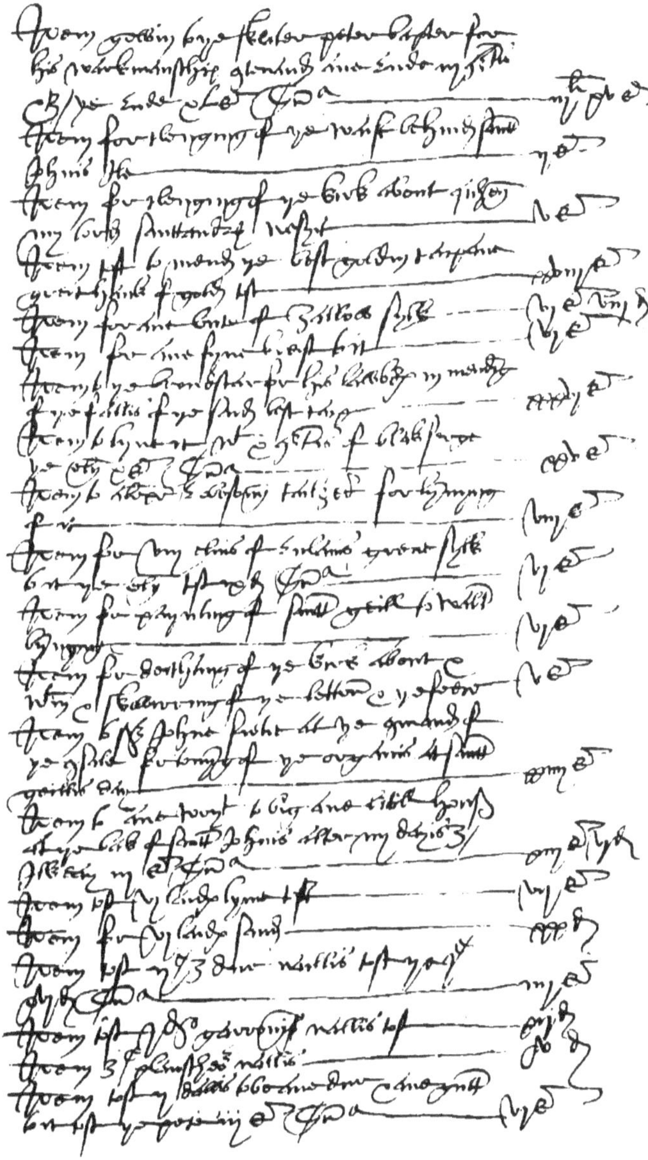

EDINBURGH ACCOUNTS :—Page 58 of old Accounts of Deans of Guild.

Item, for viij elnis of rubanis grene sylk to it, the eln cost ix^{d}; summa, . vj^{s}

Item, for paynting of Sanct Geill, to Walter Bynning, . . vj^{s}

Item, for deichting of the kirk, about and withlin, and skowerring of the lettron and the freir, ... v^{s}

Item, to Sir Johne Fietie, at the command of the counsale, for tonying of the organis at Sanct Geillis day, ... $xxiiij^{s}$

Item, to ane wrycht to big ane litill hous at the back of Sanct Johnis alter, iiij dayis ½, ilk day iij^{s}; summa, . $xiij^{s}$ vj^{d}

Item, coft vj laids lyme, cost, vij^{s}

Item, for vj laids sand, . . . xxx^{d}

Item, coft ij^{c}½ dur naillis, cost the j^{c}, xvj^{d}; summa, $iiij^{s}$

Item, coft j dosone garroun nallis, cost, . xij^{d}

Item, ½^{c} planscheor nallis, ... xv^{d}

Item, coft ij dallis to be ane dur and ane gutter to it, cost the pece iij^{s}; summa, ... vj^{s}

[59] Item, for ane loke and ane pair of bands to it, . . xj^{s}

Item, for bussumis to deycht the kirk with, the haill yeir, . vj^{s} $viij^{d}$

Item, to ane masoun thre dayis and ane half to big up Sanct Johnis windois, and the dur cheiks of it, ilk day iij^{s}; summa, x^{s} vj^{d}

Item, coft laith to theik it with, cost, . . $viij^{s}$ vj^{d}

Item, to ane sklater to theik it, ... $xiiij^{s}$

Item, to mak twa mortcaippis, xj elnis ½ Lyllis worsat, the eln $xiij^{s}$ $iiij^{d}$; summa, ... vij^{li} $xiij^{s}$ $iiij^{d}$

Item, to be orphenis to thame and huds, x quarteris blak welvet, the eln iij^{li} xij^{s}; summa, ... ix^{li}

Item, for x elnis bukrem to lyne thame with, the eln $iiij^{s}$; summa, . xl^{s}

Item, coft xiiij elnis greit sylk rubanis, the eln ix^{d}; summa, . . ix^{s} ix^{d}

Item, coft ij unce ½ blak sylk to be freinzeis to thame, cost the unce vij^{s}; summa, ... $xvij^{s}$ vj^{d}

Item, for weving of the frenzeis, ... iij^{s}

Item, for half ane quarter quhit sating to be the mort heids, $iiij^{s}$

Item, to the broudstar for wourking of the mort heids, . . . vj^{s}

Item, to Alexander Robesoun for his laubors of the saids twa caippis, and finding of silk to sew thame with, ... $xiij^{s}$ vj^{d}

JAMES CARMICHAEL, Dean of Guild, 1554-55.

Item, to the childer in drinksilver, ... xviij[d]

Item, gevin to Alexander Robesoun for mending of the kirk geir ane yeir, that is to say, frontellis, tynnakellis, caippis, westments, be secht of Patrik Tod, for his contentatioun thairof, ... xij[s]

Item, to Andro Mantioun, for his Witsondayis pentioun, as his discharge beirris thairupon, in anno [J[m] V[c]] l quinto [1555], . . . v[markis]

Item, ressavit fra Maister Johne Prestoun, thesurar, ane litill dur of the nether thevis hoill, contenit in wecht, weyit in Johne Ahannayis, vij stane xj punds.

[60] Item, mair to be the charterhous, ane dur, to compleit the samyn, of irne, xviij stane ½, the stane at viij[s]; summa, ... vij[li] viij[s]

Item, to John Ahannay, for his warkmanschip of the said dur, . iij[li] xv[s]

Item, for drinksilevr to the childer, ... xviij[d]

Item, to Thomas Pettigru for twa loks and twa keyis with thair putstoppis, iiij[li]

Item, for drinksilver to his servands that makis thame, . . . iij[s]

Item, for pynor fie of the said dur to the said loksmyth, and beirring to the kirk, and heissing up of it to the charterhous in towis, . . xxx[d]

Item, for ane tre to be cheikis, lintell, and soill to the inner dur of the charterhous, ... x[s]

Item, to Robert Finder, for making and hinging of the said dur of the charterhous, ... viij[s]

Item, for ane pair of greit bands, and iiij irne botts and naillis to the samyn, xv[s] vj[d]

Item, to ane masoun for wourking of the bott hollis, ... iiij[s]

Item, for vij punds leid to yett the saids botts, the pund vij[d]; summa, . iiij[s] j[d]

Item, coft foure stanis in Cragmillar to be the irne dur cheikis, cost, . iij[s]

Item, for cart hyre of thame, ... x[s]

Item, for pyner fie to thre warkmen to beir thame to the charterhous dur, iiij[s] vj[d]

Item, to Gilbert Cleuth for his warkmanschip of the said stane wark, and hinging of the said dur, ... xxxv[s]

Item, in drinksilver to his servands, ... ij[s]

Item, coft fra Johne Weir, powderar, to yet the gret botts xvij[li] leid, the pund vij[d]; summa, ... ix[s] xj[d]

Item, to the warkmen to serve Gilbert Cleuth, and the uther masonis, iij days, ilk day xvj[d]; summa, . . . iiij[s]

JAMES CARMICHAEL, Dean of Guild, 1554-55.

[61] Item, for watter to drauke the lyme, ... xij^{d}
Item, for mending of the thre choippis at the west end of the fute of the kirkyaird, for stray, . . xvj^{s} iiij^{d}
Item, for scheratts and devatts, . . . ix^{s}
Item, to ane wrycht to wirk the rufe spair thairof, vij^{s} vj^{d}
Item, to ane thekar to theik the thre choippis, . xij^{s}
Item, for garroun naillis and plancheor nallis, v^{s} iiij^{d}
Item, for oley to the knok all yeir, . . . xiij^{s}
Item, for keipping of the silver candilstikks, to Patrik Tod, . x^{s}
Item, to Gorge Johnestoun, all the yeir, for walks to the greit candilsteikis, xxxiiij^{s}
Item, to Patrik Gowan, for deichting of the guttars aboun the kirk all the yeir, for his fie, ... xxx^{s}
Item, for my awin fie, and my chaiplannis, . x^{li} xiij^{s} iiij^{d}
Item, to Rechard Trowp, at the command of the counsale, v^{li}
Item, to James Henrisoun, xl^{s}
Item, to Rechard Plummer, xl^{s}
Item, to David Windiyetts, xl^{s}
Item, to Patrik Weychtman, xxx^{s}
Item, to Alane Purves, . xl^{s}
Item, to James Andersoun, xl^{s}
Item, to William Cowtts, xl^{s}
Item, to Thomas Todrik, . xl^{s}
Item, to Johne Wauchlat, xl^{s}
Item, to Maister Alexander Logy, xl^{s}
Item, to Gorge Gourlay, . xl^{s}
Item, to William Nicoll, . xl^{s}
Item, to Gorge Cranstoun, xl^{s}
Item, to Thomas Hall, ... xl^{s}
Item, to Patrik Govan, for walx to the powpet all the yeir, xxviij^{s} viij^{d}
[62] Item, to Thomas Watsoun, glassinwrycht, for his yeirlie fie, . . iiij^{li}
Summa of the haill discharge, . . ij^{c}lxxxvj^{li} xv^{s} v^{d}

At Edinburgh, the vj day of Marche, the yeir of God, J^{m} v^{c} lv yeirs. The auditors of comptis under writtin, conveinit in the Tolbuith of Edinburgh, for heirring

JAMES CARMICHAEL, Dean of Guild. 1554-55.

of the compt foirsaid of James Carmichaell, dene of gyld in the yeir bygane, findis be the compt foirsaid, the charge thairof extends to iij^{c}vij^{li} xvj^{s} v½^{d}, and the discharge to ij^{c} lxxxvj^{li} xv^{s} v^{d}; and sua the compter restis awand to the town, xxj^{li} xij^{d} obolus [halfpenny], de claro.

[The report is not subscribed by the auditors. There is on the margin the following note by Mr Alexander Guthrie, town-clerk :—]

The comptar hes chargit him heirwith in his next compt, maid in anno lvj^{to}.

GUTHRE.

JAMES BARROUN, Dean of Guild. 1555-56.

[63]

THE COMPT of JAMES BARROUN, Dene of Gild in the Towne of Edinburgh, in the yeir of God ane thowsand fyve hundreth fyftie and sex yeirs, randart to the auditors undirwrittin, the xxiiij day of Februar, the yeir of God J^{m} v^{c} lvij yeirs, in the tolbuyth of the samin.

Auditores.

Maister Jhone Spens, presedent.

Maister Jhone Spens, baillie.	Jhone Dowgall.
David Forrestar.	Adam Fullertoun.
Edward Howpe.	Robert Henrysoun.
James Curle.	Thomas Reidpeth.

CHARGE.

Item, in primis, I am to be chargit with Sanct Gelis peice, on Sunday, the vj day of October, rassavit fra Robert Cuninghame and his marro,	xxxiij^{s} vj^{d}
Item, on Sunday, the xiij day of October, ressavit fra Edward Howpe and his marro,	xxxiij^{s} ix^{d}
Item, on Sunday, the twentie day of October, ressavit fra James Cranstoun and his marro,	xij^{s} iiij^{d}
Item, on Sunday the xxvij day of October, ressavit fra Johne Hammiltoun and his marro,	xxj^{s} ij½^{d}
Item, on Sunday, the xxiiij day, ressavit fra James Nicholl and his marro,	xxiiij^{s} iij^{d}

JAMES BARROUN, Dean of Guild. 1555-56.

Nouember.

Item, on Sunday, the thrid day, ressavit fra Johne Freir and his marro, xxiij^{s} ix$\frac{1}{2}^{d}$

Item, fra Edwart Litill and his marro, on the x day, . . . xxix^{s} x^{d}

Item, on Sunday, the xvij day, ressavit fra Johne Blakburne and his marro, ... xxj^{s} ij$\frac{1}{2}^{d}$

Item, on Sunday, the xxiiij day, ressavit fra James Nicholl and his marro, ... xxiiij^{s} iij^{d}

[64] December.

Item, on Sunday, the first day of December, ressavit fra William Andersoun and his marro, ... xxiij^{s} xj^{d}

Item, on Sunday, the viij day, ressavit fra Andro Stewinsoun and his marro, ... xvij^{s} viij^{d}

Item, on Sunday, the xv day, ressavit fra Alexander Kay and his marro, xxxviij^{s} viij^{d}

Item, on Sunday, the xxij day, ressavit fra Thomas Crychtoun and his marro, ... xxiij^{s} iiij$\frac{1}{2}^{d}$

Item, upone Yuill day, ressavit fra Alexander Park and his marro, iij^{li} vj^{s} iij^{d}

Item, on Sunday, the xxix day of December, ressavit fra Johne Moresoun and his marro, . xij^{s} v$\frac{1}{2}^{d}$

Januare.

Item, on Sunday, the first day, ressavit fra Alexander Masoun and his marro, ... xviij^{s} x^{d}

Item, on Sunday, the xij day, ressavit fra Maister Richard Strang and his marro, ... xxx^{s} vij^{d}

Item, on Sunday, the xix day, ressavit fra Archibald Grahame and his marro, ... xxix^{s} iij^{d}

Item, on Sunday, the xxvj day, ressavit fra Nicholl Rynd and his marro, xxiiij^{s} vj^{d}

Februare.

Item, on Sunday, the secund day, ressavit fra William Patersoun and his marro, ... xxxiiij^{s} j^{d}

Item, on Sunday, the ix day, ressavit fra Andro Henresoun and his marro, xvj^{s} vj^{d}

Item, on Sunday, the xvj day, ressavit fra Luik Wilsoun and his marro, . lv^{s} x^{d}

Item, ressavit fra William Holory and his marro, on the xxiij day, xxiij^{s} iiij^{d}

JAMES BARROUN, Dean of Guild. 1555-56.

Mairche.

Item, on Sunday, the first day, ressavit fra Jhone Gilbert and his marro, xxij^s ij^d

Item, on Sunday, the viij day, ressavit fra Alexander Bruiss and his marro, xxvj^s ix^d

[65] Item, on Sunday, the xv day, ressavit fra Adam Scott and his marro, xxiiij^s vj½^d

Item, on Sunday, the xxij day of Mairche, ressavit fra Alexander Sauchye and his marro, ... xxvij^s vij^d

Item, on Sunday, the xxix day, ressavit fra Jhone Wauch and his marro, xj^s viij^d

Apryle: Paische day.

Item, on Sunday, the first [fift] day, ressavit fra Alexander Park and his marro, ... iij^li vij^s iij^d

Item, on Sunday, the xij day, ressavit fra Cristell Eistoun and his marro, xxx^s ix^d

Item, on Sunday, the xix day, ressavit fra Jhone Inglische and his marro, xxv^s ix^d

Item, on Sunday, the xxvij day, ressavit fra Jhone Mair and his marro, . xxxij^s x^d

Maij.

Item, on Sunday, the thrid day, ressavit fra Thomas Thomsoun and his marro, ... xxxiij^s v^d

Item, on Sunday, the x day, ressavit fra William Aikin and his marro, xxvj^s iiij^d

Item, on Sunday, the xvij day, ressavit fra Alexander Russall and his marro, ... xxvij^s vj^d

Item, on Sunday, the xxiiij day, ressavit fra David Somer and his marro, xlj^s ij^d

Item, on Sunday, the last day, ressavit fra James Orwell and his marro, xvij^s v½^d

Junij.

Item, on Sunday, the vij day, ressavit fra William Houldane and his marro, ... xxiiij^s ix^d

[66] Item, on Sunday, the xiiij day, ressavit fra James Young and his marro, xiiij^s ½^d

Item, on Sunday, the xxj day, ressavit fra Jhone Charterhous and his marro, ... xxv^s ij^d

Item, on Sunday, the xxviij day, ressavit fra William Young and his marro, iiij^s vj½^d

July.

Item, on Sunday, the v day, ressavit fra William Ka and his marro, . xix^s j^d

Item, on Sunday, the xij day, ressavit fra Thome Scott and his marro, . xvj^s ix^d

JAMES BARROUN, Dean of Guild. 1555-56.

Item, on Sunday, the xix day, ressavit fra Jhone Watsoun and his marro, xx^{s} vij^{d}

Item, on Sunday, the xxvj day, ressavit fra Maister Robert Glene and his marro, . . . xx^{s}

August.

Item, on secund day, ressavit fra James Alexander and his marro, . xv^{s} viij^{d}

Item, on Sunday, the ix day, rassavit fra Andro Bartane and his marro, xxij^{s} viij^{d}

Item, on Sunday, the xvj day, ressavit fra James Gipsoun and his marro, xiiij^{s} vij$\frac{1}{2}^{d}$

Item, on Sunday, the xxiij day, rassavit fra Jhone Gray and his marro, . vj^{s} x$\frac{1}{2}^{d}$

Item, on Sunday, the penult day, rassavit fra Franciss Huntar and his marro, xv^{s}

September.

Item, the first day, quhilk was Sanct Gelis day, rassavit fra Thomas Uddart and his marro, ... xlij^{s}

[67] Item, on Sunday, the vj day of September, rassavit fra Walter Wycht and his marro, ... xx^{s} xj$\frac{1}{2}^{d}$

Item, on Sunday, the xiij day, rassavit fra Thomas Jaksoun and his marro, xxj^{s}

Item, on Sunday, the xx day, rassavit fra George Toddrik and his marro, xv^{s}

Item, on Sunday, the xxvij day, rassavit fra Jhone Stewart and his marro, xj^{s} ij^{d}

Item, on Sunday, the ferd day of October, rassavit fra James Rynd and his marro, . xij^{s} xj^{d}

Summa perticule, ... iij^{li} j^{d}

Summa of the haill charge of the peice, of this instant yeir, is . . . . lxix^{li} ij^{s} xj$\frac{1}{2}^{d}$

Item, I am to be chargit with the nomer of the Schippis, this instant yeir, quhilk extends, as the buik beris, to the nomer of the lxxvj schippis :—

Summa of the money of the haill schippis extendis to . liij^{li} iiij^{s}

Heir eftir followis James Barronis charge of Burgessis and Gild, contenit in the lokit buik :—

Item, in primis, Jhone Spoittiswod, xx^{s}

Robert Clerksoun, . v^{li}

Jhone Dolory, . v^{li}

Alexander Howstoun, v^{li}

Jhone Robesoun, . . v^{li}

James Barroun, Dean of Guild, 1555-56.

[68]

William Jowsse, .	xxxiij^{s} iiij^{d}
Jhone Auchmuithe,	xxxiij^{s} iiij^{d}
Robert Watsoun, .	xx^{s}
Jhone Prestoun, .	v^{li}
James Sommervell,	. xiij^{s} iiij^{d}
William Birny,	xv^{li}
Cudbart Murray, .	. xiij^{s} iiij^{d}
William Lawsoun,	v^{li}
William Adamsoun.	vj^{s} viij^{d}
Walter Coventre, .	. xiij^{s} iiij^{d}
Luik Wilsoun,	. xx^{s}
Hugo Browne, .	xxxiij^{s} iiij^{d}
Ritcheart Thomsoun,	x^{li} xiij^{s} iiij^{d}
William Scott, .	xxxiij^{s} iiij^{d}
William Stewinsoun,	v^{li}
Jhone Haldane,	. xiij^{s} iiij^{d}
William Moir,	. x^{li}
James Bard, . . .	xv^{li}
William Gawstoun, . .	. xiij^{s} iiij^{d}
George Stevand, . . .	xxxiij^{s} iiij^{d}
Hector Blacatar, ...	xxxiij^{s} iiij^{d}

Summa of the burgessis and gild, baith togidder, extendis to, this instant yeir, . . . j^{c} ij^{li} vj^{s} viij^{d}

Item, I am to be chargit with the Choppis of the kirk, and at the fute of the kirk yaird, of this yeir:—

Item, Jhone Gilbert,	xxx^{s}
Item, Uxor Rynd,	xxx^{s}
Item, Andro Eleis,	. xl^{s}
Item, George Turnour,	. xl^{s}
Item, Thomas Mereleiss,	xxvj^{s} viij^{d}
Item, David Bane, .	xxvj^{s} viij^{d}
Item, Jhone Broderstains,	xxvj^{s} viij^{d}
Item, George Merchell, .	. xx^{s}

JAMES BARROUN, Dean of Guild, 1555-56.

Jhone Forrest,	xx^{s}
Item, William Forsyth,	xx^{s}
Item, Marrioun Scott,	xx^{s}
Item, Nicholl Heistye,	xx^{s}
Item, Jhone Reid,	xx^{s}
[69] Item, Uxor Elwand,	xx^{s}
Item, Jhone Cunninghame,	xx^{s}
Item, Margaret Ruderfuird,	xx^{s}
Item, Alexander Andersoun,	xx^{s}
Item, William Harperfeild,	xx^{s}
Item, George Cowane,	xx^{s}
Item, Jhone Bynning,	xx^{s}
Item, Johne Neilsoun,	xx^{s}
Item, Michaell Windiyeitis,	xx^{s}
Summa of the choppis,	xxvj^{li}

Item, I am to be chargit with the Layeris of this instant yeir :—

Item, in primis, Besse Hume,	vj^{s} viij^{d}
Item, William Wach,	vj^{s} viij^{d}
Item, Besse Kar,	vj^{s} viij^{d}
Item, Jonet Quhippo,	vj^{s} viij^{d}
Item, Marioun Watsoun,	vj^{s} viij^{d}
Item, Jhone Sydsarff,	vj^{s} viij^{d}
Item, Marioun Nicholsoun,	vj^{s} viij^{d}
Item, Walter Trumbill,	vj^{s} viij^{d}
Item, David Ritchartsonis bairne,	ij^{s}
Item, Maister Jhone Robertsonis bairne,	ij^{s}
Item, Jhone Hammiltonis bairne,	ij^{s}
Summa,	lix^{s} iij^{d}

I am to be chargit with the four greit Goldin Canduilsteikis of this instant yeir :—

Item, Willam Forret,	ix^{s} vj^{d}
Item, Patrik Tennand,	ix^{s} vj^{d}
Item, Alexander Sydsarff,	ix^{s} vj^{d}

JAMES BARROUN, Dean of Guild. 1555-56.

Item, Patrik Barroun, ix^{s} vj^{d}
Item, Katheron Ephinstoun, ix^{s} vj^{d}
Item, Robert Graham, ix^{s} vj^{d}
[70] Item, Maister Andro Hay, ix^{s} vj^{d}
Item, Dame Effame Mowbray, ix^{s} vj^{d}
Item, William Gray, . ix^{s} vj^{d}
Item, Marioun Hammiltoun, ix^{s} vj^{d}
Item, Nicholl Carincorss, . ij^{s}
Item, Andro Uddart, . ij^{s}
Item, Petir Thomsonis wyff, ij^{s}
Item, Patrik Fleming, ij^{s}
Item, Alexander Scott, ij^{s}
Item, Alesoun Bannenden, ij^{s}
Item, Jhone Sydsarff, ij^{s}
Item, James Aikman, ij^{s}
Item, Sir Patrik Crychtoun, ij^{s}
Item, Gilbert Lawder, ij^{s}
Item, George Hendersoun, ij^{s}
Item, William Hendersoun, . ij^{s}
Item, Alexander Adamsoun, . ij^{s}
Summa, . . . vj^{li} xij^{d}

Item, I am to be chargit with the Silver Candelsteikis this instant yeir:—

Item, in primis, Sir Robert Hoppar, viij^{d}
Item, William Forrat, . . . viij^{d}
Item, the fraternite of Sanct Crispiniani, . iiij^{d}
Item, Maister Jhone Chepman, . iiij^{d}
Item, Maister Lawrenis Talzefeir, . . iiij^{d}
Item, William Fowllar and Maister William Foullar, viij^{d}
Jhone Perdowane, . viij^{d}
Item, Maister Henry Quhit, iiij^{d}
Item, Dame Mauchquhen, viij^{d}
Item, the fraternite of Sanct Loye, iiij^{d}
[71] Item, Nicholl Carncors, . viij^{d}

JAMES BARROUN, Dean of Guild. 1555-56.

Item, Andro Uddart,	viij^{d}
Item, the fraternite of Sanct Jhone,	iiij^{d}
Item, Maister Jhone Murray,	viij^{d}
Item, Petar Thomsonis wiff,	viij^{d}
Item, James Barroun,	iiij^{d}
Item, George Gipsoun,	viij^{d}
Item, Patrik Tennend,	xvj^{d}
Item, George Brounn,	iiij^{d}
Item, Patrik Barroun,	xvj^{d}
Item, the fraternite of Sanct Cowbart,	iiij^{d}
Item, William Rynd,	vj^{d}
Item, Patrik Fleming,	viij^{d}
Item, Jhone Bruss,	viij^{d}
Item, William Jowssy,	viij^{d}
Jhone Misy,	viij^{d}
Item, Katharene Elphinstoun,	viij^{d}
Item, Alisoun Bannetyne,	xvj^{d}
Item, Marioun Finlasoun,	iiij^{d}
Item, Maister Henry Quhit,	iiij^{d}
Jhone Sydsarff,	viij^{d}
Item, Jhone Aikman,	viij^{d}
Item, Robert Grahame,	xvj^{d}
Item, Sir Patrik Crychtoun,	viij^{d}
Item, Jhone Adamsoun,	viij^{d}
Item, George Scott,	viij^{d}
Item, Maister Andro Hay,	xvj^{d}
Maister Adame Otterburne,	viij^{d}
Item, Dame Effame Mowbray,	xvj^{d}
Item, the fraternite of Sanct Anna,	iiij^{d}
Item, the fraternite of Sanct Cristell,	iiij^{d}
Item, Gilbert Lawder,	viij^{d}
Item, Patrik Ritchartsoun,	iiij^{d}
Item, William Dik,	viij^{d}
[72] Item, William Gray,	viij^{d}

JAMES BARROUN, Dean of Guild. 1555-56.

Item, Thomas Broun, . iiij^d
Item, Thomas Windezeittis, iiij^d
Item, Sir Jhone Sinclar, . xvj^d
Item, George Hendersoun, viij^d
Item, William Hendersoun, viij^d
Item, Alexander Adamsoun, . . viij^d
Item, Edward Strachaune and Walter Blaklok, . viij^d
Summa, . . xxxiij^s vj^d

The charge of Sanct Gelis arme this yeir :—

Item, upone Relict Sonday and Sanct Gelis day, . ij^s

Unlawis :—

Item, fra Jhone Mosye, for bying of malt in the mercat, . . xl^s
Item, James Cranstoun, for breikin of the act maid for nychtborheid, xx^s
Summa, . . . iij^{li}
Summa totalis is . ij^c lxiiij^{li} ix^s v$\frac{1}{2}$^{d}

DISCHARGE.

THE EXONERATIOUN of the Dene of Gild, of this instant yeir, vj^o Octobris, anno 1555, to the fourt day of October, anno 1556 :—

Item, in primis, on the xij day of October to ane warkman, and for hadder to burne Inglische buiks on the mercat croce, . . xviij^d
Item, to Henslie, for ryngíng of the bellis on Salmes evin, . . ij^s
Item, to ane maisoun to hew the blew sliddry throuch at Sanct Salvator dure, ... ij^s
[73] Item, for ane daill and ane half to the stepill dure, vj^s
Item, for maikne of ane dur to the steippill, iij^s
Item, for bands, nalis, loks, and twa keyis to it, . . . xij^s viij^d
Item, for translaittiug of the lok of the nether dur of the stepill, ij^s
Item, for ane lok stapill, and redding of the nether kirk yaird yeitt, viij^s
Item, to warkmen to clenge round about the kirk agane Yuill, . vj^s x^d
Item, to Peit, belman, and the Doctor, . . (*blank*)
Item, for skowring of the brass laterne agane Yuill, . . . xij^d
Item, coft vj jestis to be ane tirleis to the deid banis at the south kirk dur, and to mend the maissoun luge that was decayit, . . iiij^{li} xvj^s

JAMES BARROUN, Dean of Guild. 1555-56.

Item, to iiij workmen to bring thame to the kirk dur, iij^{s}
Item, for vj dalis, to be sarkin to the massoun luge, xxiiij^{s}
For the peice warning, to Pait and the Doctor, . ij^{s}
Item, for sawing of iiij of thame, to be sarkine, ... iij^{s} iiij^{d}
Item, for sawing of iiij jestis, to be the tirleis, and to mend the massoun luge, ... iiij^{s}
Item, to Hennislie to cast the deid banis in the west teirleis, iij^{s}
Item, for iij^{c} sclait to mend the massoun luge, xxxvj^{s}
Item, for carrage of thame to the luge, . . . vj^{s}
Item, for making of the holls in the kirk wall to the terleis, iij^{s}
Item, for leid to yeit it, ... ij^{s}
Item, to ane wrycht for making of the teirleis, and mending of the massoun luge, ij oulkis, ... xxxvj^{s}
Item, for garroun nalis, plantior nalis and dur nalis to the sarkin, and ane bot irne to the terleis, ... xiiij^{s}
Item, to Thomas Barnat, sklater, for tyrring and theikin of the masoun luge, l^{s}
Item, for vj leid lyme and xxiiij leid sand to it, . xviij^{s}
Item, for watter to it, ... xij^{d}
Item, for ane chyst of Eistland buird to the Provest seittis, . ij^{s} vj^{d}
Item, to the glaissinwrycht to tak down pannells of glass on Candilmes day, and putting up of thame, ... ij^{s}
Item, for ane act rasit out of the buiks of counsale anents the weychtis and mesoris, be the command of Richart Carmichaell, bailye, . . ij^{s}
Item, for taikin doun and mending of glass pannalls in Sanct Salvator yll, contenand xx fute new glass, pryce of the fute xviij^{d}; summa, . xxx^{s}
Item, in the same yle, xxviij fut ald glass, pryce of the fute vj^{d}; summa, ix^{s}
Item, in the Jowall Hous, ix fut of new glass and ix fute ald glass, . xviij^{s}
Item, in Sanct Antonis ile, vj fut of new glass, with xxxv fute ald glass, xxvj^{s} vj^{d}
Item, in the same yle, ij fute new with v fute auld glass, . . v^{s} vj^{d}
Item, in Sanct Thomas yle, xv fut new glass in the heich round, and ix fut auld, ... iiij^{s} vj^{d}
Item, iij pannellis auld glass, contenand xiiij fute, . . . xij^{s}
Item, above the Queire, iiij panalls, mending and setting in new leid, contenand xxxvj fute, and vj fute new glass, . xxvij^{s}

JAMES BARROUN, Dean of Guild. 1555-56.

Item, the windo above the Ravestre, iij pannells contenand xxiij fute new glass, and vij fute auld, ... $xxxviij^{s}$

Item, in the Consistre yle xvj pannells, v^{xx} xij fute new glass, and the O in the heid of the said windo, contenand xxx fute new glass; summa of the haill new glass in the said windo, ... x^{li} $xiij^{s}$

[75]

Item, in the said yle xij pannalls ald, contenand iij^{xx} xvj fute, and the wast windo, contenand xiiij pannalls ald, contenand lvj fute, all set in new leid; summa, ... iij^{li} xvj^{s}

Item, in the Halyblude yle, xxxiij fute new glass, . xlix^{s} vj^{d}

and vj fute new glass, . . . ix^{s}

Item, in the same ile, iij^{xx} xiij fute ald glass, ... $xxxvij^{s}$

Item, in the queir, above the organis, xviij fute ald glass and ane fute new, x^{s} vj^{d}

Item, ane pannell above Sanct Paullis altar, contenand viij fute new glass and ij fute ald, ... $xiij^{s}$

Item, in Sanct Gabriallis yle, viij fute new glass, xxvj fute auld, xx^{s}

Item, in Sanct Johne yle, iiij fute new glass, ... vj^{s}

Item, above the quier, ix fute new glass and xx fute ald glass, . . $xxiij^{s}$ vj^{d}

Item, above the knok, ane pannall, contenand vj fute, ij syndrye tymes mendit, ... vj^{s}

Item, for $lvij^{li}$ weycht of glass bands, price of the pund, ix^{d}; summa, . $xlij^{s}$ ix^{d}

Item, for bringin of ane standart and ledders, and changein of thame to the glaissinwrycht sindry tymes, ... xv^{s}

Item, for mending of the paill that hingis befoir the hye altar, ij^{s}

Item, for mending of the powpat, . . . ij^{s}

Item, to ane warkman to cleinge the luge, ... iij^{s}

[76] Item, to Sir Jhone Symsoun, on Palme Sonday, for singing of the Passioun, ij^{s} vj^{d}

Item, to Sir Thomas Reith, ane elne of blak stemming, for the coppye of the Gild Lawis, ... $xxxvj^{s}$

Item, to Howme to buy bussomis to swepe the kirk at Yuill, Paische, and Witsonday, ... $xviij^{s}$

Item, to Pait and the Doctor on Paische day for (*blank*), . . ij^{s}

Item, for the iruis at the kirk dur, meill merkat, flesche merkat, and workmanschip, ... $iiij^{li}$ $xviij^{s}$

Item, for skowring of the brasin lettron at Paische and Witsonday, . $iiij^{s}$ ij^{d}

Item, to Pait and the Doctor, on Witsonday, for keiping of the kirk, . iiij^{s}
Item, for tawch candils, all winter, in the windois of the kirk, . xxxij^{s} iiij^{d}
Item, for cords to the skallet bells, this yeir, ... vij^{s} ix^{d}
Item, for keiping of the Sepulcur at Paische, viij dayis and viij nychtis, . viij^{s}
Item, for v half punds candills to the pane befoir the hye altar, . . x^{s}
Item, to George Jhonstoun for xj punds and ane half walx to the greit candilsteikis this yeir, . . . xxxiij^{s} iij^{d}
Item, for thre ellin of lynning to the fount, . v^{s} vj^{d}
Item, at Witsonday, for geirss, watter haids, and dow, xviij^{d}
Item, for ane cord to the lamp of the queir, vj^{d}
Item, for uly to the knok, . . xij^{d}
Item, for keiping of the font at Witsonday, ij^{s}
[77] Item, for dychting of the guitteris in the yeir, xxx^{s}
Item, for ane key to the eist kirk dur, . . xxx^{d}
Item, for ij hingand loks to the irnis at the kirk dur, . . . ij^{s}
Item, for iij^{m} ix^{c} Dundie sklaytts to the body of the kirk, fra the stepill west to the west kirk dur, price of the j^{m}, v lib., . . xix^{li} x^{s}
Item, for carcage of thame to the town, ilk thowsand xij^{s}, . . xlvj^{s} viij^{d}
Item, for bering of thame to the wark abone the kirk, . . . ix^{s}
Item, for thre dozone viij daillis to the gutters of leid and (*blank*) of the work, ... viij^{li} xvj^{s}
Item, for bringin of thame to the work, . ij^{s}
Item, for twa aikne treis to be clatts to the new thak, xxvj^{s}
Item, for aucht firne sparris to be clattis, . viij^{s}
Item, for dowbill garroun nalis to the wark, ... v^{s}
Item, for ane mast to lay under the leid, and bringing up of it out of Leyth, ... lvij^{s} vj^{d}
For sawin of it, ... ij^{s} vj^{d}
Item, for sawin of twa gestis to be clattis, and xxxij dalis to be serkne, . xlij^{s} viij^{d}
Item, for singill garroun nalis to the clattis, ... xij^{s} vj^{d}
Item, for plantiour nalis, lidne nalis, and dur nalis to the lacht, and uther wark, ... iij^{li} iij^{s}
Item, for ane wricht iiij oulkis, ... iij^{li} iiij^{s}
Item, to ane warkman to red the kepill feit, and uther labour, iij oulks, . xxvij^{s}

JAMES BARROUN, Dean of Guild. 1555-56.

Item, for v dozone viij laidis of lyme, . iiij[li] xvj[s]
Item, for xiij dozone sand and iiij ladis, . iij[li] vj[s] viij[d]
Item, for walter to the wark, ... xxij[s]
Item, for the slatters for thikne of iiij rud xxiiij eln new thak, . ix[li] viij[s]
Item, for pointing of the haill kirk, and boting of the faltis of it, . iiij[li]

[78] Item, to Jhone Werre, powdermaker, for casting of the lidne gutters, and mending of thame, ... iij[li] vj[s] viij[d]

Item, to ane masoun for rasing of the turnepyk heid, and rasing of ane gavill wall, ... lv[s]

Item, for ane Eistland buird, and bringing out of Leyth and sawing of it to mak ane new dur besyde the jowellhous, ... x[s] iiij[d]

Item, for aucht burdis to the thre west new windokis and new dur and crukis, iij slottis, with stapillis to the windois and dur, and ij crukis to the font, ... xlvij[s]

Item, to ane masoun to mak cruke holis, slott holis to the windois, dur, and font, ... v[s]

Item, for twa stane leid to the cruik holis, xvj[s]
Item, for ane lok to the new dur, . x[s]
Item, to the slateris drinksilver, ... iij[s]
Item, for sowping of the kirkyard (*blank*), wattering of it in somer to Sanct Gelis day, ... xvj[s]
Item, for clenging about the kirk at Sanct Gelis day, ij[s]
Item, for scowring of the brasin laternis, . ij[s]
Item, for painting of Sanct Geill, . . vj[s]
Item, for baring of him to the painter, and fra, . vj[d]
Item, for mending and polesing of Sanct Gelis arme, ... xij[d]
Item, to Pait and the Doctor, on Sanct Gelis day, for the keping of the kirk, iiij[s]
Item, coft viij laid lyme to paint Sanct Marye Chapell, . . xviij[s]
Item, for xxiiij laid sand, . . viij[s]
Item, for walter to it, ... xij[d]
Item, for ij[c] slatis, and bringing up of thame to Sanct Marye Wynd, . xxiij[s]
Item, for ane daill to be laucht to it, ... iiij[s]
Item, for sawing and quartering of it, ... xviij[d]
Item, to Alexander Robesoun, tailyeour, for mending of Sanct Gelis capis x[s]

JAMES BARROUN, Dean of Guild. 1555-56.

Item, for dichting and mending of the glassin windokis in the Ravestre, .	vj^s
[79] Item, deliverit to Thomas Todrik, officiar, the xij day of November, as ane act proportis, maid thairupoun, the sowme of, ...	v^{li}
Item, to Maister Alexander Logye, the xvj day of Februar, as ane act proportis, ...	xl^s
Item, for painting of the bred of Sanct Mary Wynd, .	vij^s viij^d
Item, to Doctor Drummond, for his yeris fie, . .	xx^s
Item, to Howme, that kepis the kirk, his yeris fie,	xl^s
The officeris feis :—	
Item, to Richard Trollop, at command of the counsell,	v^{li}
Item, to Alexander McGachane, . . .	iij^{li}
Item, to David Windiyettis,	iij^{li}
Item, to George Cranstoun,	iij^{li}
Item, to George Gourlay, .	iij^{li}
Item, to William Nicoll, .	iij^{li}
Item, to William Couttis, .	iij^{li}
Item, to Patrik Barroun, .	iij^{li}
Item, to James Henderson,	iij^{li}
Item, to Jhone Wachlop, .	iij^{li}
Item, to Richard Plumbar,	iij^{li}
Item, to Maister Alexander Logy,	iij^{li}
Item, to Allane Purves, . .	iij^{li}
Item, to Thomas Hall, . . .	xl^s
Item, to Thomas Watsoun, glassinwricht, for his yeris fie, .	iiij^{li}
Item, for my awin fie and my chapellres, . . .	x^{li} xiij^s iiij^d
Summa of the haill discharge is, .	ij^c xxij^{lib}

The xxvij day of Februar, the yeir of God J^m v^c lvij yeris. James Barrounis compt foresaid, dene of gild in the yeir of God J^m v^c lvj yeris, beand maid baith charge and discharge, had and considerat, the auditouris underwrettin, chosin be the presidentis and counsall thairto, findis the said comptar restand awand to the gude town the sowme of fourtie twa pundis nyne ^{s} v^d and ½. In witness of the quhilk the said comptar hes subscryvit this present before the saidis auditors, day, yeir, and place foresaidis.

JAMES BARROUN, Dean of Guild. 1555-56.

[The report is not subscribed by the auditors, nor by the "comptar." The following addition is by Mr Alexander Guthrie, town clerk :—]

Item, allowit to the compter quhilk he forzet out of this present compt throu negligence, the ordinar fee of Andro Mansioun, extending to, . x markis

And sua restis the compter awand to the gude town the sowme of threttye fvye pund sextene shillings j d obolus ; quhilk sowme wes ordanet to be deliverit and payit to James Carmichaell be ane act maid be the counsall thairupon, in part of payment of ane mair sowme restand awin to him be the gude town, as the act, maid the xxvj day of Marche 1557 yers, proportis.

GUTHRE.

JAMES CARMICHAEL, Dean of Guild. 1556-57.

[80]

JAMES CARMICHAELLIS Compt, being Dene of Gild, his entre at Mychaelmes in anno, etc., lvj to unto Mychaelmes in anno lvij o.

ONUS.

Item, in the first, the said Compter chargis him with the fute of his last Compte, maid the saxt day of Marche, the yeir of God J m v c and fiftie foure yeris, extending to, xxj li xij d ob

---

JAMES CARMICHAEL, Dean of Guild. 1556-57.

[81]

THE COMPT of JAMES CARMICHAELL, Dene of Gild in the Town of Edinburgh in the yeir of God ane thowsand fyve hundreth and fiftie sevin yeiris, randerit to the auditoris underwrettin the xxv day of Februar in the yeir of God J m v c and lvij yeris, in the Tolbuyth of the samyn; and induris to Mychaelmes lvij.

Auditores.

Maister Jhone Spenss and
Maister Thomas M c Kalzeane, presidentis.
Maister Jhone Spenss, ballie.
David Forrester.
Eduard Hoip.
James Curle.
Adame Fullertown.
Jhone Dowgall.
Robert Henrisoun.

JAMES CARMICHAEL, Dean of Guild. 1556-57.

CHARGE.

Heirefter followis the Oneratioun of the Dene of Gild comptis that he is to be chargit with, and his entres thairto wes xj Octobris, anno lvij [lvj].

The Pece Silver gottin be procuratioun in the kirk :—

Item, Sonnday, the samyn day, ressavit fra Alexander Duray and Alexander Blak, baxter, ... xvij^s iij^d

Item, Sonnday, the xviij day, ressavit fra William Ker and Richard Gray, xxiij^s ix^d

Item, Sonnday, the xxv day, ressavit fra David Levisoun and Nicolaus Ramsay, ... xij^s v^d

November.

Item, Sonnday, the first of November, ressavit fra Jhone Crechtoun and William Lambe, ... xxj^s iij$\frac{1}{2}$^{d}

Item, Sonday, the viij day of November, ressavit fra Richard Carmichaell and Maister Archibald Grahame, ... xxx^s x^d

Item, Sonnday, the xv day of November, ressavit fra Mungo Huntar and Jhone Hopper, ... xiij^s vj^d

Item, Sonnday, the xxij day of November, ressavit fra William Lausoun and Jhone Adamesoun, ... xxxix^s vij$\frac{1}{2}$^{d}

Item, Sonnday, the penult day, ressavit fra Jhone Andersoun and James Roger, ... xvj^s i$\frac{1}{2}$^{d}

Januar.

[82] Item, Sonnday, the iij day of Januar, ressavit fra Gilbert Gray and Alexander Robesoun, ... xv^s ij^d

Item, the x day of Januar, ressavit fra William Wauchop and Patrik Duik, xvj^s vij$\frac{1}{2}$^{d}

Item, Sonnday, the xvij day of Januar, ressavit fra Michaell Bassendene and Alexander Purves, ... xxij^s i$\frac{1}{2}$^{d}

Item, Sonnday, the xxiiij day of Januar, ressavit fra Jhone Nymmill and Patrik Wilsoun, ... xxj^s v^d

Item, Sonnday, the last day of Januar, ressavit fra Jhone Syme and Robert Watsoun, . xliij^s x$\frac{1}{2}$^{d}

Februar.

Item, Sonnday, the vij day of Februar, ressavit fra James Mosmann and James Cowpar, ... xiiij^s ij^d

JAMES CARMICHAEL, Dean of Guild. 1556-57.

Item, Sonnday, the xiiij day, ressavit fra Adame Allan and Jhone Davidsoun, xvj^{s} vij$\frac{1}{2}^{d}$

Item, Sonday, the xxj day, ressavit fra Jhone Mosmann and David Lyell, xviij^{s} iij^{d}

Item, Sonday, the last day, ressavit fra Jhone Purves and Thomas Todenar, xvj^{s} ij^{d}

Marche.

Item, Sonnday, the vij day of Marche, ressavit fra Thomas Ewin and Robert Gurlaw, ... xv^{s} j$\frac{1}{2}^{d}$

Item, Sonnday, the xiiij day, ressavit fra Hew Nesbet and Jhone Cunynghame, talyeor, ... xij^{s} j^{d}

Item, Sonnday, the xxj day, ressavit fra Williame Richesoun and Jhone Thomesoun, ... xiiij^{s} $\frac{1}{2}^{d}$

Item, Sonnday, the xxviij day, ressavit fra Alexander Naper and Hew Brown, . . xxviij^{s} viij^{d}

Aprill.

Item, Sonnday, the fourt day of Aprill, ressavit fra Maister Jhone Prestoun and Thomas Reppcht, . xlix^{s} j$\frac{1}{2}^{d}$

Summa lateris, . . xv^{li} iij^{s} ix$\frac{1}{2}^{d}$

[83] Item, Sonnday, the xj day, ressavit fra Williame Scot and David Touris, xvij^{s} v$\frac{1}{2}^{d}$

Item, Sonnday, the xviij day, ressavit fra David Foster and Jhone Couttis, ... iij^{li} iij^{s} j^{d}

Item, Sonnday, the xxv day, ressavit fra Jhone Aslowane and Michaell Clerk, . . xiij^{s} j^{d}

Maij.

Item, Sonnday, the secound day of Maij, ressavit fra Frances Ur and Jhone Small, ... xiij^{s} vij^{d}

Item, Sonnday, the nynt day, ressavit fra Jhone Harrat and Gilbert Carbrayth, ... xix^{s} v^{d}

Item, Sonnday, the xvj day, ressavit fra David Michell and Jhone Watt, xv^{s}

Item, Sonnday, the xxiij day, ressavit fra Eduard Litill and Alexander Achesoun, ... xxvij^{s} vj^{d}

Item, Sonnday, the penult day, ressavit fra Andro Wigholme and Niniane Baute, ... xxiij^{s} ij^{d}

JAMES CARMICHAEL, Dean of Guild. 1556-57.

Junij.

Item, Sonnday, the sext of Junij, ressavit fra Eduard Hoip and Adam Fowllartoun, ... xxvij^s vij^d

Item, Sonnday, the xiij day, ressavit fra Jhone Aikinheid and William Melvin, ... xxij^s v$\frac{1}{2}^d$

Item, Sonnday, the xx day, ressavit fra Adame Scott and Alexander Wod, xiij^s x^d

Item, Sonnday, the xxvij day, ressavit fra Patrik Edyear and his marrow, . . . xix^s iij^d

Julij.

Item, the iiij day of Julij, ressavit fra Laurence Simsoun and William Carbrayth, . . . xvij^s ij^d

Summa lateris, ... xiiij^{li} xij^s vij$\frac{1}{2}^d$

[84] Item, Sonnday, the xj day of Julij, ressavit fra James Dalzell and Thomas Troup, ... xix^s

Item, Sonnday, the xviij day, ressavit fra James Cranstoun and his marrow, ... xij^s iij^d

Item, Sonnday, the xxv day, ressavit fra Jhone Hutcheoun and Jhone Frier, ... xx^s vij^d

August.

Item, Sonnday, the first of August, ressavit fra Arthuir Grangear and his marrow, ... xiij^s v$\frac{1}{2}^d$

Item, Sonnday, the viij day, ressavit fra George Reippeth and Jhone Purves, ... xviij^s v^d

Item, Sonnday, the xv day, ressavit fra Jhone Blakeburne and his marrow, xiiij^s ij^d

Item, Sonnday, the xxij day, ressavit fra James Ingliss and Peter Turnor, xvij^s v^d

Item, Sonnday, the xxix day, ressavit fra William Patersoun and his marrow, . . xv^s j$\frac{1}{2}^d$

September.

Item, Sanct Gelis day, ressavit fra Jhone Cathkin and Eduard Jhonestoun, xxij^s ij$\frac{1}{2}^d$

Item, Sonnday, the v day of September, ressavit fra Jhone Tod and Bartilmo Somervell, ... xv^s viij^d

Item, Sonnday, the xij day, ressavit fra Alexander Perye and his marrow, . xj^s v^d

Item, Sonnday, the xix day, ressavit fra Thomas Crechtoun and his marrow, . . xv^s

JAMES CARMICHAEL, Dean of Guild. 1556-57.

Item, Sonnday, the xxvj day, ressavit fra Nicoll Young, talyeor, and his marrow, ... xij^{s} j$\frac{1}{2}$^{d}

Summa lateris, ... x^{li} ij^{s} x^{d}

Summa of the pece, with the rest, thre scoir fyftene pundis fyve schillingis, viij^{d}.

[This sum of 75^{li} 5^{s} 8^{d} includes "the rest" or balance of 21^{li} 1^{s} $\frac{1}{2}$^{d} on James Carmichael's Account 1554-55, and about 5^{li} of Pece Silver for December 1556, the particulars whereof are not given in this Account 1556-57.]

[85] Item, I am to be chargit with the noumer of the schippis of this instant yeir, quhilk extendis, as the buik beris, to the numer of lxvj :—

Summa of the schippis, . . xlvj^{li} iiij^{s}

Item, I am to be chargit with the Burgessis and Gildis, baith togidder, becauss thai ar in the lokkit buke, as the buik beris, and as heirefter followis at lenth :—

Item, in primis, Martene McKewin, talzeor,	v^{li}
Item, Mourdow Walker, .	v^{li}
Item, Jhone Patersoun,	v^{li}
Item, Thomas Lowis,	v^{li}
Item, Jhone Forrester,	v^{li}
Item, Richard Gibsoun,	. xiij^{s} iiij^{d}
Item, Richard Schankis, .	v^{li}
Item, Rolland Arneill,	v^{li}
Item, Leonard Dobby,	v^{li}
Item, Jhone Gardner,	. xiij^{s} iiij^{d}
Item, Jhone Creich,	. xiij^{s} iiij^{d}
Item, David Weir,	v^{li}
Item, Jhone McMoran,	v^{li}
Item, George Small,	v^{li}
Item, Alexander Sauchy, .	x^{li}
Item, Walter Brown, . .	. xiij^{s} iiij^{d}
Summa of the burgessis, . .	lxvij^{li} xiij^{s} iiij^{d}

I am to be chargit with monye allowit and ressavit for certane of the brassin pillars :—

[86] Item, ressavit fra Andro Murray of Blakbarrony for onputting of his armis upoun the pillar, ... iiij^{li}

Item, ressavit fra Maister Henry Fowlis for onputting of his armes upoun the pillar, in monye, ... iiij^{li}

Item, for my awin pillar, the quhilk I put on my armes, . iiij^{li}

Summa of this charge, . xij^{li}

[87] I am to be chargit with Choppis of the kirk and at the futt of the kirk yaird, of this instant yeir:—

Item, Thomas Mereleiss, .	xxvj^{s} viij^{d}
Item, Williame Harperfeild,	xxvj^{s} viij^{d}
Item, Jhone Broderstanis,	xxvj^{s} viij^{d}
Item, Jhone Bynning,	xl^{s}
Item, George Merschell,	xx^{s}
Item, Jhone Forrest,	xx^{s}
Item, Williame Fausyd,	xx^{s}
Item, Allen Scott,	xx^{s}
Item, Nicoll Haistie,	xx^{s}
Item, William Haistie,	xx^{s}
Item, Jhone Chepman,	xx^{s}
Item, Jhone Cunynghame,	xx^{s}
Item, Margret Richardsoun,	xx^{s}
Item, Jhone Reid, .	xx^{s}
Item, Alexander Adamesoun,	xx^{s}
Item, Jhone Neilsoun,	xx^{s}
Item, George Cowan, .	xx^{s}
Item, Michaell Windeyettis,	xx^{s}

The kirk choppis.

Item, Jhone Gilbert,	xxx^{s}
Item, George Turnor,	xl^{s}
Item, Andro Eless,	xl^{s}
Item, George Turnor, . .	xxx^{s}
Summa of this charge is, .	xxvij^{li}

JAMES CARMICHAEL, Dean of Guild. 1556-57.

I am to be chargit with the Layaris of the kirk this instant yer :—

Item, for Jhone Watsoun,	vj^{s} viij^{d}
Item, Jhone Chartoris servand,	vj^{s} viij^{d}
[88] Item, Besse Dicsoun,	vj^{s} viij^{d}
Item, Deim Gawstoun,	vj^{s} viij^{d}
Item, Alexander Hewin barn,	ij^{s}
Item, Jhone Young barn,	ij^{s}
Item, Cristill Estoun,	vj^{s} viij^{d}
Item, Jhone Smyth wyff,	vj^{s} viij^{d}
Item, Elen Ross,	vj^{s} viij^{d}
Item, James Andersoun,	vj^{s} viij^{d}
Item, Jonet Hoppringill,	vj^{s} viij^{d}
Item, Alexander Chaip barn,	ij^{s}
Summa of this charge is,	iij^{li} vj^{s}

I am to be chargit with the Silver Candilstikkis of this instant yeir :—

Item, Sir Robert Hopparis derige,	iiij^{d}
Item, Harbart Maxwellis wyff,	xvj^{d}
Item, Jhone Dowglace wyff,	xvj^{d}
Item, the fraternitie of Sanct Crispinane,	iiij^{d}
Item, Thomas Otterburn derige,	iiij^{d}
Item, Jhone Fowlar,	iiij^{d}
Summa particule,	iiij^{s}
[89] Item, Maister William Fowler,	iiij^{d}
Item, Maister Jhone Chepman,	iiij^{d}
Item, King James the Thrid,	viij^{d}
Item, Nicoll Carnecorss,	viij^{d}
Item, the fraternitie of Sanct Lowy,	iiij^{d}
Item, Janet Gelis,	viij^{d}
Item, Maister Henry Quhyt,	viij^{d}
Item, Sir Williame Lyntoun,	viij^{d}
Item, Walter Chepman,	iiij^{d}
Item, Dame Gaustoun,	viij^{d}
Item, Jhone Bruce,	viij^{d}

JAMES CARMICHAEL, Dean of Guild. 1556-57.

Item, Alexander Fausyde,	xvj^d
Item, Alexander Young, . .	xvj^d
Item, the fraternitie of Sanct Howbart,	iiij^d
Item, George Gibsoun,	viij^d
Item, Robert Barton, .	viij^d
Item, Maister William Meldrum, .	xvj^d
Item, Jhone Perdowanis wyff,	viij^d
Item, George Brown, .	iiij^d
Item, Thomas Uddart wyff,	viij^d
Item, Jhone Symsoun, .	xvj^d
Item, George Hammiltoun,	viij^d
Item, Robert Simsoun, .	viij^d
Item, Agnes Freg, .	viij^d
Item, Alesoun Cokburne, .	viij^d
Item, Makoum Porteuss, .	viij^d
Summa lateris,	xviij^s
[90] Item, for Cristell Eistoun,	viij^d
Item, Sir Patrik Crechtoun,	viij^d
Item, Thomas Bischop,	viij^d
Item, Robert Chepman, .	viij^d
Item, Jhone Smyth wyf, .	viij^d
Item, Sir Adame Otterburne,	viij^d
Item, Katherin Rig, .	viij^d
Item, William Craik, . .	xvj^d
Item, Maister Richard Strangis wyf,	xvj^d
Item, Sir Jhone Kerss, . .	iiij^d
Item, the fraternitie of Sanct Ann,	iiij^d
Item, the fraternitie of Sanct Cristell,	iiij^d
Item, Jsebell Rynd,	xvj^d
Item, Gilbert Lauder, .	viij^d
Item, Gilbert Lauderis wyff,	xvj^d
Item, Jonet Dowby, .	viij^d
Item, Andro Quhit, .	iiij^d
Item, Allane Windeyettis,	iiij^d

JAMES CARMICHAEL, Dean of Guild. 1556-57.

Item, Thomas Brown, iiij^{d}
Item, James Reid, viij^{d}
Item, James Nicoll wyff, . xvj^{d}
Item, Andro Cor, . . viij^{d}
Item, Jhone Wichtis wyff, viij^{d}
Item, Alexander Adamesoun, iiij^{d}
Item, George Hendersoun, viij^{d}
Item, William Hendersoun, viij^{d}
Item, Jonet Hoppringill, viij^{d}
Item, Besse Faussyd, . . viij^{d}
Summa lateris, . xix^{s} viij^{d}
Summa totalis, ... xli^{s} viij^{d}

[91] I am to be chargeit with the Greit Chandelaris of this instant yeir :—
Item, in primis, Jhone Dougall wyff, . ix^{s} vj^{d}
Item, Alexander Faussyd, ix^{s} vj^{d}
Item, Alexander Young, ix^{s} vj^{d}
Item, Robert Bartane, ix^{s} vj^{d}
Item, Thomas Boyiss, ix^{s} vj^{d}
Item, Jhone Symssoun, ix^{s} vj^{d}
Item, Harbert Maxwell wyff, ij^{s}
Item, Nicoll Carnecorss, . ij^{s}
Item, King James the Thrid, ij^{s}
Item, Jhone Bruce, . ij^{s}
Item, Thomas Uddertis wyff, ij^{s}
Item, Robert Chepman, ix^{s} vj^{d}
Item, Kathern Reig, ix^{s} vj^{d}
Item, William Craik, ix^{s} vj^{d}
Item, Janet Grahame, ix^{s} vj^{d}
Item, Janet Dowby, . . ix^{s} vj^{d}
Item, Maister Richard Strangis wyff, ix^{s} vj^{d}
Item, Isobell Rynd, . . ix^{s} vj^{d}
Item, Gilbert Lauderis wyff, ix^{s} vj^{d}
Item, James Nicollis wyff, ix^{s} vj^{d}
Item, Alexander Kais wyff, ix^{s} vj^{d}

Item, Besse Faussyde,	ix^s vj^d
Summa lateris,	ix^{li} xij^d
[92] Item, Cristell Eistoun,	ij^s
Item, Jhone Smyth wyff,	ij^s
Item, Gilbert Lauder,	ij^s
Item, Jhone Wichtis wyff,	ij^s
Item, George Hendersoun,	ij^s
Item, Williame Hendersoun,	ij^s
Item, Jhone Craig,	ij^s
Summa particule,	xiiij^s
Summa totalis,	ix^{li} xv^s
Summa of the haill charge is,	ij^c xliij^{li} v^s viij^d

[93] THE EXONERATIOUN of the Dene of Gild of this instant yeir, the xij day of October 1556.

Item, in primis, coft ane greit irne padill to padill the kirk, cost,	vi^s
Item, coft ane spunge to spunge the claith of the hie alter, cost,	viij^d
Item, to Thomas Henslie for rynging of the bellis upoun Saulmess evin,	ij^s
Item, coft four faddome of cordis to the bell of the hie alter, cost,	xvj^d
Item, the xj day of November, put up in Sanct Antanis Iill, thre pannellis of new glass, contenand ilk pannell vj fut new glass and four fut auld glass, the fut new glass xviij^d, and fut auld glass set in new leid vj^d; summa,	xxxv^s iij^d
Item, coft thre glass bandis weyand sex lib wecht to the saidis windokis, the stane at xij^s; summa,	iiij^{li} vj^d
Item, coft to big our Lady Iill xij gestis, the price of the pece xj^s; summa,	vj^{li} xij^s
Item, for pynor fie in Leyth,	iij^s
Item, for cairt hyir,	xvj^s
Item, for inbaring of thame in the kirk yaird,	xxx^d
Item, mair coft the samin tyme vj greit gestis, cost the pece xviij^s; summa,	v^{li} viij^s
Item, for pynor fie of thame in Leyth,	ij^s
Item, for cairt hyir of thame,	xviij^s
Item, for bering of thame in the kirk yaird,	xviij^d
Summa lateris,	xvj^{li} xij^s ix^d

JAMES CARMICHAEL, Dean of Guild. 1556-57.

Item, coft, maij, sex gestis of xxxiiij fut lang, cost the pece xxiiij^{s}; summa, . . . vij^{li} iiij^{s}
Item, for pynor fie in Leyth and bering of thame on the Schuir, . . . iiij^{s}
Item, for cairt hyir of thame, ... xxj^{s}

[94] Item, for inbaring of thame in the kirk yard to the workmen, . . . ij^{s}
Item, coft the samyn tyme v dosone knappald dowble, cost, . . . xxxv^{s}
Item, for upbringing of thame furth of Leyth, ... iij^{s}
Item, coft v quarteris bukren to lyne the apparalingis of twa standis at the Hie Alter, ... v^{s} vj^{d}
Item, to Alexander Robesoun for mending of the saidis standis and lyning of the apparalingis, ... iiij^{s}
Item, for ane slot of irne to the north kirk dur, cost, . . . iij^{s}
Item, to ane warkman to big up the dure in the nether kirk yaird, . . . xviij^{d}
Item, for clengeing of the eist still in the kirk yaird of irne, . . . iij^{s}
Item, for bussowmes to sowp the kirk at Yowll, ... vj^{d}
Item, for ane pynor fie of ane greit standart ladder furth of the Abay to the kirk wendowis, ... xviij^{d}
Item, for ane cheinze of irne to the bell of the Hie Alter, . . . xxviij^{d}
Item, to the warkmen to carye xviij gestis furth of the kirk yaird to the nether Tolbuyth, ... viij^{s}
Item, for careing of sex greit gestis to the nether Tolbuyth, to the workmen, ... iij^{s}
Item, for outtaking of thame agane and having to the saweris, . . . ij^{s}
Item, for mending of the bell of Our Ladye Alter, . . . xij^{d}

Summa lateris, ... xij^{li} iiij^{s} iiij^{d}

[95] Item, for sawing of xviij gestis anis throw, to the sawars, . . . xviij^{s}
Item, to four warkmen to carye thame to the nether Towbuyth, . . . vj^{s}
Item, coft fra Jhone Smyth, twelf pillaris of brass, weyand lij stane xij lib., cost the pound xiiij^{d}; summa, ... xlix^{li} iiij^{s} viij^{d}
Item, for pynor fie to carye thame to David Rowanis werkhowss, . . . iiij^{s}
Item, to David Rowane for mending of four of the pillaris at wes brokin and making of sex schildis to thame and grating of the haill xij pillaris, for his lauboris, ... x^{li}
Item, coft mair to eik thame out with v stane brass, the pund cost xvj^{d}; summa, . . . v^{li} vj^{s} viij^{d}

Item, to ane warkman to beir the red at the eist end of the kirk dur, thre dayis, ilk day xvj^{d}; summa, . iiij^{s}

Item, for sawing of thre geistis, xxx^{d}

Item, for pynour fie of thame, ... xij^{d}

Item, to lyne the greit stand of damess of the hie alter viij ellis ½ bukren, the ell iiij^{s}; summa, ... xxxiiij^{s}

Item, coft nyne ellis of reid silk ribbonis, cost the ell viij^{d}; summa, vj^{s}

Item, coft thre quarteris unce silk, cost, . . v^{s} iij^{d}

Item, for warkmanschip, to David Richardsone, . . . vj^{s} viij^{d}

Item, coft fra William Robesoun, xxj Januarii, to the perpell wallis, twa dosone worschot, the price of the pece vij^{s}; summa, . viij^{li} viij^{s}

Summa lateris, . lxxxvij^{li} vj^{s} ix^{d}

[96] Item, for cairt hyir of thame, v^{s} iiij^{d}

Item, for pynour fie, ... viij^{d}

Item, for sawing of xviij of the saidis burdis to be pannellis to our Ladye Iill, ... ix^{s}

Item, for careing of thame to the sawer and bringing hame agane of thame to the nether Tolbuyth, ... xij^{d}

Item, coft sex pund glew, cost the pund xviij^{d}, to glew thame; summa, . ix^{s}

Item, for mending of the loke of the south kirk dur, . . . xviij^{d}

Item, to ane wricht to mend and rung all the ledderis in the stepill, and making of indass bellis, ... vj^{s}

Item, for mending of ane band to the box of the comoun scill, ij^{s}

Item, for clengeing of the nether Tolbuyth, to twa warkmen, . . ij^{s}

Item, tane down twa pannellis of glass in Prestonis Iill, contenand vij futt new glass and v fut auld glass, the fut of new glass cost xviij^{d}, and the fut of auld glass vj^{d}; summa of baith togidder, . . . xiij^{s}

Item, coft j stane thre pund candill to the workmen in the nether Tolbuyth, cost the stane xij^{s}; summa, ... xiiij^{s} iij^{d}

Item, for sawing of sex draucht of wanschot, viij^{d} raw tymmer, . . vj^{s} viij^{d}

Item, for sawing of xxxiij draucht of greit tymmer, ilk draucht x^{d}; summa, xxviij^{s} vj^{d}

Summa lateris, ... iiij^{li} xvij^{s} ix^{d}

[97] Item, gevin to Robert Farder and his colligis for workmanschip of twa perpell wallis to our Ladye Iill, ... xxiiij^{li}

JAMES CARMICHAEL, Dean of Guild. 1556-57.

Item, gevin to David Richardsoun to lyne the stand of quhit dames at the hie alter and to lyne crame of welvot vestment, xj ellis new blak bukren, the ell iiij^{s}; summa, ... xlxiiij^{s}

Item, for xvj ellis rubbonis and freinzeis of silk, ane unce and ½ to mak the knoppis and to sew thame with; summa, . . . xxxij^{s} vj^{d}

Item, to David Richardsoun, for his werkmanschip of thame, xxxv^{s}

Item, for drink silver, ... xviij^{d}

Item, for pynour fie for the inbringing of the wark to the kirk of our Ladye Iill, ... iiij^{s} vj^{d}

Item, for drink silver to Robert Findaris servandis, . v^{s}

Item, for clengeing of freir and lectroun, ... v^{s}

Item, coft sevin ellis rubonnis to the reid stand, cost the ell ix^{d}; summa, v^{s} iij^{d}

Item, coft to be ane waill to the hie alter in lentron to hing afore the queir, xxviij ellis ½ of bartane cauves, cost the ell iiij^{s}; summa, . . v^{li} xiiij^{s}

Item, coft ane pund ane ½ of quhit birge threid to be bandis and lachattis to it, at the price of the pound vj^{s}; summa, ... ix^{s}

Item, to ane sewstar for sewing of it and sewin of ane cross in the middis of it, of holmwark, . xxiiij^{s}

Summa lateris, . . . xxxviij^{li} v^{s}

[98] Item, for frenzeis of quhit threid to eik it with, ... v^{s}

Item, for wesching and saip to it, ... v^{s}

Item, for baring of the pillaris furth of David Rowannis to the kirk, . iij^{s}

Item, coft sex laid lyme to grownd the work of Our Ladye Iill, cost the laid xv^{d}; summa, ... vij^{s} vj^{d}

Item, coft ane dosone ½ sand, cost the dosone v^{s}; summa, . . vij^{s} vj^{d}

Item, to Gilbert Cleuch and four masonis to raiss the throchis in our Lady Iill, and to hew a pairt thairof and lay thame in order agane, . xviij^{s}

Item, to thre masonis thre dayis therefter to lay the perpell wallis ground, ilk day iij^{s} the man; summa, ... xxvij^{s}

Item, for stanis to the said perpell wallis, ... xvij^{s}

Item, to thre werkmen thre dayis to beir stanis, riddell lyme and sand to serve the werkmen, and to beir away the rede, ilk man on the day xvj^{d}; summa, ... xvj^{s}

Item, for walter, ... iiij vj^{d}

Item, to Walter Bynning for painting of twa trene pillaris, . . viij^{s}
Item, Fryday and Setterday xx^{o} Marcii, to Howm and Hainslie to beir the red furth of the kirk, . . v^{s} viij^{d}
Item, for sawing of tymmer to be half pillaris, . . . v^{s} viij^{d}
Item, to Thomas Petticreif, smyth, for sex bandis to the iiij half durris, . vj^{li}
Item, for drinksilver to his childer, . . iij^{s}
Item, to him for blind nalis, ... vij^{s} viij^{d}
Item, for twa gret bottis irne, weyand ij stane $\frac{1}{2}$, the stane at xi^{s}; summa, ... xxvj^{s} ij$\frac{1}{2}$^{d}
Summa lateris, ... xiiij^{li} viij^{s} ij$\frac{1}{2}$^{d}
[99] Item, coft to the bot hollis, sex pundis leid, the lib vij^{d}; summa, . xlij^{d}
Item, for irne werk to the turnyng stullis to the warkmen, . . xij^{s} vj^{d}
Item, to the warkmen at the upsetting of the werk, daner and nown schankis, ... xij^{s} iiij^{d}
Item, coft to point the kirk, xviij laidis lyme, the dosone cost xvj^{s}; summa, xxiiij^{s}
Item, coft iij dosone $\frac{1}{2}$ of sand, cost the dosone v^{s}; summa, . . xvij^{s} vj^{d}
Item, coft ane reddell, cost, . . . xij^{d}
Item, for vj dosone walter, . . . v^{s}
Item, for redling and drawin of it, ... ij^{s} viij^{d}
Item, to Thomas Pettycreif for twa slott lokkis to the ground of the durs in our Ladye Iill, . . . xj^{s}
Item, for bussomes at Pasche to sowp the kirk, xij^{d}
Item, for clengeing of the kirk about, . v^{s}
Item, for skowring of freir and the lecteroun, ... v^{s}
Item, the xviij day of Aprill, to the saweris for sawing of the gret tymmer to the daskis of our Ladye Iill, . . vij^{s} viij^{d}
Item, for pynor fie, ... xviij^{d}
Item, for pynor fie of ij standart leddis to the glassin windokis, . . xiiij^{d}
Item, coft ane pair gogillis to ane workman, ... ij^{s}
Item, coft ij dosone hadder bussomes to sowp the mouswalbis our all the kirk and wallis and windokis, ... xxxij^{d}
Item, to thre werkmen for thair lauboris of sowping of all the kirk and queir, for thair laubouris, . . . xxxiiij^{s}
Summa lateris, . vij^{li} ix^{s} v^{d}

JAMES CARMICHAEL, Dean of Guild. 1556-57.

Item, for skowring of our Ladye Pillaris, ... xxx^{d}

Item, put up at Sanct Stevinis Alter, xxvij Aprill, twa pannellis glass, contenand of new glass ix fut and of auld glass set in new leid viij fut, the fut new glass xviij^{d} and the fut auld glass vj^{d}; summa of baith togidder, ... xvij^{s} vj^{d}

[100]

Item, put up the samin tyme in Sanct Annis Iill ane gret pannell, contenand xj fut new glass, the fut xviij^{d}; summa, . . . xvj^{s} vj^{d}

Item, ane uther pannell set in new leid and auld glass, contenand ix fut ½ auld, with thre fut new glass, the fut auld glass vj^{d}, the fut new glass xviij^{d}; summa, ... ix^{s} iij^{d}

Item, in Walter Chepmannis Iill, ane heid pannell, contenand vj new glass, the fut xviij^{d}; summa, ... ix^{s}

Item, Sanct Gabreallis Iill, ane pannell new glass, contenand ix fut ½, the fut xviij^{d}; summa, ... xiiij^{s} iij^{d}

Item, coft fra Thomas Pettecreif, twa greit slottis to our Lady Iill durris, v^{c} stapillis, ... xxij^{s}

Item, coft fra Sir William McDowgall xvj vinschot to the seittis, cost the pece vj^{s} iiij^{d}; summa, ... v^{li} xvj^{d}

Item, for pynor fie in Leyth, . . vj^{d}

Item, for cairt hyir, . . . iij^{s} iiij^{d}

Item, for puttin in of thame in the luge, . iiij^{d}

Item, at Witsunday, for bussomes, . . vj^{d}

Item, for skowring of the freir and lecteroun, . . v^{s}

Item, for ane dow, garss and walter, ... xviij^{d}

Item, Monunday, the xvj day of Julij, for baring of thame furth of the luge to the nether Tolbuyth, ... xvj^{d}

Item, for sawing of xvj winshot to our Ladye Stallis, . . . vij^{s}

Summa lateris, ... x^{li} xj^{s} x^{d}

[101] Item, for sawing of ane lang geist, and ane greit sex draucht corbell, ... v^{s} ij^{d}

Item, coft iiij lib glew, the lib xviij^{d}; summa, . . vj^{s}

Item, for ane dosone of sparris to be streinzeoris, cost, v^{s}

Item, coft thre pottis to melt glew in, ... xij^{d}

Item, coft maij, v dosone knappald, cost xxxv^{s}, to the stallis.

JAMES CARMICHAEL, Dean of Guild. 1556-57.

Item, coft mair fra William Robesoun, to the stallis, ane dosone wanschot, cost the pece, vij^{s}; summa, . . iiij^{li} iiij^{s}
Item, for pynour fie in Leyth, vj^{d}
Item, cairt hyir, . . . iij^{s}
Item, upbringing of the knappald, ... xxx^{d}
Item, mair, coft to the fluring and settis of the said stallis ane dosone daillis, cost, ... xxx^{s}
Item, for cairt hyir and pynour fie, . . xl^{d}
Item, the xx of August, for sawing of foure burdis, . . . xxx^{d}
Item, for twj^{c} blind nalis to Thomas Petticreif, the hundreth xviij^{d}; summa, ... iij^{s}
Item, may, ij^{c} ½ of greit blind nalis, the j^{c}, xxviij^{d}; summa, v^{s} x^{d}
Item, for sawing of thre wanescot, ... xv^{d}
Item, to Thomas Pettycreif, for ix bottis to the bak of our Ladye Stallis, wyand ane stane and ix lib, the staue cost xij^{s}; summa, . . xviij^{s} ix^{d}
Item, coft to yet the bottis xv lib leid, cost the lb vij^{d}; summa, . viij^{s} ix^{d}
Item, to ane masoun to mak the bott holis, twa dayis, . . iiij^{s}
Summa lateris, ... x^{li} xix^{s} vij^{d}

[102] Item, for sawing of iiij burdis to the Quenis Seit, . . xx^{d}
Item, coft to the werk iij^{c} ½ planschcor nalis, the j^{c}, xxviij^{d}; summa, . viij^{s} ij^{d}
Item, to four werkmen to beir in the haill stallis and to serve the wrichtis at the upputting of the werk, . . . vj^{s}
Item, for clengeing of the kirk about at Sanct Gelis day, . v^{s}
Item, for skowring of the freir, the lectrowns and our Ladye pillaris, vj^{s}
Item, for painting of Sanct Geill, ... vj^{s}
Item, to the glassinwricht servandis to thair drink silver, efter the mending of haill windokis about the kirk, ... v^{s}
Item, to the wrichtis servands drink silver for putting up of the stallis, . vj^{s}
Item, for sawing of twa burdis to be mallours and twa peces of treis, . xix^{d}
Item, to ane workman to mak morter and to lift the ledderis about the kirk windoks, ilk day of iij dayis xvj^{d}; summa, . iiij^{s}
Item, for sawing of iiij wanschot, ... xx^{d}
Item, for sawing of ane daill, . . xiiij^{d}
Item, for ane pair of bandis to the Quenis Stall, . iiij^{s}

JAMES CARMICHAEL, Dean of Guild. 1556-57.

Item, for inbering of it, ... xvj^{d}

Item, put up ane pannell of glass of Sanct James Alter, contenand viij fut ½ new glass, the price of the fut xviij^{d}; summa, . . . xij^{s} ix^{d}

Item, ane uther pannell of auld glass sett in new leid, contenand xij fut, the fut vj^{d}; summa, ... vj^{s}

Summa lateris, ... iij^{li} xvj^{s} iiij^{d}

[103] Item, put up above the west kirk dure, ane pannell of glass v fut new glass and aucht fut auld glass, the fut of new glass xviij^{d}, the fut auld glass vj^{d}; summa, ... xj^{s} vj^{d}

Item, coft ane dosane knaphald, cost, vij^{s} to the mellaris.

Item, ane ^{li} glew, ... xviij^{d}

Item, coft vij ladis lyme, cost the leid xxij^{d}, to the allering; summa, xij^{s} x^{d}

Item, coft ij dosen sand, cost the dosen v^{s}; summa, ... x^{s}

Item, to Petter Baxter, slater, for poynting of the haill allering of the kirk, xxiiij^{s}

Item, for drink to the boyis, ... xviij^{d}

Item, to Robert Fendar for warkmanschip of the haill sklatis and the Quenis Sait, ... xiij^{li} iiij^{s}

Item, to the belman for keping of the Sepulture, . . . viij^{s}

Item, to ane fallow to wesche the kirk thre moneth in winter, . xiiij^{s}

Item, for singing of the Passioun, . . xxx^{d}

Item, for xij faudome of cordis to the wolt, ... iij^{s} vj^{d}

Nota; to be dischargit. Item, to Andro Mantioun, for his yeris pensioun as his act proportis, vj^{li} xiij^{s} iiij^{d}

Item, to Thomas Watsoun for his pensioun, conforme to his act, . . iiij^{li}

Item, to Thomas Howme for keping of the kirk ane yeir, . . iij^{li}

Item, to Robert Drummond for his yeris fie, ... xx^{s}

Item, to Patrik Gawen for dichting of the guttaris, for his yeris fie, . xxx^{s}

Item, for tawch candill in the middis of the kirk all winter, to Patrik, xxxiij^{s} iiij^{d}

Item, for ule dolie to the knok, ... xij^{s}

Summa lateris, ... xxxvj^{li} ix^{s}

[104] Item, for wax to the poulpat all the yeir as ane act beris, to Patrik Gawin, ... xxvj^{s} viij^{d}

Item, to Patrik Tod for keping of the silver werk, his yeris fie, . . x^{s}

Item, to George Jhonestoun for xvij^{li} ½ wax to the greit chandillaris all the yeir, the ^{li} iiij^{s}; summa, ... iij^{li} x^{s}

JAMES CARMICHAEL, Dean of Guild. 1556-57.

Item, coft to mend the kirk, iiij^{c} sklatis, cost the j^{c}, xij^{s}; summa, xlviij^{s}
Item, for upbringing of thame furth of Leyth, ... viij^{s}
Item, for bering in of thame in the luge, ... viij^{d}
Item, coft, to thik the Sang Schole, xxv thraves of stra, cost the threif ij^{s}; summa, ... l^{s}
Item, for stowbis, . . viij^{s} vj^{d}
Item, for devattis, ... xiiij^{s} iiij^{d}
Item, to ane thekar for his workmanschip and his servand, . xvj^{s}
Item, for ane lok and ane key to the Sacrament almerye, . . v^{s}
Item, coft to mak symound to calphat the guttaris abone upoun the kirk, v^{li} wax, cost the ^{li} iiij^{s}, ... xx^{s}
Item, mair, xiij ^{li} rosat, cost the ^{li} viij^{d}; summa, . . viij^{s} viij^{d}
Item, foure ^{li} brontstane, the ^{li} xxx^{d}; summa, x^{s}
Item, sex pundis cordis, cost, ... xviij^{d}
Item, to Gilbert Cleuch and Jhone Anderson, and ane servand with thame, ... xxvj^{s} viij^{d}
Item, to ane warkman to serve thame, ... vj^{s}
Item, in Halibluid Iill, ane pannell of glass contenand xij fut new glass, the fut xviij^{d}; summa, ... xviij^{s}

Summa lateris, ... xvij^{li} viij^{s}

[105] Item, ane uther pannell, contenand iiij fut new glass and viiij fut auld glass, the fut new glass xviij^{d}, and the fut auld glass vj^{d}; summa, . x^{s}
Item, gevin for iij laiddis pettis to the workmen to calphat the guttar, and the leid xvij^{d}; summa, . iiij^{s} iij^{d}
Item, thre laiddis collis, . . vij^{s} viij^{d}
Item, coft twa ledis hadder, cost, ... iiij^{s} viij^{d}
Item, ane pannell of glass in Lausounis Iill, contenand vj fut new glass and twa fut auld glass, the fut new glass xviij^{d}, and the fut auld glass vj^{d}; summa, ... x^{s}

Officeris feis.

Item, gevin to Richard Trollop, conforme to his auld uss for his burgeschip, v^{li}
Item, to James Hendersoun, ... iij^{li}
Item, to David Windizettis, . . iij^{li}
Item, to Maister Alexander Logye, . iij^{li}

JAMES CARMICHAEL, Dean of Guild. 1556-57.

Item, to Richard Plumber, iij^{li}
Item, to William Cowtis, . . iij^{li}
Item, to William Nicoll, . . iij^{li}
Item, to Jhone Wauchlop, . iij^{li}
Item, to George Gowlay, . . iij^{li}
Item, to George Cranstown, . iij^{li}
Item, to William Dowglass, . iij^{li}
Item, to Allane Purves, . . iij^{li}
Item, to Patrik Barrown, . iij^{li}
Item, to Thomas Hall, . . . xl^{s}
Item, for my awin fie and my chaiplanis, . . x^{li} xiij^{s} iiij^{d}

Summa lateris, ... lv^{li} ix^{s} xj^{d}

Summa of the haill discharge is iij^{c} v^{li} xviij^{s} x^{d}; sua restis to the compter thre scoir twa ^{li} xiij^{s} ij^{d}

[106] The xxv day of Februar, the yeir of God J^{m} v^{c} lvij yeris, the dene of gild, James Carmichaell, produceand his comptis of his intromissioun and charge and discharge fra the Michaelmes in lvj yeir of God onto the Michaelmess J^{m} v^{c} lvij yeris, he is found superexpendit be the auditors underwritten the sowme of lxij^{li} xiij^{s} ij^{d}.

[Unsigned.]

JAMES CARMICHAEL, Dean of Guild. 1557-58.

THE COMPT of JAMES CARMICHAELL, Den of Gild, the x day of October, anno 1557.

CHARGE.

[107] [The Pece Silver gottin be procuratioun in the Kirk.]

Item, in primis, ressavit fra Alexander Masoun and Jhone Young, . xxj^{s}
Item, Sonnday, the xvij day, ressavit fra Archibald Grahame and Peter Dowglass, ... xx^{s} v^{d}
Item, Sonnday, the xxiiij day, ressavit fra Robert Crage and Maister Johnne Hamyltoun, ... xvj^{s} ij^{d}
Item, Sonnday, the last day, ressavit fra Robert Lun and Gilbert Armour, xj^{s} j$\frac{1}{2}^{d}$

JAMES CARMICHAEL, Dean of Guild. 1557-58.

November.

Item, Sonday, the sewint day, ressavit fra Maister James Lindesay and Alexander Hume, ... xvij^s viij$\frac{1}{2}^d$

Item, Sonday, the xiiij day, ressavit fra Johnne Gemmill and Johnne Auchmuty, ... xij^s j^d

Item, the xxj day, ressavit fra Adam Gray, his alane, . . . ix^s j^d

Item, Sonday, the xxviij day, ressavit fra Johnne Henrisoun and his marrow, ... xiiij^s j^d

December.

Item, Sonnday, the vj day, ressavit fra Cuthbert Murray and his marrow, xviij^s iiij^d

Item, Sonnday, the xiij day, ressavit fra Mungo Napeir and Mungo Russall, ... xx^s ij$\frac{1}{2}^d$

Item, Sonnday, xix day, ressavit fra Robert Fynder and Williame Ra, . xiiij^s

Yuill day.

Item, ressavit fra Johnne Dowgell and William Patersoun, . iij^{li} xviij^d

Item, Sonnday, the xxvj day, ressavit fra Johnne Halyday and Johnne Grahame, . . xx^s j^d

Januar.

Item, Sonnday, the secund day, ressavit fra Johnne Eistoun and Arthur Carnmir, ... xiij^s

[108] Item, Sonnday, the ix day, ressavit Archibald Leiche and Williame Ury, xx^s v^d

Item, Sonnday, the xvj day, ressavit fra Johnne Duray, his alane, . v^s

Item, Sonnday, xxiij day, ressavit fra Alexander Bruce and James Joussye, ... xxiij^s vj^d

Item, Sonnday, the penult day, ressavit fra Alexander King and Hector Blacader, ... xxxij^s v^d

Februar.

Item, Sonnday, the vj day, ressavit fra Adam Scott and Andro Henrysoun, xiij^s ij^d

Item, Sonnday, the xiij day, ressavit fra William Harlaw and Johnne Henrisoun, ... xvj^s vj^d

Item, Sonnday, the xx day, ressavit fra Johnne Inglis, his alane, . ix^s j^d

Item, Sonnday, the penult day, ressavit fra James Huntair and Johnne Foster, . . . xiiij^s ij^d

JAMES CARMICHAEL, Dean of Guild. 1557-58.

Marche.

Item, Sounday, the vj day, fra Nicholl Fyldour and his marrow, . . xiijˢ vijᵈ
Item, Sonnday, the xiij day, fra James Barton and Frances Lintoun, . xixˢ ixᵈ
Item, Sonnday, the xx day, ressavit fra James Aikman and Johnne Robertsoun, ... xxvˢ ijᵈ
Item, Sonday, the xxvij day, ressavit fra Johnne Gilbert and Robert Dalgleisch, . . xijˢ jᵈ

Apryle.

Item, Sonnday, the thrid day, ressavit fra Johnne Litill and Luk Wilsoun, xxvˢ vijᵈ
Item, Sonnday, the x, Peasche day, ressavit fra Thomas Thomesoun and Maister Archibald Grahame, ... lvˢ ijᵈ
Item, the xvij day, ressavit fra Alexander Moresoun and Johnne Mar, . xvˢ
Item, the xxiiij day, ressavit fra Alexander Thomsoun and David Corsbie, xixˢ iijᵈ

Maij.

Item, the first day of Maij, ressavit fra William Aitkin and James Hoppringill, ... xxjˢ j½ᵈ
Item, the viij day, ressavit fra Alexander Sauchy and Williame Henrisoun, xxˢ iijᵈ
Item, the xv day, ressavit fra Maister Robert Glen and Newy Bruschet, xiiijˢ vjᵈ
Item, the xxij day, ressavit fra Johnne Calderwod, his lane, . . viijˢ vᵈ
Item, the xxix day, ressavit fra Andro Sklatter and David Kinloche, xxxvjˢ iijᵈ

Junij.

[109] Item, the v day, ressavit fra James Mure and Peter Marteine, . xvijᵈ
Item, the xij day, ressavit fra Thomas Vass, his lane, . . xˢ ijᵈ
Item, the xix day, ressavit fra James Young and Thomas Purves, xvˢ iiijᵈ
Item, the xxvj day of Junii, ressavit fra Patrik Schang and Thomas Mow, vˢ jᵈ

Julij.

Item, the thrid day, ressavit fra William Huchesoun and Archibald Maw, vˢ xᵈ
Item, the x day, ressavit fra James Curll and David Symmer, . . xxvjˢ vᵈ
Item, the xvij day, ressavit fra Johnne Gibsoun and Alexander Wod, . ixˢ
Item, the xxiiij day, ressavit fra Johnne Watsoun, and James Alexander wes seik, ... viijˢ iijᵈ
Item, the last day, ressavit fra James Alexander and the Ingliss bowar, ixˢ iijᵈ

JAMES CARMICHAEL, Dean of Guild. 1557-58.

August.

Item, the vij day, ressavit fra Alexander Bartilmo and Johnne Robesoun,	x^s vij^d
Item, the xiij [xiiij] day, ressavit fra James Brown and his marrow,	ix^s j^d
Item, the xxj day, ressavit fra Adam Rannaldsoun and his marrow,	vij^s iiij$\frac{1}{2}^d$
Item, the xxviij, ressavit fra James Hunter and Johnne Ramsay,	vj^s j^d

September.

Item, upone Sanct Gelis Day, ressavit fra Andro Bartane and George Todrik,	xij^s viij^d
Item, the fourt day, Hercules Methuen and Andro Makilwrayth wald not gang,	(*blank*)
Item, the xj day, ressavit fra Hercules Methwen and Andro Makilwrayth,	iij^s iiij$\frac{1}{2}^d$
Item, the xviij day, ressavit fra Andro Gibsoun and Walter Wycht,	xj^s vj^d
Item, the xxv day, ressavit fra Williame Grantoun and his marrow,	viij^s j^d

October.

Item, the secund day, ressavit fra James Arnott and William Dempster,	ix^s j^d

[110] Item, I am chargit with the nummer of the schippis of this instant yeir, quhilk extendis as the buik beris to the nomber of lxxvj :—

Summa of the schippis, (*blank*)

Item, I am to be chargit with the Burgessis and Gildis, bayth togidder, becauss thai ar in the lokkit buik as the buik beris and as heirefter followis at lenth :—

Item, in primis, Andro Armistrang,	x^{li}
Item, Henry Kyuloche,	xxxiij^s iiij^d
Item, George Hopper,	xx^s
Item, Johnne Stoddert,	xxxiij^s iiij^d
Item, William Mathesoun,	xxxiij^s iiij^d
Item, Andro Pumphray,	vj^s viij^d
Item, Nicholl Ramsay,	xxxiij^s iiij^d
Item, Johnne Eistoun,	xxxiij^s iiij^d
Item, James Craig,	xiij^s iiij^d
Item, Johnne Carwod,	xiij^s iiij^d
Item, Williame Galloway,	v^{li}

Item, James Johnnestoun,	v^{li}
Item, James Mosmann,	xx^{s}
Item, David Brown,	xiij^{s} iiij^{d}
Summa is, ...	(*blank*)

I am to be chargit with the Choppis of the kirk and at the fut of the kirk yaird of this instant yeir:—

Item, Thomas Murcleiss,	xxvj^{s} viij^{d}
Item, William Happerfeild,	xxvj^{s} viij^{d}
Item, Johnne Broderstanis,	xxvj^{s} viij^{d}
Item, Johnne Bynning,	xl^{s}
Item, George Marschell,	xx^{s}
Item, Johnne Forrest,	xx^{s}
Item, Williame Fausyde,	xx^{s}
Item, Adam Scott,	xx^{s}
Item, Nicholl Haistie,	xx^{s}
Item, William Haistie,	xx^{s}
Item, Johnne Chepman,	xx^{s}
[111] Item, Johnne Cunninghame,	xx^{s}
Item, Margaret Ruthirfurd,	xx^{s}
Item, Johnne Reid,	xx^{s}
Item, Alexander Andersoun,	xx^{s}
Item, Johnne Neilsoun,	xx^{s}
Item, George Cowane,	xx^{s}
Item, Nicholl Wyndegaittis,	xx^{s}

The kirk choppis.

In primis, Johnne Gilbert,	xxx^{s}
Item, George Turnour,	xl^{s}
Item, Andro Eleiss,	xl^{s}
Item, Cristell Galbrayth,	xxx^{s}
Item, George Turnour,	xxx^{s}

I am to be chargit with the Silver Candillstikkis:—

In primis, Sir Robert Hopper,	iiij^{d}
Item, James Bannantyne bairn,	viij^{d}

JAMES CARMICHAEL, Dean of Guild. 1557-58.

Item, the fraternite of Crispiniane, iiij^{d}
Item, Johnne Foular, iiij^{d}
Item, Nicholl Carncross, . viij^{d}
Item, Maister William Foular, iiij^{d}
Item, Maister Robert Heriott, xvj^{d}
Item, Maister Chepman, . iiij^{d}
Item, Maister Laurence Taillicfer, iiij^{d}
Item, Thomas Young, . viij^{d}
Item, Johnne Douglass wyf, viij^{d}
Item, Johnne Mosmann, . viij^{d}
Item, Sir George Roger, . viij^{d}
Item, the fraternitie of Sanct Eloy, iiij^{d}
Item, Jonet Rynd, . iiij^{d}
Item, Katherene Sympsoun, viij^{d}
Item, Thomas Craig, . viij^{d}
Item, Bartilmo Somerwell, viij^{d}
Item, Mungo Huntaris wyf, viij^{d}
Item, William Newtounis wyf, viij^{d}
Item, Maister Henry Quhyt, . iiij^{d}
Item, to the fraternitie of Sanct Jhonne, . iiij^{d}
Item, Walter Chepman, . iiij^{d}
Item, Alexander Elphinstoun, iiij^{d}
Item, the Abbot of Newbotle, . xvj^{d}
Item, the fraternitie of Sanct Mungo, iiij^{d}
Item, Johnne Bruce, . . viij^{d}
[112] Item, the fraternity of Sanct Anthone, viij^{d}
Item, Maister Johnne Murray, viij^{d}
Item, David Grame, . iiij^{d}
Item, Maister Adam Galbrayth, . viij^{d}
Item, Thomas Marioribankis, ij^{s}
Item, Johnne Layng, viij^{d}
Item, James Barroun, . . iiij^{d}
Item, the fraternitie of Sanct Chowbert, . iiij^{d}
Item, George Gibsoun, viij^{d}

*

JAMES CARMICHAEL, Dean of Guild. 1557-58.

Item, Katherene Howtoun,	viij^{d}
Item, George Brown,	viij^{d}
Item, James Bronis wyif .	xvj^{d}
Item, David Forestair,	viij^{d}
Item, Patrik Flemyng,	viij^{d}
Item, Alexander (*blank*), .	iiij^{d}
Item, Sir Johnne Symsoun,	viij^{d}
Item, Margaret Finlasoun,	iiij^{d}
Item, Maister Henry Quhyt,	iiij^{d}
Item, Sir Thomas Maxwell,	iiij^{d}
Item, Maister Richard Lawsoun, .	iiij^{d}
Item, William Craig,	viij^{d}
Item, Johnne Davesoun,	viij^{d}
Item, Patrik Durhame,	viij^{d}
Item, Sir Johnne Kerss, .	iiij^{d}
Item, the fraternitie of Sanct Ann,	iiij^{d}
Item, Thomas Brown,	iiij^{d}
Item, Sir William Broun, .	iiij^{d}
Item, the Bischop of Galloway,	iiij^{s}
Item, Walter Blaklok,	iiij^{d}
Item, Patrik Heriott,	iiij^{d}
Item, Adam Strawchane, ...	iiij^{d}
Summa of the silver candilstikis of this instant yeir,	(*blank*)

I am to be chargit with the Candillstickis that standis in the Queir and about the beir, of this instant yeir:—

In primis, Nicholl Carncorss,	ij^{s}
Item, Johnne Dowgallis wyf,	ij^{s}
Item, Johnne Mosman,	ij^{s}
Item, Katharene Symsoun,	ij^{s}
Item, Johnne Bruce, .	ij^{s}
Item, Maister Robert Heriot,	ix^{s} vj^{d}
Item, Thomas Craig, .	ix^{s} vj^{d}
[113] Item, Maister Richard Hopper,	ix^{s} vj^{d}
Item, the Abbot of Newbotle,	ix^{s} vj^{d}

JAMES CARMICHAEL, Dean of Guild. 1557-58.

Item, Maister Adam Galbrayth, . ix^{s} vj^{d}
Item, Maister Thomas Marioribankis, ix^{s} vj^{d}
Item, James Barronis wyf, ix^{s} vj^{d}
Item, William Craik, ij^{s}
Item, Johnne Andersoun, . ij^{s}
Item, the Bischop of Galloway, . . ix^{s} vj^{d}
Summa of the goldin candilstickis, ... (*blank*)

I am to be chargit with the [Layaris] in the kirk this instant yeir :—

Item, in primis, Sir Johnne Ormistoun, vj^{s} viij^{d}
Item, Robert Wardlawis wyf, vj^{s} viij^{d}
Item, Bartilmo Somervell, vj^{s} viij^{d}
Item, James Curllis servand, vj^{s} viij^{d}
Item, Andro Symsonis wyff, vj^{s} viij^{d}
Item, Issobell Boyis, . vj^{s} viij^{d}
Item, Ane Monk of Balmerynoch, vj^{s} viij^{d}
Item, Besse Lowrie, vj^{s} viij^{d}
Item, Margaret Grinlaw, . vj^{s} viij^{d}
Item, Thomas Grayis wyf, vj^{s} viij^{d}
Item, Patrik Kemis barn, ij^{s}
Item, Gilbert Hayis barn, ij^{s}
Item, Sir Robert Johnestoun, vj^{s} viij^{d}
Item, Thomas Maben, . vj^{s} viij^{d}
Item, Johnne Cuthbertsonis wyf, . vj^{s} viij^{d}
Item, Alexander Peris barne, ... ij^{s}

I am to be chargit with the rest of ane compt maid be James Barroun, extending to the sowme of xxxv^{li} xvj^{s} j$\frac{1}{2}^{d}$.

The oneratioun [exoneratioun] of James Carmichaell, Den of Gild of this instant yeir :—

Item, restis awand to me of my last compt maid the xxv day of Februar the yeir of God J^{m} v^{c} lvij yeris, the soume of, . iij^{xx} ij^{li} xiij^{s} ij^{d}

[114] THE EXONERATIOUN of the Dene of Gild of this instant yeir, as eftir followis :—

Item, coft ane gryt sloit to the kirk dure, cost, ... iij^{s}
Item, coft viij faddomis of towis to the pann in the myddis of the kirk, price of the faldome viij^{d} ; summa is, . . v^{s} iiij^{d}

JAMES CARMICHAEL, Dean of Guild. 1557-58.

Item, to Hanslie for ringing of the bellis upone Salmess evin, . ij^{s}
Item, for mending of ane leddir of the powpate, and rungis to it, . x^{d}
Item, the ix day of Nouember, coft to mend and poynt the queir iij^{c} and ane half sklatts, cost the hundreth xj^{s}; summa, . . xxxviij^{s} vj^{d}
Item, coft the samin tyme, xxvij laids of lyme, cost the dosone xiiij^{s}; summa is, ... xxxj^{s} vj^{d}
Item, coft the samin tyme, v dosone of sand, cost the dosone v^{s}; summa, xxv^{s}
Item, coft twa hundreth and ane half of naillis, cost the hundreth xviij^{d}; summa. . . . . iij^{s} ix^{d}
Item, to Peter Baxter, sklatter, for his lawbors, . xxiiij^{s}
Item, at Yuill, for cleyngeing of the kirk about, . . . iij^{s}
Item, for skowring of brassing work of the queir and our Ladye Ile, . iij^{s}
Item, for pynour fie of twa grit standert ledderis to the kirk wyndois, the xxij day of Januar, ... xij^{d}
Item, the same tyme put up abone the queir in the heych wyndois ane pannale of glass in the west south windok, contenand of new glass vj fut, and of auld glass ix fut, price of the fut of new glass xviij^{d} and the fut of auld glass vj^{d}; summa of bayth togidder, . . . xiij^{s} vj^{d}
Item, the samin tyme put up in our Ladye Ile ane heid pannale of glass, contenand vj fut and ane half of new glass, price of the fut xviij^{d}; summa is, ... ix^{s} ix^{d}
Item, the xxij of Merche, put up in the twa eist windowis on the south syde, abone the queir, twa grit pannallis of glass, contenand of new glass viij fut and ½, and of auld glass xxv fut, price of the fut of new glass xviij^{d}, and of the fut of auld vj^{d}; summa is, . . . xxv^{s} iij^{d}
Item, put up at Sanct Markis Alter, on the north syd of the queir, ane pannale of glass, contenand iij fut of new glass and v fut of auld glass, price of fut of new glass xviij^{d}, and of auld glass vj^{d}; summa is, . vij^{s}
Item, coft twa glass bandis, price, ... iij^{s} viij^{d}
Item, coft twa glass lockettis to the glass vyndockettis of the queir, fra Thomas Pettecio, ... iij^{s} vj^{d}
Item, coft thre dosone of lockit nailles, price of the dosone xij^{d}; summa is, iij^{s}
[115] Item, coft be Patrik Gowane vij faldome of cordis to the wall of the queir, price of the faldome vj^{d}; summa is, . . iij^{s} vj^{d}

JAMES CARMICHAEL, Dean of Guild. 1557-58.

Item, on Palme Sonnday, for byssomis to dicht the kirk, . . . vj^d

Item, to the preistis of the queir for singing of the Passioun on Palme Sonnday, ... ij^s vj^d

Item, for clengeing of the kirk about and taking of the red away fra the west end thairof, ... iiij^s

Item, for keping of the Sepulcre viij dayis and viij nychtis in the tyme of Peasche, ... viij^s

Item, for twa gryt ledderis to ane sklatter with Gilbert Clewth to vesy the gryt wyndow at the eist end of the queir gavill, to ane wrycht to put up ane prop of tymmer and the casting doun of the stane of the window, ... vj^s

Item, to foure werkmen for furth bering of the Quenis Sait fra Our Lady Altar to the Hie Altar and bering agane to Our Lady Altar, . . xij^d

Item, the xxiij day of Apryle, anno, etc., lviij^o, for stanis to byg up ane window abone the croce kirk upone the west syd of the samin, . ij^s

Item, to ane masoun for his workmanship, and to ane werkman to serve him, ... v^s

Item, put up in the samin wyndok ane pannale of glass, contenand vij fut of new glass, price of the fut xviij^d; summa, . x^s vj^d

Item, coft fra Johnne Hanna twa gryt glass bands, weyand v punds and vj unces, cost the stane xj^s; summa, . . . v^s ij$\frac{1}{2}$^{d}

Item, for drinksilver to the grassinwrichtis servandis at the grathing of the haill windokis, ... ij^s

Item, the vij day of Maij, put up ane pannale of glass in Sanct Thomas Ile, contenand vij fut of auld glass and iij fut of new glass; summa, viij^s

Item, coft twa small glass bandis, cost, . . . iij^s

Item, the xv day of Maij, for paynting of ane brod, to Johnne Sampsoun, paynter, to hing at the Hie Altar, ... vij^s

Item, to James Feild for ane dosone of sand to mixt lyme to poynt thir windokis abone the queir and the rest of the haill kirk wyndowis, cost, v^s

Item, at Witsonday for cleyngeing of the kirk about, . iij^s

Item, for bussommis to sowp the kirk, . . . vj^d

Item, for cleyngeing of the brassing work of the Queir and our Lady Ile pylaris, ... iij^s

JAMES CARMICHAEL, Dean of Guild. 1557-58.

[116]

Item, at Witsonnday for ane dow, fyr and wattir to the kirk, . .	xviij^d
Item, for keping of the Funt viij dayis and viij nychts and cover thairof,	ij^s
Item, for mending of the lok of the Revestre dure, ...	xij^d
Item, for ane irne, to Mungo Huntair, to put in the lamp of the queir, with ane chenze of irne, ...	iiij^s
Item, the xxviij day of Junij, gevin for sklattis, lyme and sand to theik fyve new choppis at the fut of the kirk yaird, and the losing and poynting and mending, and to ane sklatter for his wermanship of the haill choppis, ...	x^li xj^s
Item, coft to the saidis choppis iij gryt geistis to be rynnpannis and stuttis to the saidis choppis, price of the pece xvij^s; summa is, .	lj^s
Item, for kart hyr, . .	iiij^s vj^d
Item, for pynour fe, . .	iij^s
Item, to the sawars for sawing of v drauchtis, . .	iiij^s ij^d
Item, coft to be sarkin to the saidis choppis iij daills, cost the pece iij^s; summa, ...	ix^s
Item, to the sawars for sawing of thame, . .	ij^s vj^d
Item, mair, coft ane gryt wyne pype to be layth, cost, . . .	v^s
Item, to iij werkmen to help the wrychts to feis the saids choppis to put in stuttis and the rynnpannis, twa days, ilk man in the day xvj^d; summa is, . . .	viij^s
Item, coft ane schule to the masoun, cost, ...	xij^d
Item, to Robert Fynder, wrycht, for his werkmanschip of the saidis choppis, and twa werkmen with him, ...	xviij^s
Item, to ane masoun ane wolk and foure dayis to big the durrs and windoks of all the haill choppis at the fut of the kirk yaird his wage in the wolk xvj^s; summa is, . .	xxiiij^s
Item, for ane dozone of lyme, price, .	xvj^s
Item, ij dosone of sand, price of the dosone v^s; summa, . . .	x^s
Item, to ane werkman to serve to ridle and drauk the lyme, ilk day xvj^d; summa is, ...	xiij^s iiij^d
Item, for mending of the lockis, bandis and sloitts of the durris and windowis of the saidis choppis, . . .	xv^s viij^d
Item, for ane new lok to Cowanis buith dure, .	iij^s

JAMES CARMICHAEL, Dean of Guild. 1557-58.

Item, the thrid day of Julij, to twa werkmen to gand to the Abbay and feche viij to the Processioun of the Sacrament quhen the Quenis Grace wes maryit, ... xij[d]
Item, to Hanslie, in drink silver, for ringing of the bells, ij[s]
Item, for mending of the wattir stop at the revestrie dur, . xij[d]
Item, the xxv day of Julii, gevin for selettis, lyme and sand, and to ane workman for poynting and mending of the Hospitele of Sanct Mary
[117] Wynd and mending of the chymnay heid of the samin, lj
Item, for drink silver, ... xij[d]
Item, gevin, for mending of ane lok to the dure of the organis, and for mending of the drauchtis of the samin, ... iiij
Item, gevin, at the command of ane precept maid be the president, baillies and counsale for reformation of the south styll at the eist end of the kirk, to Thomas Jaksoun, masoun, he furnessand stane, lyme, sand and werkmanschip to the said styll, . iiij [merks]
Item, to the calsay maker for his werkmanschip, . iiij
Item, to ane werkman to await upon the grassinwrycht at the poynting of the kirk windowis and mending thairof, carying of ledderis, rydling of lyme and sand, ilk day of ix dayis, price of the day viij[d]; summa is, vj
Item, at Sanct Gelis day, for skowring of the brassin werk in the queir and of our Lady pillaris, . . . iij[s]
Item, for dychting of our Lady styll and round about the kirk, . iij
Item, for bowsomes to soup the kirk, . . . vj[d]
Item, to David Richardson for mending of the haill standis at the hie altar, frontellis and westamentis thairof all the yeir, . xiiij
Item, for tauche candill in the myddis of the kirk in wynter, xxxij vj[d]
Item, for walx candill to George Johnnestoun till find the grit candilstikkis all the yeir, x punds walx, price of the pund iiij[s]; summa, . xl[s]
Item, for walx candill to pollpatt all the yeir, . . xxvj[s] viij[d]
Item, for olldoling to the knok all the yeir, . . . xij[s]
Item, to Patrik Tod for his yeirs fee for keping of the silver werk, . x[s]
Item, to Doctour Small for keping of the kirk, wattering and sowping of the samin, ilk viij dayis somer and ilk xv dayis winter, iij[li]
Item, to Robert Drummond for his fie, . xx[s]

JAMES CARMICHAEL. Dean of Guild. 1557-58.

Item, to Patrik Gowane for cleyngeing of the guthreis abone the kirk xxx^s

Item, gevin to Hanslie for ringing of the bell at ix horis to convene the Lordis to the Tolbuith, ... xx^s

Item, gevin to Maister Johnne Spens, baillie, at the command of ane precept maid be the president and counsale, in money, ... v^{li}

[118] Item, to Andro Mensioun for his yeiris pensioun, conforme to his act, vj^{li} xiiij^s iiij^d

Item, to Thomas Watsoun, glassinwrycht, for his yeiris pensioun, conforme to his act maid thairupone, iiij^{li}

Item, to Richard Trohop, ... v^{li}

Item, coft, that is lyand in the luge, dressit, twa hundreth and ane half of sklaittis quhilk suld have mendit ane houss in the body of the kirk, cost the ^{c}, xj^s: summa is, ... xxvij^s vj^d

Item, coft, that is liand in the luge, vj laidis of lyme, cost the laid xviij^d; summa is, ... ix^s

Item, mair, vj laids sand, liand in the luge, ij^s vj^d

Officiariis feis.

Item, to David Wyndegattis, iij^{li}

Item, to Maister Alexander Logy, iij^{li}

Item, to Richard Plimber, iij^{li}

Item, to Williame Cowttis, iij^{li}

Item, to Williame Nicholl, iij^{li}

Item, to Johnne Wauchlot, iij^{li}

Item, to George Gourlay, . iij^{li}

Item, to George Cranstoun, iij^{li}

Item, to Williame Dowglass, iij^{li}

Item, to Alane Purves, iij^{li}

Item, to Patrik Barroun, . iij^{li}

Item, to James Henrysoun, iij^{li}

Item, to Thomas Hall, xl^s

Item, to Niniane Maw, . . . xxx^s

Item, for my fie and my chaiplannis, . . x^{li} xiij^s iiij^d

Item, the compter is to be dischargit with the chop maill of Johnne Chepmann, quha is fugityve at the weiris, and na thing poindable, extending to, ... xx^s

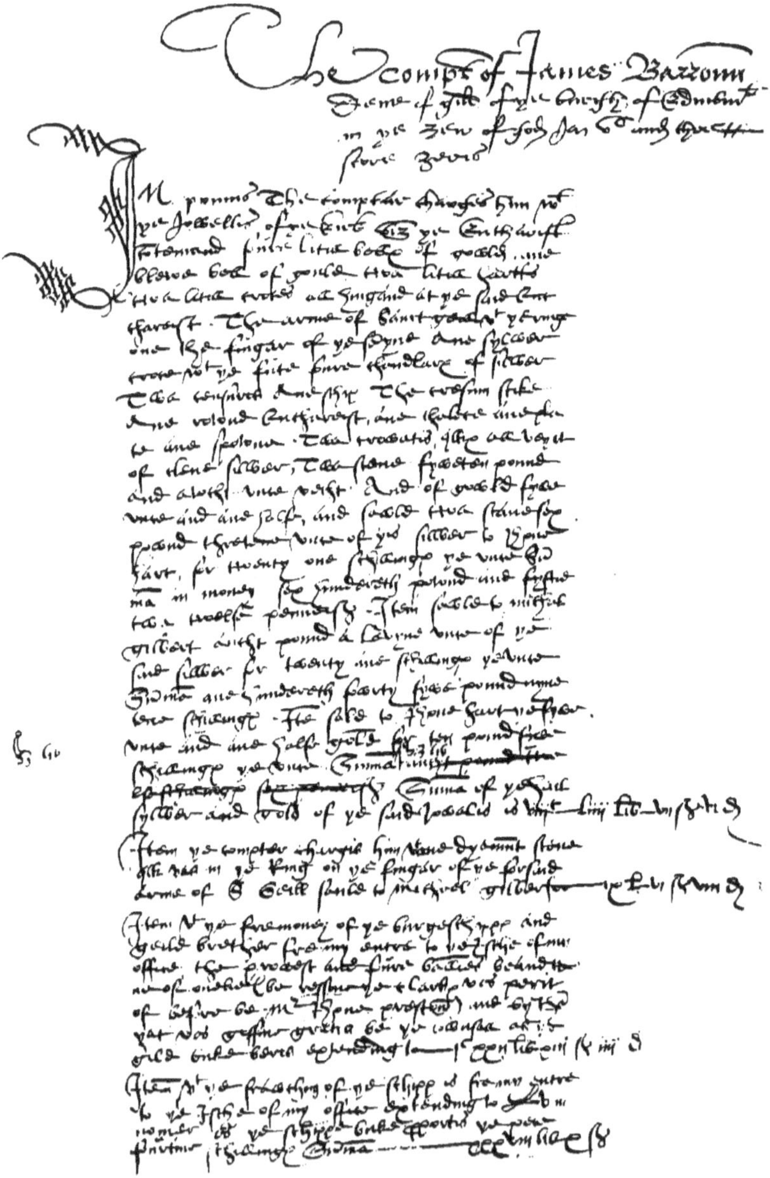
The compt of James Barroun

EDINBURGH ACCOUNTS:—Page 121 of old Accounts of Deans of Guild.

JAMES CARMICHAEL, Dean of Guild. 1557-58.

Decimo tertio Januarii 1558.

The quhilk day the auditoris of comptis underwritin hes sene and considderit the compt afoir writin, charge and discharge thairof, quairby thai find the Dene of Gild, compter, restand awand to the guid town the sowme of fyfteen li aucht s. sex d and ane obolus.

[Unsigned.]

Item, of this rest, allowit to James Carmychaell threty s for Niniane Mawis half fie, quha enterrit at half terme of James Hendersoun, officer, wes slane; and sua restis be the said James Carmychaell threttene pundis xviij s vj d, quhilk is payit to James Barroun, Dene of Gild, at command of the Counsale, and the said Barroun to be chargit thairwith. Et eque.

GUTHRE.

[THE ACCOUNT OF THE DEAN OF GUILD (John Charteris, Dean,) for the year 1558-59, is wanting.]

JAMES BARROUN, Dean of Guild. May to October, 1560.

121] THE COMPT of JAMES BARROUN, Dene of Gild of the Burgh of Edinburgh, in the yeir of God J m v c and thrie score yeris.

IN PRIMIS, THE COMPTAR CHARGES HIM WITH THE JOWELLIS OF THE KIRK, VIZ.:—

The Eucharist contenand foure litill bellis of gowld, ane blewe bell of gould, twa litill hartts, twa litill croces, all hingand at the said Euchareist: the Arme of Sanct Geill with the Ring one the fingar of the samyne, ane silwer croce with the fute, foure chendlaris of silwer: twa censuris, ane schip: the cresum stike and ane rownd Euchareist, ane chelece, ane plate, ane spowne: twa crowatis: quhilkis all weyit of clene silwer, twa stene fyweten pound and awcht unce wecht; and of gowld fyve unce and ane halfe; and sawld twa stane sex pownd thretene unce of this silwer to Jhone Hart, for twenty one schillingis the unce; summa in money, sex hundereth pownd and fyftie twa [pound] twelfe penneiss; Item, sawld to Michal Gilbert, aucht pound alavyne unce of the said silwer for twenty ane schillingis the unce; summa, ane hundereth fowrty

JAMES BARROUN, Dean of Guild. May to October, 1560.

fywe pound nynetene schillingis; Item, sald to Jhone Hart the fyve unce and ane halfe gold for ten pound fyve schillingis the unce; summa 53 lib.; Summa of the haill Sylwer and Gold of the said Jowalis is, viij^c liiij^{li} vij^s vj^d

Item, the compter chargis him with ane Dyament stane quhilk was in the Ring on the fingar of the foresaid Arme of S. Geill, sauld to Michael Gilbert for, ... ix^{li} vj^s viij^d

Item, with the fre money of the Burgeschippis and Geild Brether, fre my entre to the ische of my office, the prowest and foure ballies beand chesne of onelie (be ressone the clarkis wes payit of before be Maister Jhone Prestoun), and by thame that wes giffin gratis be the cownsale, as the gild buke beris, extending to, ... j^c xxij^{li} xiij^s iiij^d

Item, with the frawching of the Schippis, fre my entre to the ische of my office, extending to lv in nomer as the schyppe buke proportis, the pece fourtine schillingis; summa, ... xxxviij^{li} x^s

[122] Item, with the mallis of the Cordinaris Choppis, extending in this yeire to, xxj^{li}

The Choppis above the kirke.

Adam Denum, xxx^s

Jhone Gilbert, . xxx^s

George Turnouris chope, . xxx^s

George Turnouris stand, xl^s

Andro Heleis stand, . xl^s

Latteris, . ij$^{c\ li}$

Cristall Calbraith for his chope, ... xxx^s

Item, resavit be the compter fre Jhone Chartouris the rest of his compt, liij^{li}

Item, fre Jamis Carmichaell the rest of his compt, . . xiij^{li} xviij^s viij^d

Item, ressavit be the compter fre Cowper at the fute of the Over Bow for ane nychburheid, ... xl^s

Item, fre William McMoran for his nychburheid, ... xx^s

Summa, . lxxij^{li} viij^s viij^d

[123] EXONERATIO.

The money debursit upon the Wark and Warkmen of the Kirk, fre the first day of Maii (*blank*) the (*blank*) of Junii (*blank*).

Item, in primis, to ten warkmen quha wrocht be the space of nyne dayis

JAMES BARROUN, Dean of Guild. May to October, 1560.

for takine doun of the hail Allteris of the Kirk, of the Rude Loft, for bering of the red and stanes thairof away, . . xj^{li} xv^{s}

Item, for the lok to the kirk dore at the stinkand styl, . . viij^{s}

Item, for the rasin of the trowchis of the kirke, ... xviij^{s}

Item, for ane stok lok and ane cate band and ane hingand lok to the south kirk dor, price of all, ... xij^{s}

Item, for fyve stane of irne to be thre gewlokis, ilk stane viij^{s}; summa, xl^{s}

Item for making of thame, ... iij^{s}

Item, for bering of v ledders fra Sanct Paulis warkis to the kirk. xvj^{d}

Item, twa glaspis of irone to ane brokine stule, vj^{d}

Item, ane newe dore to the revestry, . ij^{s} iiij^{d}

Item, for the mending of ane brokine gewlok, . iij^{d}

Item, charpine of twa matolkis and grindine of one, vj^{d}

Item, twa schowlis with the irons to thame, v^{s}

Item, ane newe pik with the chaft, vij^{s} iiij^{d}

Item, twa scanze of threid to be lynis, ... x^{d}

Item, ane lok and bandis to ane almere in the revestrie to keipe nalis in, . . vj^{s}

Item, ane tre blok, ... iij^{d}

Item, for beringe of stanis fre the Gray Freris to the new kirk dore, vj^{s}

Item, to Patrik Gowan, belman, for olie to the bellis, xvij^{s}

Item, to ane papir buk to vreit my compt in, . . . vj^{d}

Item, to the warkmen that laid over the tymmar in the Tolbuith, iiij^{d}

Item, to Doctor Drummond for salping and waltering of the kirk at syndry tymes, ... vj^{s}

Item, for ane uther scanze threid to be ane lyne, ... vj^{d}

Item, for bering of the tymmer and auld wark of the stanis furth of the Tolbuith to the kirk, . . . iiij^{s}

Item, twa schullis with the irons to thame, . viij^{s}

Item, for ane new bar to the kirke dore, ... thre ^{s}

Item, to Jhone Wallace to produce the Townis Commissioun affor the Lordis of Parlament, ... x^{s}

The nomere of the calk bocht by me: v^{xx} xiiij stane gottine fre James Lyndesay.

JAMES BARROUN, Dean of Guild. May to October, 1560.

[124]

Item, xiiij^{xx} stanis calk, bocht fre Andro Lambe for viij^{d} the stane; summa, ... ix^{li} vj^{s} viij^{d}

Item, for grinding of thir xiiij^{xx} stanis and Maister James Lyndsayis vj^{xx} xiiij stane, ilk stane grinding x^{d}; summa, ... xvj^{li} viij^{s}

Item, bocht fre Jhone Wilsoun ij^{c} stane of calke for viij^{d} the stane; summa, viij^{li}

Memorandum: this twa ^{c} stane wes grund be ouwle.

Item, for bringing of this calk [fra] Leyth, ... xxxj^{s}

Item, for walter to the laying of the kirk flure, spargen of the kirk, grinding of the calke, theking and poynting of the kirk, and weschin of the flure thairof ilk prechinge day, ... iiij^{li} xx^{d}

Item, for fowre wyne punscheonis that servit for walter to the laying, and to put the ground calk in, ... xx^{s}

Item, twa half punscheonis to pitt ground calk in. vj^{s}

Item, twa meikill bukattis for the said calk, . v^{s}

Item, vj small bukattis, pryce, ... x^{s}

Item, for v dosone and ane halfe of bussumyis for scoupping of the kirk flure and to serve the spargenaris and crelmen, pryce xviij^{d} the dosone; summa, ... viij^{s} iiij^{d}

Item, for twa schanze of threid to bind thar skeppis on thar haidis feschine of thar bussumis, ... x^{d}

Item, for small towis, ... ij^{s} vj^{d}

Item, for twa large moreiss pikis to put one thar bussumis for spargyne of the kirk, ... viij^{s}

Item, for bering thame fra Leyth, ... iiij^{d}

Item, to Walter Bynniege, painter, for painting grene of the xxiij pillaris, and the loft estimit to be 2 pillaris, ilk pillar aucht schillings; summa, x^{li}

Item, vj ells of awld canvess to lay about the pulpit heid quhen thai wesche the kirk, ... viij^{s}

Item, to Mungo Huntare for ane lok and pare of bandis and thre keis to the pulpit, ... xij^{s}

Item, for ane lok and ke to the rewestrie dor, ... vij^{s}

Item to twenty pyners quha bure the gret schipe maist fre Leith to the kirk, ... xxvj^{s}

Item, thre dosone garon nalis to this maist, price of dosone ij^{s}; summa, . vj^{s}

JAMES BARROUN, Dean of Guild. May to October, 1560.

Item, iij dosone garron nalis to the cran; summa, . v^{s}

Item, for xviij faddom of ane gret cobill tow to the wyndais that drew owpe the cradill, ... xlviij^{s}

Item, ane pound wecht of small towis to spaiss the gret towe with, xij^{d}

Item, xvij faddom of towis to the armis of the wyndaiss that held thame in mesour, ... xiij^{s} iiij^{d}

Item, x faddom of towis to the heid of the cradill, . . xxiij^{s} viij^{d}

Item, for fyve faddom of towis that past with the cheiff and was layd to the cabill, ... vj^{s} viij^{d}

Item, ix faddom small towis to draw owpe the calk to the cradill, iiij^{s} vj^{d}

Item, viij faddom of tow to the pillie on the maist heid that drew owpe the cradill, ... xj^{s} viij^{d}

Item, x faddom towe to the b (*blank*) at the maist heid that drew owe the samyn, ... v

Item, viij faddom small towis to twa lang ledderis that wysche the pillaris, ... iiij^{s}

Item, v faddom to twa schort ledderis, ... xx^{d}

[125] Item, for iij^{xx} ix laid of lyme to the kirk flure, spargine the samyn, sklating and pointing thairof, and to do all uther necessaris concerning the said kirke affor the v day of October, . . v^{li} xix viij^{d}

Item, for xij dosone and viij laid of sand to mix the lyme, serve the kirk flure, spargyn, pointing, and theking thairof, pryce of the dosone viij^{s}; summa, ... v^{li}

Item, boucht fre Allexander Parke xx stane of irone to be ane part of the standdarttis of the brand windo on the south syd of the kirk, price of the stane, ... (*blank*)

Item, for xxxiiij^{xx} vj fute and ane half newe glass to the said windo, pryce of ilk fute xviij^{d}, ... lj^{li} ix^{s} ix^{d}

Item, for making of ten score xvj fute of auld glass to the iij maid windokis above the queire, ilk fute vj^{d}; summa, ... v^{li} viij^{s}

Item, to George Baxter for bindinge the skaffalding of the windok, xv faddom towe, pryce, ... xv^{s}

Thymmar.

In primis, for xxxviij corbellis, pryce thairof the peice x^{s}; summa, xix^{li}

JAMES BARROUN, Dean of Guild. May to October, 1560.

Item, iij^{xx} Eistland burds, pryce thairof the peice vij^{s} vj^{d}; summa, xxij^{li} x^{s}
Item, foure gret geistis, . . iiij^{li}
Item, for the [maist] of the schippe, vj^{li}
Item, for xxiij geistis, . (*blank*)
Item, ane uther gret geist, . xxxvj^{s}
Item, xxij gret geistis for, xxiiij^{li} iiij^{s}
Item, xxiij schortar geistis. xvj^{li}
Item, xxiiij corbellis, xij^{li}
Item, twa geistis, . . xxxvij^{s}
Item, twa dosone garronis, xlviij^{s}
Item, sex rufe sparris, . xxiiij^{s}
Item, xv plankis of ane schippe, . l^{s}
Item, v dosone daills, the dosone xlviij^{s}; summa, xij^{li}
Item, twa dosone daills, the dosone iij^{li}; summa, . vj^{li}
Item, vij dosone of daills, the dosone xxxviij^{s}; summa, . . . xij^{li} xix^{s}
Item, for xij draucht of this thymmer fre the Newhevin to this burgh, ilk draucht viij^{s}; summa, . iiij^{li} xvj^{s}
Item, to for men that landid thir cartts, . . iiij^{s}
Item, to for pynerss that bure this timmer to the kirk, . . . iiij^{s}
Item, for thre score of drauchtis of this tymmer, furthe of Leith to this burgh, ilk draucht v^{s}; summa, ... xv^{li} ij^{s} vj^{d}
Item, to pure men that bure the thimmer in Leith to the carttis and ladint the samyne, ... xix^{s} viij^{d}
Item, to foure pynors that bure this to the kirk, . . viij^{s}
[126] Item, iij dosone and ane half of daills, at xxxvj^{s} the dosone: summa, . vj^{li} vj^{s}
Item, iij dosone and ane half of daills, the dosone xxxvij^{s}; summa, vj^{li} ix^{s} vj^{d}
Item, for sawing four draucht in ane geist, iiij^{s}
Item, for sawing four draucht in ane geist, ... iij^{s}
Item, for twenty ij pound glew to the kirk doris pannellis bownd wark, and to the mixteine of the calk, pryce of the pound xxij^{d}; summa, xxxvj^{s} viij^{d}
Item, for xiij dosone killing sundis to my and this glew, the dosone x^{d}; summa, ... x^{s} x^{d}
Item, ij laid of collis to melt and seith it with, v^{s} vj^{d}
Item, for piggis to melt the glew in, . v^{s}

Item, for bering of xij ledderis fre Sanct Geilis kirk to Sanct Pawlis wark, iiij[s] JAMES BARROUN, Dean of Guild. May to October, 1560.

Item, to Henry Hatte for symont to lay on the guttaris of the kirk, above umquhille Sanct Anthonis Ile, . vj[s] viij[d]

The expensis and money debursit be the compter upon Leide to the kirk :—

In primis, boucht v[xx] xv stane of clayth leid to the platforming of the steipill, pryce of the stane viij[s] ; summa, . . . xlvj[li]

Item, to the braid wyndo in Sanct Anthonis Ile, boucht xviij stane twa pounds leid, for x[s] the stane, ... ix[li] xv[d]

Item, boucht xxvij stane leid to zet the boltis of the pulpet, new sluttis, loft crowkis of the newe durris, and kirk yeard durris, pryce of the stane vij[s] ; summa, ... ix[li] ix[s]

Item, to Jhone Weire for his laboris, and twa servandis be the space of xiiij dayis, in dressing and platforming off the steipill, solding of the hail guttaris of the kirk quhair ony falt was, and mending of the rest of platformis of the samyne, iiij[li]

The money debursit be the comptar upon the Irone warke, lokks, bandis, nalis, and warkmenschipe of the samyne within the kirk :—

In primis, to Jhone and Henery Smith for xv stane xv pound made wark in twa flaillis, six bandis and twa boltis to the new kirk durre, xxviij glass bands, thir glaiss bandis, pryce of the stane xiij[s] ; summa, xj[li] ij[s] iiij[d]

[127] Item, to the said Jhone for xvj stane foure pound made wark in vj corss bandis to the meikill wyndo heid, and four crukis to the new kirk dure, pryce of the stane xiij[s] ; summa, ... x[li] xj[s] viij[d]

Item, to him for j[c] naillis to the durris and scaffaldis, ilk pece j[d] obolus ; summa, ... xv[s]

Item, coft and ressavit fre David Duncan, smyth, lix stane nyne pound mad wark, in vj bolltis, vj farebottis and vj sparis to the quhelis of the cran, xij stane to the samyne quhelis, twa doubill strakis, twa stirreppis to the creddill, thre boltis to the new loft, ane pare of bandis and ane pare of new crukis to the samyne, for bolltis to the pulpet, thre lang wedis to the pulpet heid, foure boltis to the fute ; and keeing of uther

JAMES BARROUN, Dean of Guild. May to October, 1560.

foure bolltis to the samyne fyve boltis to the mariage saittis; crukis, bandis and boltis to the twa braid yetts in the kirk yeard, sex standartis to the glaspe bandis and sex dosone wedgis to the mikill braid windo, pryce of the stane xiij^{s}; summa, . . . xxxviij^{li} xiiij^{s}

Item, to him for ij^{c} leid nalis, . . . vj^{s}

Item, for ij^{c} plancheour nalis to the fluring of the loft, vj^{s}

Item, iij dosone doubill garroun nalis to the cran, . . . ix^{s}

Item, thre dosone and ane half singill garron nallis to the cran, the dosone ij^{s}; summa, ... vij^{s}

Item, xl planscheour nalis to the fluring of the loft, xij^{d}

Item, j^{c} blynd nail garron nall schank to the saittis, . . . iiij^{s}

Item, j^{c} blynd nale durre nal chank to the heid of the pulpet and sylouring, ij^{s}

Item, j^{c} nalis to scho the cran, . . iiij^{s}

Item, ij^{c} planscheour nale to the loft, . . vj^{s}

Item, xvj nalis to set on the bandis of the new durre to the loft, ij^{s}

Item, xxxij nalis to the pulpet, ... ij^{s} viij^{d}

Item, maire, ij^{c} blynd nale garroune nale schank to the saittis, iiij^{s} the hunder, viij^{s}

Item, v^{xx} nalis to the twa yetts in the kirk yeard, pryce, . v^{s}

Item, maire, ij^{c} leid nalis to the platforme, pryce, . vj^{s}

Item, mair, j^{c} blynd nale garroun nale schank to the saittis, iiij^{s}

Item, j^{c} nalis, maire, to the leid, ... iij^{s}

Item, maire, iiij^{c} blynd nalis garroun nale schank to the saittis, . xvj^{s}

Item, ij^{c} durre nale schank to the saittis, . . . iiij^{s}

[128] Item, maire, xxiiij dowbill garroun nalis to the crann, . . iiij^{s}

Item, maire, viij^{c} iij^{xx} durre nale at twa schillings the hunder to the smal warke and skaffalding; summa, . xvj^{s}

Item, ij^{c} xxxiij garroun nalis at vj^{s} the hunder; summa, . . xiij^{s} vj^{d}

Item, xxj^{c} planscheour nalis at iij^{s} iiij^{d} the hunder; summa, . iij^{li} xj^{s} ix^{d}

Item, to the said David Duncan for ane lok and ten keis to the new kirk durre of the last, ane rang, ane roiss, ane swek, swek heid and ane keper, price of the haill, . . . xx^{s}

Item, for uther twelfe keis to the said kirk durre, . . . xvj^{s}

Item, ane lok and ane pare of bandis to the durre quhare the wrychtis warks, . . . vj^{s}

JAMES BARROUN, Dean of Guild, May to October, 1560.

Item, for ane stok lok to the steipill, . iij^s
Item, for mending of the nether lok durre in the steipill, . . xij^d
Item, for ane ke and slot and twa stapillis to the durre of the howss above the sowth kirk dur, ... iiij^s
Item, ane pare of corslet bandis to the dure of the steipell, . . iij
Item, for ane spar and furlok to the credill and dressing of the bell to it, ij^s
Item, twa scraperis to the spargeris and twa virrellis to the cradill, iij^s
Item, for mending of ane mattok and thre pound irone, pryce thairof, ij
Item, ane sweik and sweikheid and the keiper of it wes pittine on the new sait in the kirk dure, ... iij^s
Item, ane new scheif to the pillie, weyand xxx lib wecht, pryce, . . xxvj iij^d
Item, for mending of ane lok to the steipell, . . . ix^d
Item, to Jhone Bankis, smyth, for xiiij glaiss bandis, weyand thre stane of iron and twa pound and ane halfe to thre wyndokis above the queire, pryce of the stane xiiij^s; summa, . . . xl iij^d
Item, mare, for foure gless bandis to the braid wyndo, pryce of the stane xiij^s, weyand thre stane vj pound; summa, ... xliij^s x^d
Item, v score lokit pynnis to the said windo, weyand ane stane and thre pound, pryce of the stane xiij^s; summa, . . . xv^s x^d
Item, for vij pound of irone and warkmanschipe in eiking of lxxx glaiss bandis to the said windo, ... iiij^s
[129] Item, for v pound of irone and eiking of viij new bandis and twa auld bandis to the windokis in the queire, ... iij^s iij^d
Item, for glaiss bandis iroune betwix windo, weyand foure pownd and fouertyne unce, pryce, ... iiij
Item, ane pare of bandis to beire owpe the ard to Jhone Carns kneis and the rest to the samyne, and the irone to the pulpit that the bassyng standis on, pryce of all, ... xxx^s
Item, ane lok and twa keis to the meikill kirk durre, ane grait ring and ane roiss and ane smal ring and ane roiss with ane bar, pryce of all, xliiij^s
Item, for twa bandis and twa crukis of irone to the Haly Blud Ile, . iij^s
Item, maire, foure boltis of irone, weyand xx lib, to the new loft, the stane xiiij^s; summa, ... xvij^s vj^d
Item, thre stok lokis with the keis to the steipill, xij^s

JAMES BARROUN, Dean of Guild. May to October, 1560.

Item, xvij pound wecht of maid boltis, . xv^{s}
Item, foure grait garroun nalis to the pulpet, vj^{d}
Item, ij^{c} singill garroun nalis, pryce, ... viij^{s}
Item, for thre corsstalit bandis and ane chek lok with iiij keis with ring, roiss and nalis to the saitt at Sanct Annis alter, pryce, . . xx^{s}
Item, iiij^{xx} glaiss bandis, contening in wecht foure stane and twelfe pound, to the meikil windo, pryce of the stane xiij^{s}; summa, . . . iij^{li} j^{s} ix^{d}
Item, for ane standert and thre thertouris with thar lokkis and thar sweikis in thame to the grait windo, contenand aucht stane and twa pound wecht, pryce of the stane xiij^{s}; summa, . . . liij^{s}
Item, for the furnesing of foure durris to the saittis with roissis nalis and swelkis, ... xxxij^{s}
Item, iiij^{c} laissand nalis to the kirk dur, pryce of the hunder xx^{s}; summa, iiij^{li}

[130] The Expensis mad upoun masonns, barromen, wrychtis, sawaris and spargenris fre the xvj day of Junii 1560, reparelling of the kirk to the (*blank*) of (*blank*) at the quhilk Maister James Watsoun, Deine of Gild, enterit thairto:—

In primis, to Gilbert Gray, masoun, xxx^{s}
Item, to William Barre, masoun, . xxx^{s}
Item, to Robert Crumme, masoun, xxx^{s}

Barromen.

Item, to Jhone Symsoun, . xij^{s}
Item, to William Boncle, . xij^{s}
Item, to William Walker, xij^{s}
Item, to Robert Drummond, xij^{s}

Wrichtis.

Item, to George Baxter, . xxx^{s}
Item, to Andrew Williamsoun, xxx^{s}
Item, to David Williamsoun, xxx^{s}
Item, to George Williamsoun, xxiiij^{s}
Item, to David Mure, . xxiiij^{s}
Item, to Allexander Fyndar, xxiiij^{s}

James Barroun, Dean of Guild, May to October, 1560.

Item, to David Carsam, sawer, for iij dayis wadgis, precedand the xxix day of Junii, ... xij^{s}

Item, to David Lawresoun, his marrowe, for the said iij days laubouris, . xij^{s}

The oulkis wadgis precedand Sonnday the xxx day of Junij :—

Massouns.

In primis, to William Barre, masoun, xx^{s}

James Masoun, xx^{s}

Robert Crumme, . xx^{s}

David Kippill, xx^{s}

Jhone Phyllope, xx^{s}

Barromen.

Patrik Maxwel, xij^{s}

Jhone Symsoun, xij^{s}

Williame Boncle, . xij^{s}

Jhone Craige, . xij^{s}

[131] Robert Drowmond, . . . xij^{s}

Item, for thar soupper on Satterday at evin, ij^{s}

Wrychtis.

George Baxter, . xxvj^{s}

Andro Williamsoun, xxvj^{s}

David Williamsoun, xxvj^{s}

David Mure, . xx^{s}

George Williamsoun, . xx^{s}

Allexander Fyndar, ... xx^{s}

Item, for thar soupperis on Setterday at elvin, the xxix day of Junij, x^{s}

Sawaris.

Item, to Allexander McCalpye and his marrowe, to ilk one of thame on the day be the space of ij dayis, iij^{s}; summa, . xvj^{s}

The wagis peyit to the masounis, barromen, wrychtis for the oulk immedewlie precedand Sonnday the vij of Julj 1560 :—

Masounis.

James Masoun, xxiiij^{s}

James Barroun, Dean of Guild, May to October, 1560.

Williame Barre, .	xxiiij^s
Robert Croumie, .	xxiiij^s
David Kippill,	xx^s
Jhone Philippe,	xx^s

Barromen.

Patrik Maxwel,	xij^s
Jhone Symsoun, .	xij^s
William Boncle,	xij^s
Jhone Craige,	xij^s
Robert McBrair, .	xij^s
Andro Connell, .	xij^s
Robert Drowmund, . . .	xij^s
Item, for thir barromenis soupper on Setterday the saxt of Julii,	iij^s

Wrychtis.

George Baxter, .	xxvj^s
Andro Williamsoun,	xxvj^s
George Williamsoun,	xxiiij^s
David Williamsoun,	xx^s
David Mure, .	xx^s
Allexander Fyndar, .	xviij^s
Item, for thir wrychtis supper the said Setterday,	x^s

[132] The Expense of the masonis, barromen and wrychtis of the oulk immediatlie precedand Setterday the xiiij day of Julii 1560 :—

Masonis.

James Masoun, .	xxiiij^s
Williame Barre,	xxiiij^s

Barromen.

Patrik Maxwel, .	xij^s
Jhone Symsoun,	xij^s
Andro Connell,	xij^s
Jhone Craige, .	xij^s
Robert Drowmund, ...	xij^s
Item, for thir barromenis supparis on Setterday the xiiij day of Julii,	ij^s

JAMES BARROUN, Dean of Guild. May to October, 1560.

Wrychtis.

George Baxter, .	xxvj^s
Andro Williamsoun,	xxvj^s
George Williamsoun,	xxiiij^s
David Williamsoun,	xx^s
Donald Mure, ...	xx^s
Item, Thomas Keinede for ij dayis lauboris, . .	viij^s
Item, for thir sex wrychtis supparis on Setterday forsaid,	x^s

The masounis, wrychtis, barromen and sawaris wadgis, preceedand Setterday the xxj day of Julii 1560 :—

Masounis.

James Masoun,	xxiiij^s
Williame Barre, .	xxiiij^s

Barromen.

Patrick Maxwel, .	xij^s
Jhone Symsoun,	xij^s
Andro Connell,	xij^s
Jhone Crage, ...	xij^s
Item, for thair supparis on Setterday last,	ij^s

Wrychtis.

George Baxter, .	xxvj^s
Andro Williamsoun,	xxvj^s
George Williamsoun,	xxiiij^s
Item, for thair soupper,	v^s

Sawaris.

[133] Item, to Allexander Makcalpie for four dayis laboris,	xx^s
Item, to his marro,	xx^s

The oulkis wadgis, preceedand Sonnday the xxviij day of Julii 1560 :—

Masounis.

Jamis Masoun,	xxiiij^s
Williame Barre, .	xxiiij^s

James Barroun, Dean of Guild, May to October, 1560.

Barromen.

Patrik Maxweil,	xij^s
Jhone Symsoun,	xij^s
Jhone Craige,	xij^s
Andro Connell,	xij^s
Robert Drummound,	xij^s
Item, thar soupparis on Setterday 27 day of Julii,	ij^s

Wrychtis.

George Baxter,	xxvj^s
Andro Williamsoun,	xxvj^s
George Williamsoun,	xxvj^s

Spargearis.

Fynale Maquhannane,	xviij^s
Allaster Smyth,	xvj^s
Robert Pawle,	x^s

The oulkis wadgis, precedand Sonnday iiij Agust :—

Masounis.

Henery Bawte,	xxiiij^s
Johannes Mar, his servand,	xx^s
Williame Barre,	xxiiij^s

Barromen.

Patrik Maxwel,	xij^s
Jhone Symsoun,	xij^s
Jhone Crage,	xij^s
Andro Connell,	xij^s
Robert Drowmund,	xij^s
Item, for thair supparis on Settarday iij Agust,	ij^s

Wrychtis.

[134] George Baxter,	xxvj^s
David Dronar, his man,	xx^s
Andro Williamsoun,	xxvj^s

JAMES BARROUN, Dean of Guild. May to October, 1560.

George Williamsoun,	xxiij^{s}
Item, thar supparis,	x^{s}

Spargenaris.

Finlay Marquhannan,	xviij^{s}
Allaster Smyth,	xvj^{s}
James Schawe,	x^{s}

Warkmennis wadgis debursit in the owlk precedand Sonday the xij of August 1560 :—

Massounis.

Henery Bate,	xxiiij^{s}
Thomas Mure, his man,	xx^{s}
James Masoun,	xxiiij^{s}
Andro Gede, his servand,	xx^{s}
Williame Barre,	xxiiij^{s}

Barromen.

Patrik Maxwell,	xij^{s}
Jhone Symsoun,	xij^{s}
Jhone Craige,	xij^{s}
Andro Connell,	xij^{s}
Marteine Pawle,	xij^{s}
Williame Gibsoun,	xij^{s}
Jhone Cunninghame,	xij^{s}
Gilbert McMillane,	xij^{s}
Robert Drummownd,	xij^{s}
Item, thar supparis on Setterday the xj day of Agust,	iiij^{s}

Wrichtis.

George Baxter,	xxvj^{s}
Henery Andersoun, his servand,	xx^{s}
Andro Williamsoun,	xxvj^{s}
Francis Weir, his servand,	xx^{s}
Andro Williamsoun,	xxvj^{s}
Patrik Schang,	xxvj^{s}

JAMES BARROUN, Dean of Guild. May to October, 1560.

George Do, his servand, xx^{s}
Adam Schang, . . xx^{s}
William Ra, servand to Jhone Cunynghame, xviij^{s}
Henery Kok, servand to Robert Moffet, . xviij^{s}
Item, for thar supparis, x^{s}

[135]

Spargenaris.

Item, to Finla McQuhannan, xviij^{s}
Item, to Allaster Smyth, . xvj^{s}
Item, to Thomas Thomsaine, viij^{s}

Sawaris.

Item, to Allexander McCalpie for fyve days in sawing of tymmar, xxv^{s}
Item, to David Jhonistoun his compenzeoun that helpit to serve him in sawing of the said tymmer be the said space of fywe dayis, xxv^{s}
Item, for turning of the standart that beris owpe the new loft, viij^{s} vj^{d}

The oulks wadgis precedand xx August 1560 :—

Masounis.

Henery Bawtre, . xxiiij^{s}
William Mar, his servand, xx^{s}
Jamis Masoun, xxiiij^{s}
George Hendersoun, his servand, . xx^{s}
William Barre, xxiiij^{s}

Barromen.

Patrik Maxweill, xij^{s}
Jhone Symsoun, xij^{s}
Jhone Craige, xij^{s}
Andro Connell, . xij^{s}
Item, to Marteine Paule, . xij^{s}
William Gibsoun, . xij^{s}
Jhone Cunnynghame, xij^{s}
Gilbert McNellan, . xij^{s}
Robert Drummound, xij^{s}
Item, thar supparis, iiij^{s}

JAMES BARROUN, Dean of Guild. May to October, 1560.

Wrichtis.

George Baxter,	xxvj^s
Robert Boyman, his servand,	xx^s
Andro Williamsoun,	xxvj^s
Henery Roust, his servand,	xx^s
David Williamsone,	xx^s
Thomas Kenulde,	xxvj^s
Robert Moffet,	xxvj^s
Jhone Ged, his servand,	xviij^s
Patrik Schang,	xxvj^s
Thomas Tod, his servand,	xx^s
[136] Adam Schang,	xx^s
David Maw, servand to Jhone Cunnynghame,	xviij^s
Item, for thar supparis on Setterday xviij Augusti,	x^s

Spargenaris.

Item, Finlai McQuhannan,	xviij^s
Item, to Jhone McConnell, his servand,	xvj^s
Item, to Jhone Droner quha servit thame,	x^s

Sawaris.

Allexander McCalpe,	xxv^s
Item, his marrowe,	xxv^s

The expensis made upon masounis, barromen, wrichtis, painteris, sauaris, in the oulk immediatlie precedand Sounday the xxv of August 1560:—

Masounis.

Henery Bate,	xxiiij^s
Jamis Tod, his servand,	xx^s
Jamis Masoun,	xxiiij^s
Henery Cant, his servand,	xx^s
William Barre,	xxiiij^s

Barromen.

Patrik Maxwel,	xij^s
Jhone Symsoun,	xij^s

JAMES BARROUN, Dean of Guild. May to October, 1560.

Jhone Craige,	xij^s
Andro Connell,	xij^s
Martene Pawl,	xij^s
William Gibsoun, .	xij^s
Jhone Cunnynghame,	xij^s
Gilbert Makmillane,	xij^s
Robert Drummound, . .	xij^s
Item, for thar supparis, xxiiij Augusti,	iiij^s

Wrichtis.

George Baxter, . .	xxvj^s
Cudbert Dik, his servand,	xviij^s
Alexander Furd, .	xx^s
Andro Williamsoun, .	xxvj^s
Robert Clark, his servand,	xviij^s
David Williamsoun,	xx^s
Thomas Kinnede, .	xxiiij^s
Robert Moffet, . .	xx^s
Thomas Broun, his servand,	xviij^s
George Williamsoun,	xx^s
Adam Schange, .	xx^s
Item, for thar supparis,	x^s

[137]

Paynteris.

Jhone Sampsoun, . . .	xx^s
James Schange, his servand,	xij^s
Jhone Watsoun,	xvj^s

Sawaris.

Item, to Allexander McCalpye, . .	xxiiij^s
Item, to Jhone Lowresoun, his marrow,	xxiiij^s

The oulkis wagis precedand Sonnday the first of September:—

Masounis.

Henery Bate, masoun, . .	xxiiij^s
James Rynd, his servand,	xx^s

James Masoun, . . xxiiij^s

Thomas Todener, his servand, xx^s

JAMES BARROUN, Dean of Guild, May to October, 1560.

Barromen.

Patrik Maxweill, .	xij^s
Jhone Symsoun,	xij^s
Andro Connell,	xij^s
Martene Paule,	xij^s
William Gibsoun, .	xij^s
Gilbert McMellane,	xij^s
Robert Drummound,	xij^s
Item, for thar supparis,	iiij^s

Wrichtis.

George Baxter, . .	xxvj^s
Robert Bate, his servand, ...	xviij^s
Item, to Jhone Banx, his uther servand, of the said George, for four dayis,	xij^s
Andro Williamsoun, . .	xxvj^s
Jhone Young, his servand,	xviij^s
Item, to Robert Moffet	xx^s
Jhone Scott, his servand, .	xvj^s
Thomas Kennede, iij dayis laboris,	x^s
Item, for thar supparis, .	x^s

Spargenaris.

Fynlai McQuhannan, . .	xv^s
David Mar, his servand, the space of fyve dayis, .	x^s

Payntteris.

Jhone Sampsoun, thre dayis lauboris,	x^s
Jhone Blythman, his servand, thre dayis, .	vij^s

Sawaris.

Item, to Allexander McCalpye for thre dais,	xv^s
Item, to Robert Tod, his helpar, .	xv^s

JAMES BARROUN, Dean of Guild. May to October, 1560.

[138]

The oulkis wagis immediatlie precedand the aucht day of September the yeir of God 1560 :—

Masounis.

Henery Bawte, . .	xxiiij^s
David Gray, his servand, .	xx^s
Jamis Masoun,	xxiiij^s
His servand,	xx^s

Barromen.

Patrik Maxweill, .	xij^s
Jhon Symsoun,	xij^s
Andro Connell,	xij^s
Martene Paule,	xij^s
William Gibsoun, .	xij^s
Gilbert McMyllane,	xij^s
Robert Drummound, ...	xij^s
Item, for thar supparis on Setterday the vij day of September,	iiij^s

Wrichtis.

George Baxter, .	xxvj^s
Robert Boyman, his servand, .	xviij^s
William Ra and ane servand of his,	xx^s
Andro Williamsoun,	xxvj^s
Andro Ker, his servand,	xviij^s
Robert Moffet,	xx^s
Jhone Mure, his servand, .	xvj^s
Thomas Kennede, .	xx^s
Item, for thar supparis,	x^s

Spargenaris.

Fynlai McQuhannan, .	xviij^s
David Gray, his servand, . .	xij^s
Item, to Robert Weir that servit thame, .	viij^s

Painteris.

Jhone Symsoun, . . .	xx^s
Jhone Banx, his servand, .	xiiij^s

JAMES BARROUN, Dean of Guild. May to October, 1560.

Jhone Forster,	xviij^s
Jhone Watsoun, .	xiiij^s

Sawaris.

Item, to Allexander McCalpie for foure dayis laubors,	xx^s
Item, to Robert Kyle, his marrow,	xx^s

The oulkis wagis precedand Sonnday the xv of September 1560 :—

Henery Bate, .	xxiiij^s
Jhone Grahame, his servand,	xx^s
Arthur Hammyltounis servand,	xvj^s
Jamis Masoun, . .	xxiiij^s
Robert Stuthie, his servand,	xviij^s

Barromen.

[139] Patrik Maxweill, .	xij^s
Jhone Symsoun,	xij^s
Andro Connell,	xij^s
Marten Paule, .	xij^s
Robert Drummound, .	xij^s
William Gibsoun, twa dayis lauboris,	ij^s vj^d
Andro McMyllane, twa dayis labor,	ij^s vj^d
Item, thar supparis of Setterday 14 of September,	iij^s

Wrichtis.

George Baxter, .	xxvj^s
William Adamsoun, his servand, .	xviij^s
Andro Williamsoun, .	xxvj^s
Jhone Geddrek, his servand,	xviij^s
David Hoip, ane uther servand, .	xviij^s
Robert Moffet, . .	xx^s
Thomas Lang, his servand,	xvj^s
Thomas Kennede, his servand,	xx^s
George Williamsoun,	xviij^s
Item, thar supparis,	x^s

JAMES BARROUN, Dean of Guild. May to October, 1560.

Spargenaris.

Fynlai McQuhannan, . xviij^s
James Blakwod, . . xiiij^s
Thomas Quhyt, that servit thame, viij^s

Paynteris.

Jhone Symsoun, . . . xx^s
Henery Guthre, his servand, xiiij^s
Jhone Forster, xx^s
Andro Watsoun, . xiiij^s

Sauaris.

Item, to Allexander McCalpie and his marrow for thre dayis wagis, xxx^s

The oulks wagis precedand Sounday the xxij day of September, debursit upon the warkmen wirkand in the Kirke of Edinbrogh 1560 :—

Masounis.

Henery Bate, masoun, xxiiij^s
Jhone Scott, his servand, . xx^s
Jamis Masoun, . xxiiij^s
Robert Parke, his servand, xviij^s

Barromen.

Patrik Maxweil, . xij^s
Jhone Symsoun, xij^s
Martein Paule, xij^s
Andro Connell, xij^s
Item, for thar supparis, ij^s

Wrichtis.

[140] George Baxter, . . . xxvj^s
Jamis Walker, his servand, xviij^s
George Williamsoun, . xviij^s
Andro Williamsoun, . xxvj^s
David Mwte, his servand, xviij^s
Robert Moffet, xx^s

JAMES BARROUN, Dean of Guild. May to October, 1560.

William Reidpeth, his servand,	xvj^s
Thomas Kennede, .	xx^s
Item, thar supparis, . . .	x^s

Spargenaris and Paintteris.

Fynlai McQuhannan, . .	xviij^s
Jamis Blakwod for four dayis lauboris,	viij^s
Jhone Sampsoun, . . .	xx^s
Jhone Forster, .	xx^s
Andro Watsoun, . . .	xiiij^s
David Younge, Jhone Sampsonis man,	xiiij^s

Sawaris.

Item, to Allexander McCalpie and his marrow for foure day laboris, .	xl^s

The wagis debursit upon the warkmen in the oulk immediatlie precedand Sonnday the xxix day of September 1560 :—

Masounis.

Henry Bate, . .	xxiiij^s
Andro Gray, his servand, .	xx^s
Jamis Masoun, . .	xxiiij^s
William Lowre, his servand,	xviij^s

Barromen.

Patrik Maxweill, .	xij^s
Jhone Symsoun,	xij^s
Martene Paule,	xij^s
Andro Connell, .	xij^s
Item, for thar supparis, .	ij^s

Wrichtis.

George Baxter, . .	xxvj^s
William Wauche, his servand,	xviij^s
Andro Williamsoun,	xxvj^s
Robert Foster, his man,	xviij^s
Thomas Kennede, .	xx^s
George Williamsoun, .	xviij^s

JAMES BARROUN, Dean of Guild. May to October, 1560.

Robert Moffet twa dayis lauboris,	vj^s viij^d
Andro Borl, his man,	xvj^s
For thar supparis,	x^s

Spargenaris and Paynteris.

Fynlay McQuhannan,	xviij^s
Jhone Symsoun,	xx^s
David Kie, his servand,	xiiij^s
Jhone Forster,	xx^s
Jamis Blakwod,	xij^s

Sawaris.

[141] Item, to Allexander Makcalpie and his marrow for four days lauboris, . xl^s

The warkmenis wagis of the oulk immediatlie precedand the sext of October 1560 :—

Masounis.

Jhone Patersoun thre days wagis,	xij^s
Henery Bate,	xxiiij^s
Robert Craik, his servand,	xx^s
Jamis Masoun,	xxiiij^s
Jamis Lowrie, his servand,	xviij^s

Barromen.

Patrik Maxweill,	xij^s
Jhone Symsoun,	xij^s
Martein Paule,	xij^s
Andro Connell,	xij^s
Item, for thar supparis,	ij^s

Wrichtis.

George Baxter,	xxvj^s
Cudbert Dic, his servand,	xviij^s
Andro Williamsoun,	xxvj^s
Jhone Clark, his servand,	xviij^s
Thomas Kennede,	xx^s
George Williamsoun,	xviij^s

JAMES BARROUN, Dean of Guild. May to October, 1560.

Robert Moffettis servand, . xvj^{s}
Jhone Cunnynghame, . xx^{s}
Robert Aitken, his servand, xviij^{s}
Item, thar supparis, . x

Spargenaris, Paintereis.

Jhone Sampsoun, . . xx^{s}
Williame Myrreleis, his servand, . xiiij^{s}
Jhone Forster, xx^{s}
Jamis Blakwod, . xij^{s}
Fynlaj M'Quhannan, xviij^{s}

Sawaris.

Item, to Allexander Makcalpie and his marrow for foure dayis and ane halt, xlv^{s}

The Officiaris.

In primis, to the xij officiaris of this burgh for thare burgeschippis. . xxxvj^{li}
Item, his fee, . vj^{li} xiij^{s} iiij^{d}
Item, his servandis fee, ... iiij^{li}
Item, Thomas Hall, Javolour, his burgeschippe, v^{li}
Item, Richard Troup, his burgeschippe, . . v^{li}
Item, to Thomas Watsoun, glassynwricht, for his yeiris fie, . . iiij^{li}
Item, at the counsellis command, to Jhone Knox, minister, for his half yeiris stipened precedand the moneth of Februar instant, . . ij$^{c\,li}$
[142] Item, mar, at the counsellis command, upoun the vij of Februar instant, awant to him his quarters fie, . j^{li}
Item, to him to by howsald geire, ... xxj^{li}
Item, to Margaret, his barne, the relict of umquhill Patrik Irland, for the said Jhonis howss maill at the heving thereof, . . x^{mark}
Item, to Jhone Carnis, be ane precept of the daitt iij^{o} Januarii 1560, . xl^{s}
Item, be ane precept of the counsallis of the dait the aucht of September be Maister Jhone Spens, baillie, the dewyss of ane burgeschippe in recompence of his pains and laubors tane this last yeire, . . v^{li}
Item, to David Somer, be ane precept of the counsellis of the daitt the xx day of September 1560, for his laboris in lyk maner, the dewte of ane burgess and gildschippe, . . . v^{li}

*

JAMES BARROUN, Dean of Guild. May to October, 1560.

Item, thar was tynt be the Ingliche layit money ressavit be Patrik Browne, officiar, in uptakine of the malis, cordineris chopis and standis about the kirk, ... iiij^{li} x^{s}

Item, (*blank*) to bellmen for keiping of the kirk, . . . ij^{li}

Item, to him for deichtine of the gutters, . . . xxx^{s}

Item, to him for the gild serwandschippe, . . . xxx^{s}

Item, for the ringing of the bells to the lordis at thar convening, . . . xx^{s}

Summa of the comptaris hale discharge, . . . j^{m} ij^{c} lxxiij^{li} x^{s} vij^{d}

And sue the compter is superexpendit his charge, quhilk is, j^{m} j^{c} xxvj^{li} xvj^{s} ij^{d}— j^{c} xlvij^{li} xv^{s} v^{d}

[143] The xx day of Februar the yeire of God J^{m} v^{c} lx yeiris, the compt of Jamis Barroun, Dene of Gild, quhais entre to the said office was in the monethe of Maij, in the yeire of God J^{m} v^{c} and lx yeiris, as said is, the office being refusit be Thomas Uddert. The said Jamis charge and discharge be the auditors underwretine have seine and considerit. The charge extending to ane thowsand ane hunderethe twenty sex poundis xvj^{s} ij^{d}. And his discharge to ane thousand twa hunderethe thre scor fouertin poundis xj^{s} vij^{d}. And sue the said comptar superexpendit, the quhilkis restis awand him be the guid toun, the soum of j^{c} xlvij^{li} xv^{s} v^{d}.

Ita est. David Symmer.
Jamis Adamsoun.
Thomas Thomsoun.
Jamis Thomsoun.
Louk Wilsoun, with my hand led be Alex^{r} Guthre, clark.
Thomas Reidpeth, with my hand led be the said clark.
Alex^{r} Smyth, with my hand led be the said clark.
Allex^{r} Guthre, Scriba Civitatis de Ed^{r}.

Memorand: I haif left out of this compt xv^{c} sclatis, cost xj crouns the hundereth; summa, ... viij^{li} v^{s}

And for bringing of thame fre Leith, . xxij^{s}

Yit to the sclater that wroucht upon the kirke mending and poyntin it, viij^{li} JAMES BARROUN, Dean of Guild. May to October, 1560.

Item, peyit to the quariors that wroucht at the Gray Freiris for sertane stains to the newe durr, . xviij^{s}

Summa, ... xviij^{li} v^{s}

Memorand: Jamis Barroun is to be chargit with xxvj^{li} xvj^{s} viij^{d} quhilk Maister Jhone Prestoun haiss debursit in maner following:-

Item, the tyme of the absence of the Faythfull at the fortafeing of Leyth befor the incuming of Inglish Arme the said Maister Jhone, elect Deine of Gild, ressavit in his tyme befoir Jamis Barroun was chosine, for xiij schippis, ... ix^{li} ij^{s}

Item, for burgeschippis as the particular compt beris, xj^{li} xiij^{s} iiij^{d}

Summa Exonerationis, . xx^{li} xvj^{s} iiij^{d}

[144] Item, ij^{o} Martii 1559, to the xij officiaris and the javilior, ilk ane of thame to ane compt of burgeschippe xl^{s}: summa, . . . xxvj^{li}

Item, at the Quenyis command for munting of ane new powpet, placing of the stallis in the awld maner and sicce uther wikitness, . xvj^{s} viij^{d}

Summa Exonerationis, ... xxvj^{li} xvj^{s} viij^{d}

And sue is the compter superexpendit vj^{li} xvj^{s} vj^{d} peyit to him be the said Jamis Barroun.

And sue the forsaid xviij^{li} v^{s} foryet be the said Jamis Barroun in his compt allowit to him, the said Maister Jhone peyit his rest forsaid. The said Jamis Barroun restis awand to the guid toun xxxv^{s} becawss this rest, befor the compter subscryvit, is payit to him be Lowk Wulsoun.

---

[145] THE CHARGE of Maister JAMIS WATSOUN, Dene of Gild of the burgh of Edinburgh, in the yeire of God 1560 yeiris, and entres thereto the vj day of October, yeire forsaid. JAMES WATSOUN, Dean of Guild. 1560-61.

In primis, the comptar chargis him with thre belleces of the orgains, coft be Jhone Mosman for, ... vj^{li}

Item, the xiij day of Januar, resavit be the comptar of sylwer wark, viz.,

JAMES WATSOUN, Dean of Guild. 1560-61.

ane croce and ane chellice of the Holy blud olim, and ane uther of Sanct Anthone, weyand all to gidder in presence of Allexander Guthre, David Symmer and Michael Gilbert, quha coft the samyne for xxiij schillingis the unce, iiij^{xx} xj unce; summa in money, ... j$^{c\,li}$ xiiij^{s}

Item, the comptar chargis him with x^{xx} xviij stane of brassine pyllars with the men and the lectrone of brass, and of iiij^{xx} xiij stane xij lib weicht quhilk I wes causit to sell for xviij^{s} the stane to Adam Fullartoun, bailye, be the counsall, extending in money, . . ij^{c} iiij$^{xx\,li}$ xj^{s} vj^{d}

Item, the comptar chargis him with the burgess and gildschippis as the lokkit buik proportis, extending to the soum of, . . vij^{c} xl^{li} vj^{s} viij^{d}

Item, in lykwyiss of the frauchting of the schippis that past furth of Leith this yeire, xiiij^{s} ilk schipe, as the buk of entery proportis; summa, iij^{xx} ix^{li} viij^{s}

Item, the comptar chargis him with the malis of the cordinaris choppis, extending to, ... xxj^{li}

Item, with the choppis about the kirk, viz.:—

Adame Denonne, .	xxx^{s}
Jhonne Gilbert, .	xxx^{s}
George Turnoris choppe,	xxx^{s}
George Turnoris stand,	xl^{s}
Andro Heleis stand, .	xl^{s}
Cristell Galbraithis choppe, .	xxx^{s}
Summa of thir choppis, .	x^{li}
Summa totuis Onerationis,	j^{m} ij^{c} xxvij^{li} xvij^{s}

[146] THE EXPENSIS made be me, the said Compter, upone the said masounis, wrychtis, barromen, sawaris, spargeouris, glassinwrychtis, quariuris, pynnoris, and uther necessaris pertenning to the kirk and reparaling thairof, fre the vj day of October in the yeire of God J^{m} v^{c} lxj yeiris:—

Monunday, vij Octobris.

Item, for vj laid Costland lyme to thre sklatars that theikit the kirk and poynt it, iij^{s} the laid; summa, . . xviij^{s}

Item, for xij laid sand, vj^{d} the laid; summa, . vj^{s}

Item, for twa skeppis to the bodie of the pulpet, . v^{s}

JAMES WATSOUN, Dean of Guild, 1560-61.

Tuisday, viij of October.

Item, for 4 laid lyme, xxxiiij^{d} the laid; summa, . xj^{s} iiij^{d}
Item, for viij laid sand, ... iiij^{s}
Item, to vj pynoris for carying of thre throwchtis fre the freiris, vj^{s}
Item, to sex pynoris for carying of xj throwchis fre the freiris, . . xxij^{s}
Item, to ij quarioris for wynninge of thame and cutting of thame in the middis, thre dayis wagies, ... xx^{s}
Item, for four gret candil for putting owpe of the glass in the gret windo, xvj^{d}
Item, to Alan Purvess for j^{c} calk, for ix^{d} stane; summa, . . iiij^{li} x^{s}

Wedinsday, ix of October.

Item, for candill at mornyng for removinge the mast, vj^{d}
Item, for four laid of lyme, for iij^{s} the laid; summa, xij^{s}
Item, for awcht laid sand, ... iij^{s}
Item, to xij pynoris for helping to remowe the mast, sex ^{d} the pece; summa, vj^{s}
Item, to twa warkmen for fowsing the kirk yard, ij^{s} the pece; summa, . iiij^{s}

Turisday, x Octobris.

Item, for four laid lyme, . . . xij^{s}
Item, for aucht laid sand, ... iiij^{s}
Item, for candill at mornyng, . . . vj^{d}

Fryday, xj Octobris.

Item, for four laid lyme, . . . xij^{s}
Item, for aucht laid sand, ... iiij^{s}

Satterday, xij Octobris.

Masounis.

Henery Bate, . . xxvj^{s}
Item, to his servand, xviij^{s}
Item, to Jamis Masoun, xxvj^{s}
Item, to his servand, . xviij^{s}
Item, to Jhone Patersoun, . xxiiij^{s}

Wrichtis.

George Baxter, ... xxvj^{s}
Allexander Fyndar, his servand, . . xviij^{s}

JAMES WATSOUN, Dean of Guild, 1560-61.

Andro Williamsoun,	xxvj^s
David Murray, his servand,	xviij^s
Jhone Cunnynghame,	xxvj^s
Thomas Kennede,	xx^s
Edward Lowre, his servand,	xviij^s
Michael Thomsoun, servand,	xviij^s
George Williamsoun, servand,	xviij^s
Item, to thame in drink sylver,	x^s

Spargenaris.

Johnne Sampsoun,	xx^s
Johnne Froster,	xx^s
Johnne Norwell,	xiiij^s
Fynlaj Balquhannan,	xviij^s
Jamis Blakwod,	xij^s

Barromen.

Andro Connell,	xij^s
Martein Paule,	xij^s
Johnne Symsoun,	xij^s
Patrik Maxwell,	xij^s
Item, to thame in drink sillwer,	ij^s

Sawaris.

William Ekkalis and Allexander McCalpye x^s on the day; summa,	iij^{li}
Item, to the walter wyffe,	iij^s
Item, to the Inglischmen for fywe leddars,	l^s; x^s the pece
Item, for condill at even,	viij^d
Summa this oulk precedand Sounday the xiij day of October, is,	xl^{li} iiij^d

Sonnday xiij day of October.

Monnday.

Item, for four laid of lyme,	x^s viij^d
Item, for awcht laid sand,	iiij^s
Item, for candill at evning and mornyng,	xij^d
Item, to twa men for biggin owpe of the yettis and durris with lowss stanis of the ludgyng in the kirk yeard,	iij^s

JAMES WATSOUN, Dean of Guild. 1560-61.

Tuisday.

[148] Item, for candill at mornyng, viij^{d}
Item, for four laid of lyme, xij^{s}
Item, for aucht laid of sand, ... iiij^{s}
Item, for thre elnis and ane half of Frenche grein to covre the ministers burd, xij^{s} the elne; summa, ... xiij^{s}
Item, to the wrichtis officiar that cersit the towne with Johnne Cunnynghame and me quhen the tymmer was stowne, . ij^{s}
Item, for condill at evin, ... viij^{d}
Item, to twa warkmen for helping the fowseis of the kirk yeard, iiij^{s}

Wedinsday.

Item, for ane pype lok to the south kirk dorre, vj^{s} viij^{d}
Item, for candill, mornyng, at eining, . xij^{d}

Thurisday.

Item, for ane Frenche lecteron buk to Johnne Knox, xx^{s}
Item, for candill at morning, . . . vj^{d}
Item, for candill at evin for taking doun of the mast, xij^{d}

Fryday.

Item, for candill mornyng and eining, xij^{d}
Item, for twa laid of lyme, . vj^{s}
Item, for four laid of sand, . ij^{s}

Setterday.

Item, for twa men that walkit the kirk sene Tysday the tymmer wes stowine, ilk nycht ij^{s}; summa, ... viij^{s}
Item, coft fre Andro Lambe in Leith ij^{c} calk for viij^{d} the stane; summa, iiij^{li}
Item, for bryning owpe of it, ... vj^{s}
Wrichtis: this nyt I tuk doune thar wagis and x^{s} of drink silver upon ane premiss with Johnne Cunnynghame.
Item, to Johnne Cunnynghame, . xx^{s}
Item, to George Baxter, . . xx^{s}
Item, to Andro Williamsoun, . . xx^{s}
Item, to George Tod, . . xx^{s}

JAMES WATSOUN, Dean of Guild. 1560-61.

Item, to William Kennedy,	xx^{s}
Item, to thar v servandis, ilk ane xiiij^{s}; summa,	iij^{li} x^{s}
Item, for glew to the pannellis,	iiij^{s}
Item, for ane band of iron to join twa standertis togidder,	xvj^{d}
Item, to George Baxter for j^{c} blynd nall,	ij^{s}

Masounes.

[149] Item, to the masounes, as said is,	v^{li} xij^{s}

Spargenaris.

Item, to the spargenaris, as said is,	iiij^{li} iiij^{s}
Item, for twa bent skeppis to thame,	xx^{d}
Item, for takkettis,	vj^{d}

Sawaris.

Item, to the twa sawars,	iij^{li}
Item, to four warkmen this oulk,	xlviij^{s}
Item, in drink sillver to thame,	ij^{s}
Item, to Jok for candill he coft by me this oulk,	ij^{s}
Item, to twa masouns, efter thar laboris wes done, for making of bothollis in the pillar,	xij^{d}
Item, for ij dosone watter this oulk,	iij^{s}
Item, for lokkis, bandis and (*blank*) to the ministers ludging,	xv^{s} x^{d}
Item, to the sklater for poynting ane parte of his howss and cleinging gutters,	xxvj^{s}
Item, for twa laid of lyme to him,	ix^{s}
Item, for vj laid sand,	iij^{s}
Summa of this oulk precedant the xx day of October,	xxviij^{li} ij^{s} vj^{d}

Sonday, xx day of October.

Item, for twa laid lyme,	v^{s} iiij^{d}
Item, for four laid sand,	ij^{s}
Item, to Johnne Watsoun for iij^{c} small blynd nale,	vj^{s}
Item, for thre hunder blind plancheoris nallis, iij^{s} iiij^{d}; summa,	x^{s}
Item, for ij^{c} plancheoris nalle,	vj^{s}
Item, for candill,	xij^{d}

Tysday.

Item, for twa laid of lyme, vj^{s}
Item, for foure laid of sand, . ij^{s}
Item, for candill morning and evyning, . xij^{d}

Wedinsday.

Item, for twa laid lyme, . . vj^{s}
Item, for foure laid sand, ... ij^{s}
Item, for ane j^{c} doubill garron naill to the mast and scaffetting to the windois, iiij^{d} the pece; summa, . xl^{s}
Item, for candill, . xij^{d}

Thurisday.

Item, for twa laid lyme, . v^{s} viij^{d}
Item, for foure laid sand, . ij^{s}
Item, for candill, . xij^{d}

[150] Fryday.

Item, for twa laid lyme, v^{s} viij^{d}
Item, for foure laid sand, . ij^{s}
Item, for candill, . xij^{d}

Setterday.

Wrichtis.

Item, to the wrichtis, as said is, . viij^{li} x^{s}
Item, for glewe to the pannellis, . ij^{s}

Masounis.

Item, to the masounis, as of befor, v^{li} xij^{s}
Item, for takkates, . . vj^{d}

Spargeonaris.

Item, to the spargeonaris, as said is, . iiij^{li} iij^{s}
Item, for ane j^{c} stane of calk, to Andro Lamb, iiij^{li}
Item, for careing owpe of it, . . vj^{s}
Item, to George Baxster for j^{c} blynd naill, ij^{s}
Item, for ane uther band of iron to him, . xvj^{d}

JAMES WATSOUN, Dean of Guild. 1560-61

Sauaris.

Item, to the twa sawaris, as said is, iij^{li}
Item, to foure barromen, . xlviij^{s}
Item, to the walter wyfe, ... iij^{s}
Summa of this oulk precedend the xxvij day of October, xxxiij^{li} xiiij^{s} vj^{d}

Sonnday, xxvij day Octobris.

Monunday.

Item, for candill, morning and evning, xij^{d}

Tuysday.

Item, for ij laid lyme, vj^{s}
Item, for foure laid sand, ij^{s}
Item, for candill, morning and evening, . xij^{d}

Wedinsday.

Item, for ane laid lyme, ij^{s} viij^{d}
Item, for twa laid sand, . . . xij^{d}
Item, for candill, morning and evining, . xij^{d}
Item, for ane chopine ule to the bell, ... viij^{d}
Item, for ane pound of Orknay butter for the mast and yetting the botts, xvj^{d}

Thurisday.

Item, for twa laid lyme, vj^{s}
Item, for foure laid sand, . ij^{s}
Item, for candill, . xij^{d}

Fryday, sumtyme callit Alhaloweday.

Item, to Johnne Watsoun, smyth, for ij^{c} blynd plancheour naill,. vj^{s}
151] Item, for thre hunder blynd dur naill for Eistland burde, vj^{s}
Item, for ij^{c} plancheour naill, . . . vj^{s}

Setterday.

Wrichtis.

Item, to the wrichtis, as said is, . . viij^{li} x^{s}

JAMES WATSOUN, Dean of Guild, 1560-61.

Masounis.

Item, Henery Batie and Jamis Masoun wer with my Lord Dewk ij days, and tuke ane laid of lyme with thame furth of the kirk, quhilk extendit with thar wages to x^s, that being deducit thai gatt bot, v^{li} ij^s

Sawaris.

Item, thai sawit bot thre dayis, . . xxx^s

Spargeonaris.

Item, Johnne Sampsoun wos with my Lord Dewk ij dayis, deducent vj^s viij^d therfor thai gat, ... iij^{li} xvj^s iiij^d

Item, to iij barromen that cariit the dedmennis baneis and made ane fowsie to put tham in, and I tuk the branders of thame and made stagis to the pillaris, ... xxxvij^s

Item, for butter and stringis to the mast, xv^d

Item, for walter this oulk, . . . iij^s

Item, for ane elne of Frauche grein to the pulpet, xij^s

Item, to Williame Harlawe for grathing of it, ... xij

Summa of this oulk precedent the thrid of Nouember, xxiiij^{li} vij^s iij^d

Sonnday, iij Nouember: Monday.

Item, coft fre Henery Wedhell in Leith viij plankis for the tabillis and traistis for the Communione for ix^s the peice; summa, iij^{li} xij^s

Item, for bringing owpe of thame, . . iiij^s

Tuysday, Wedinsday, Thurisday, Fryday, Setterday.

Item, to the wrichtis, as said is, ... viij^{li} x^s

Masounis.

Item, to the masounis, as said is, . . v^{li} xij^s

Spargeonaris.

Johnne Sampsoun, Johnne Froster and ane servand, this oulk, . . liiij^s

Item, for candill to the masounis for hewing of the stanis to the windois; by the principall masounis, . . . iij^s vj^d

Item, to the watterwyffe this oulk, . iij^s

Item, for ane lange stray skeppe to the loft, iiij^s

Item, to thre warkmen, ... xxxvj^s

Summa of this oulk precedent the x Nouember, xxij^{li} xviij^s vj^d

JAMES WATSOUN, Dean of Guild. 1560-61.

Sounday the x Nouember: Monunday, Tuysday.

Item, coft fre the said Henery Michaell foure mo planks for viij^s the peice; summa, . . xxxiij^s

[152] Item, for bringing oupe of thame, ij^s

Item, for thre laid of lyme, . ix^s

Item, for vj laid sand, iij^s

Wendnisday, Thurisday and Fryday.

Item, for glewe to the pannellis, . iiij^s vj^d

Item, payit to Jok for ane laid collis, . . iiij^s

Item, for caryinge of xiij treis fre the but to the kirk, iiij^s 3^d

Setterday.

Item, to Johnne Cunnynghame, xx^s

Item, to his servand, . xij^s

Item, to George Baxster, . xx^s

Item, to Andro Williamsoun, xx^s

Item, to George Tod, xx^s

Item, to his servand, xij^s

Masounis.

Item, to the masounis dischargeandis, ... iij^l 4^s

Item, to the warkmen for orderyng the kirk and serving the masounis and wrichtis, ... xxxvj^s

Item, to ij men for walkinge the kirk this oulk be ressoun of takine doune of the pend in the north kirk durre, vj nycht; summa, . . xij^s

Item, to the watter wyfe, ... ij^s

Item, to Jok for candill this oulk, . . iij^s

Item, to George Baxster for doune taking of the mast, . x^s

Item, for iij laid of lyme, ... ix^s

Item, for vj laid of sand, ... iij^s

Summa of this oulk precedent xvij day of Nouember, . xv^li xxij^s

Sonnday, xxvij Nouembris: Monunday, Tuysday, Wedinsday, Thurisday, Fryday.

Item, for twa laid lyme, . . vj^s

JAMES WATSOUN, Dean of Guild. 1560-61.

Item, for iiij laid sand, ij^{s}

Setterday.

Item, to the wrichtis as befor, $v^{li}\ x^{s}$

Masounes.

Item, to the masounes as befor, $iij^{li}\ iiij^{s}$
Item, to the watter wyffe, ij^{s}
Item, to iij warkmen, ... $xxxvj^{s}$
Item, to David Litstar, beyond the brige, for ane hunder calk, $iiij^{li}$
Item, for bringing owpe of it, ... vj^{s}
[153] Item, for $vj^{c}\ ^{xx}\ iiij^{x}$ stainis carying to the kirk yeard, for iij^{d} the peice, xix^{s} the hundereth; summa, . $x^{li}\ 2^{s}\ 3^{d}$
Item, to Jok for candill this oulk, by me, xx^{d}
Item, to twa men that walkit the kirk this oulk, . . . xij^{s}
Summa of this oulk precedent xxiiij of Nouember, $xxv^{li}\ xv^{s}\ xj^{d}$

Sonnday, xxiiij Nouember: Monunday, Tuysday.

Item, to iij men that broucht iij trouchis fre the freiris, ij^{s}; the uther thre men that helpit thame wer our owine.
Item, to ane quarior that wan thame and cuttit thame in the middis, $iij^{s}\ 4^{d}$

Wednisday.

Item, for ane laid of lyme, iij^{s}
Item, for ij laid of sand, . xij^{d}

Thurisday, Fryday, Setterday.

Item, to the masounis as of befor, $iij^{li}\ iiij^{s}$
Item, for ij laid of lyme, . vj^{s}
Item, for iij laid of sand, ... ij^{s}
Item, for twa lokkis to the twa durris of the pulpit, and iij keis thairto, x^{s}
Item, to iij warkmen this oulk, . . . $xxxvj^{s}$
Item, to the watter wyffe, . . . ij^{s}
Item, for candill, ... vj^{d}
Summa of this oulk precedent the first of Desember, . $vj^{li}\ ix^{s}\ x^{d}$

JAMES WATSOUN, Dean of Guild. 1560-61.

Sonnday, primo Desembris:
Monunday, Tuysday.

Item, for ane laid of lyme, iij^{s}
Item, for twa laid sand, xij^{d}
Item, for candill, . . vj^{d}

Wedinsday.

Item, to the stane men for twa hunder stanis, xxx^{s} the hundereth ; summa, iij^{li}

Thurisday: Glaschingwrichtis.

Item, peyit to Jhone Watsone for iij glass wyndois on the north syd of the queire, aboune wolt, conteinnane x^{xx} xvj fute, vj^{d} the fute ; summa, v^{li} viij^{s} vj^{d}
Item, to Jok for candill, ... xij^{d}

Fryday.

Item, for candill mornyng and ennyng; and making of the wark houss at the west end of the kirk, ... xij^{d}
Item, to ij masoun boyis efter sex hours for making of bothollis in the pillar, xij^{d}

Setterday.

Item, to the masounis, as said is, . iij^{li} 4^{s}
Item, to iij warkmen for this oulk, xxxvj^{s}
[154] Item, to the sawaris this oulk, vj^{li}
Item, to the watter wyffe, . xij^{d}
Item, for candill, ... iiij^{d}
Item, to the quariors for wynning stanis iij dayis, . x^{s}
Item, for iij^{c} xx stanis, ... iiij^{li} xv^{s}
Summa of this oulk precedent viij of Desember, xxij^{li} xv^{s} iiij^{d}

Sonnday, viij Desembris: Monunday, Tuysday, Wedinsday, Thurisday.

Item, ane laid of lyme for myntzellis of the south windois, . iij^{s}
Item, for ij laid sand, ... xij^{d}
Item, to (*blank*) Hattmaker, for thre braid corbellis for braidnes of the settis of the south pillar, ... xlviij^{s}
Item, for candill to Jhone Inglis for hewing the windois at mornyng and evining, ... xvj^{d}
2^{d} the peice

Fryday.

Item, for candill to the masounis, xvj^{d}
Item, for ane laid of lyme, iij^{s}
Item, for twa laid sand, xij^{d}

Setterday: Wrichtis.

Item, to Johnne Cunnynghame, xx^{s}
Item, to his twa servandis, xxiiij^{s}
Item, to George Baxster, . xx^{s}
Item, to his twa servandis, xxiiij^{s}

Masounis.

Item, to Jhone Inglis, . xxvj^{s}
Item, to Gilber Cleuch, . . xxvj^{s}
Item, to thar iiij servandis, . . . iiij^{li}
Item, to ij masounis to ragell the north pillar, ij dayis, . xiij^{s} iiij^{d}

Sawaris.

Item, to thame this oulk, . iij^{li}
Item, to thre warkmen, xxxvj^{s}
Item, to the walter wyfe, . . . iiij^{s}
Item, to the quariour for stanis wynning this oulk, xx^{s}
Item, peyit to the stane men for iij^{c} stanis, iiij^{li} x^{s}
Item, for candill mornyng and evning, . . . xiiij^{d}
Item, to ij for walking the kirk this oulk, becauss the south windois wes doun, ... xiiij^{s}
Item, coft j^{c} small schellis for the mynzellis, . . . ij^{d}
Summa of this oulk precedent xv of Desember, xxv^{li} xvij^{s} 6^{d}

[155] Sonnday, xv day December.

Monnday.

Item, for ane burding of colis to melt leid with to the pillar, xvj^{d}

Tysday, Wednisday, Thurisday.

Item, to iiij servand masouns to ragill the bak syd of the pillar, ane quart aile and ane laiffe, ... xvj^{d}

JAMES WATSOUN, Dean of Guild. 1560-61.

Fryday, Setterday.

Item, to Jok for candill this oulk, . viij^{s}

Wrichtis.

Item, to the wrichtis as of befor, . . . iiij^{li} viij^{s}

Masounes.

Item, to the masouns as of befor, . vj^{li} xij^{s}

Item, to the sawaris this oulk, ... iij^{li}

Item, the masounis feit uther ij serwandis for haisting of the windois, their wageis, ... xl^{s}

Item, to the quariors for wynning stanis to the ledaris, . xx^{s}

Item, to 2 that walkit the kirk this oulk, . xiiij^{s}

Item, to the stane men for iiij^{c}, ... vj^{li}

Item, for j tung to the bell of Sanct Paulis Wark, and ane string and putting upe of it, ... vj^{s} viij^{d}

Summa of this oulk precedent xxij day December, xxiiij^{li} xj^{s} 4^{d}

Sounday, xxij day December: Monnday.

Item, to ane masoun for dressing the pillar, ij dayis, . . vj^{s} vij^{d}

Wedinsday, sumtyme callit Yule day; Thurisday, Fryday, Setterday.

Item, to the wrichtis as saidis, . iiij^{li} viij^{s}

Item, to ij warkmen, . xiiij^{s}

Item, for walking the kirk, xiiij^{s}

Item, to the quarioris, . xx^{s}

Item, for ij^{c} stanes, . . iij^{li}

Item, for mending of the loft dur, and twa keyis, iiij^{s} iiij^{d}

Item, for ane lok to Jhonn Knox yet, and twa keyis, vj^{s}

Item, to him for mending of ane throwch lok, and ane new key, . ij^{s}

Item, for putting in of ane stepill to his chek lok, and leid, . xij^{d}

Item, to Jhonne Cunninghame be ane dress maid betwix him and me as of befor is mentionat the tyme I tuk doune thair wageis fre xxvj^{s} in the oulk to xx^{s}, and becauss the leife consent thairto, my apoyntment was to give him xxij^{s} and for his twa servandis xxxij^{s}, quhar the rest gat bot xij^{s}, sua it extendis to viij oulkis till iiij^{li}, viz., x^{s} for ilk oulk he

JAMES WATSOUN, Dean of Guild. 1560-61.

wantit and lykwayis I hold thame x^s thai gat ilk oulk of befor in drink silver, ... iiij^li

[156] Summa of this oulk precedent the xxix of December, . xv^li v^s

Sonnday, xxix December: Monnday, Tuysday, Wednisday, Thurisday, Fryday, Setterday.

Item, to the wrichtis, as said is, . iiij^li x^s
Item, to ane warkman, . . . xij^s
Item, for walking the kirk, ... xiiij^s
Item, to ane mason that maid botholis and regeleit ane quarner of the pillar and soupleit the regeleing of windo, for cutting of the glass bandis, ane dayis wageis, iij^s iij^d
Item, for candill this oulk, . . iij^s
Item, for ane gret corbell to put under the loft. xvj^s
Item, for bringing oupe of it, ... xj^d
Summa of this oulk precedent the fyft day of Januar, vj^li xvij^s 4^d

Sonnday, v of Januar: Mounday, Tuysday, Wednisday, Thurisday, Fryday, Setterday.

Item, for walking the kirk, ... xiiij^s
Item, for foure gret candill for putting up of the westmast south wyndo, . xvj^d
Item, to ij warkmen for transporting the tymmer and putting of it in the wark howss and cutting of the leid fre the bak of the wyndois, vj^s
Item, to ane turnour for turning the stoupe under the loft, x^s
Item, for upbringing of it fre the Cannogeit, ... iiij^d
Item, for ane laid of lyme for putting one the wyndois efter the glasching of thame, . . iij^s
Item, for ij laid sand, ... xij^d
Item, to the glaschinwrycht for xij fute of new glass to Johnne Knox, xviij^d the fut; summa, ... xliiij^s
Item, for xiij fut of auld glass for his chalmer windo, vj^s
Item, for iij panellis abov the kirk dur, xx fute, . x^s
Item, for ij panellis in Sanct Johnnes Ile, of xx fute, x^s
Item, xij fute abone the stepel dur, . vj^s
Item, for cleikis and one to the tabellis, . xij^s

JAMES WATSOUN, Dean of Guild. 1560-61.

Item, for ane lok to the westmest part of trevice and ij pare of bandis, iij keis, ... xvj^s

Item, to Johnne Alhannayis servandis and Jhone Bankis for heisting the iron wark for the ij south windois, ... x^s in drink

Summa of this oulk precedent the xij of Jauuar, . vj^{li} iij^s $viij^d$

Sonnday, xij Januarii : Monunday, Tuysday, Wednisday, Thurisday, Fryday, Setterday.

Item, to Jhone Cunninghame and his twa servandis for making of vj lang formes and short for serwinge the tabellis, ij dayis labour, . . xvj^s

[157] Item, for xxviij elnis of braid blechit bartan clayth of bartanze to cover the tabillis, vj^s the elne ; summa, ... $viij^{li}$ $viij^s$

Item, efter that, to the said Johnne and his ij servandis, ij dayis labour, for making and hinging of iij durris above the woltis, and taking doune of two stages fornent the pulpet, with uther small jottis, . xvj^s

Item, the flitting of the foir faice of the south trevice, for the mare eisment to the tabellis, and for candill thereto, . vj^d

Item, to iij pynouris for removing of the samyne, . $xviij^d$

Item, ane masoun for taking doune furth of the south pillar, vj^d

Item, for ane lettroun making to the clarkis chalmer, v^s

Item, for bandis and lokis tharto, ... $xiij^s$

Summa of this oulk precedent the xix of Januar, x^{li} xix^s xij^d

Sonnday, xix Januar.

Item, this nycht I causit to walk the kirk becauss of the steiling of glass bandis of the south windois, ... ij^s

And restis to Monunday the xvij day of Februar.

Moninday the xvij day Februar.

Item, in drink silwer to the childer that made the glass bandis, weyand ix stane and xx lib, ... vj^{li} vj^s ix^d

Tuysday, Wednisday, Thurisday, Fryday, Setterday.

Item, for walking the kirk this oulk, ... xij^s

Item, bowcht in this oulk for the wall of the west end of the kirk x dozone lyme for xij^s the dosone, of Southhowss, of lyme ; summa, . vj^{li}

Item, for xij dosone, as said is, for vj^{d} the laid; summa, . iij^{li} xiij^{s}
Item, for ane bassing and ane lawer, ... xl^{s}
Item, for ij laid of lyme and ij laid of sand, and for poynting the windois efter the breking, . . . viij^{s}

Summa of this oulk precedent the xxiij day of Februar, xix^{li} ij^{s} x^{d}

Sonnday, xxiij Februarii: Moninday, Tysday, Wednisday, Thurisday, Fryday, Setterday.

Item, to Hercules Meffan for vj^{xx} breid for 4^{d} the pece; summa, xl^{s} to the communion.
Item, to Johnne Cunnynghame for ordering the kirk, setting tabillis and removing of thame agan, . . vj^{s}
Item, for ane j^{c} plancheor nallis, ... iij^{s} 4^{d}
Item, to Jok and ane uther to helpe him to carie the tymmer, . . ij^{s}
Item, taking in this oulk v dosone lyme of Southowss, xij^{d} the laid; summa, iij^{s}
[158] Item, of sand iij dosone, vj^{d} the laid; summa, xxxvj^{s}
Item, for walking the kirk this oulk, ... xij^{s}
Item, for dichting the north kirk durris and putting of filth away, xij^{d}
Item, for candill that nycht, ... vj^{d}
Item, to iij men for biging of the fald for keping the lyme and sand, thre dayis labor, ... xij^{s}
Item, to the Communion viij gallons of wyne and ane half for xij^{d} the pynt; summa, ... iij^{li} viij^{s}
Item, for caryinge of the wyne to the kirk, iiij^{d}
Item, to Jok for ule to the bell, . . . xvj^{d}

Summa of this oulk precedent the secund of Merche, xij^{li} 2^{s} vj^{d}

Sonnday, ij of Merche, the Communone ministrat be Johnne Knox in the Hie Kirk of Edinburgh: Monunday, Tuysday, Wedinsday, Thurisday, Fryday, Setterday.

Item, bowcht in this oulk iiij dosone of lyme for xij^{d} the laid; summa, . xlviij^{s}
Item, for x dozone sand, ... iij^{li}
Item, for walking the kirk, ... xij^{s}

Summa of this oulk precedent the ix Merche, vj^{li}

JAMES WATSOUN, Dean of Guild. 1560-61.

Monunday, Tuysday, Weddnisday, Thurisday, Fryday, Setterday.

Item, for vj dosone of lyme, ... iij[d] xiij[s]
Item, for x dosone of sand, . . iij[li]
Item, walking the kirk, ... xij[s]
Summa of this oulk precedent the xxiij day of Merche, . vij[li] iiij[s]

Sonnday, xxiij of Merche: Monunday; Tuysday, xxv, yeir of God 1561 yeire, sumtyme callit our Lady day in Lentron; Wednisday, Thurisday, Fryday, Setterday.

Item, tane in this oulk v dozone lyme, iij[li]
Item, xij dozone sand, . . iij[li] xij[s]
Item, for walking the kirk, . xij[s]
Item, for ij puncheons to hald watter in, . x[s]
Item, for ane riddill, . . . xviij[d]
Item, for iij skanzis of pak threid, . . xij[d]
Item, for ij ule barellis to mak tubbis to hald mortare, . . . vij[s]
[159] Item, to ij warkmen for removing of the warkhouss and carying of the tymmer to the revestre, . . xij[s]
Item, to Johnne Inglis, ... v[li]
Item, the ballies causit me red the Fische marcatt and cary away the red and tuk the wall stanis thereof to the kirk and hade thre men wirkand this oulk for xx[d] on the day; summa, ... xxx[s]
Item, giving to Jhone Inglis servand to take doune the heid of the Croce, v[s]
Item, to ij warkmen that furnist watter to steipe the lyme and mix it with sand, this, ... xx[s]
Item, to Jok for dewyding the lyme and sand apart sene the inbringing thairof, ... v[s]
Item, for vj dosen of helis of sklattis and schellis, for ij[d] the creil, this oulk, ... xij[s]
Item, for sex horss for carying of wall stanis fre the Freiris, ilk laid ij dozone ilk day xxxiiij gange, extending to vij[xx] iiij laid in the day, in the oulk vij[c] xxiiij laid; in mony cometande to, . . vij[li] iiij[s]
Item, the quariour that wan thame, ... xx[s]
Summa of this oulk expensis precedent the xxx day of Merche, ... xxiiij[li] xvij[s] vj[d]

Sonnday, xxx Merche: Monunday, Tysday, Weddinsday, Thursday, Fryday, Setterday.

Item, for vj dosone lyme of Straitton, xij^{d} the laid; summa, iij^{li} xij^{s}

Item, for vj dozone sand, ... xxxvij^{s}

Summa of this oulk precedent the vj of Apryl, v^{li} viij^{s}

Sounday, vj Aprilis, sumtyme callit Peasche day: Monunday, Tuysday, Weddinsday, Thurisday, Fryday, Setterday.

Item, for ij dosone Costland lyme for ij^{s} ij^{d} the laid; summa, liij^{s}

Item, for ij dosone Straiton lyme for xiiij^{d} the laid, xxvj^{s}

Item, for vij dosone sand, . . . xliij^{s}

The letter end of this oulk, for ij dayis.

Item, to Johnne Inglis, ... xv^{li}

Item, to iiij warkmen that broucht wall stanis fre the Fische markat to the kirk as I wes commandeit be the ballies, ... xl^{s}

Item, to iij uther men that rasit the stanis with mattoks and caryit the grummell away, ... xxx^{s}

Item, sex horss, as said is, for vij^{xx} iiij laid the day, in the oulk vij^{c} xxiiij led, extending in money to, . vij^{li} iiij^{s}

[160] Item, to the quarior, ... xx^{s}

Item, to Jok and Watsoun for furnisching of sklettis and schellis this oulk, ... xx^{s}

Item, for walking the kirk, ... xij^{s}

Summa of this oulk precedent xiij Apryle, xxxiij^{li} iiij^{s}

Sonnday, xiij Apryl: Monunday, Tuysday, Wednisday, Thurisday, Fryday, Setterday.

Item, for my expens in ryding to Drumfermeling and the Lyme killis, and coft xx chalder, iij dayis furth, ... xl^{s}

Item, for ane boit of lyme, and v chalder, ilk chalder xvj schillings at the kill; summa, . . . iiij^{li}

Item, ilk chalder in fraucht to Leith v^{s}; summa, . xxv^{s}

Item, for carying of ilk chalder to the kirk vj^{s}; summa, . xxx^{s}

Item, to ane pynor that fillit the seves, . . ij^{s}

JAMES WATSOUN, Dean of Guild, 1560-61.

Item, for my expenssis, horss and servand, ... v^{s}
Item, to Jok and his marrow for casting the lyme aparte from the sand, ane dayis wagis, ... iiij^{s}

Fryday.

Item, ane uther boit of lyme come ouer of v chalder, as said is, extending in all chargeis to, ... vij^{li} vj^{s}
Item, boucht in this oulk vij^{xx} iiij led laid staneis, as said is, extending to, vij^{li} iiij^{s}
Item, to the quarior, ... xx^{s}
Item, to iiij men that broucht staneis fre the Fische marcat, as said is, . xl^{s}
Item, David Fullurton and David Symer made appoyntment with thei iij men for taking away of the hail waire for iij lib; summa, . iij^{li}
Item, to Jok and his marrow for walking the kirk, xij^{s}
Item, for x dosone sand, ... iij^{li}

Summa of this oulkis expenss precedent the xx Apryl, xxx^{li} viij^{s}

Sonnday, xx Apryl: Moninday, Tuysday, Weddinsday, Thurisday.

Item, the iij boit of lyme come in al chargeis as of befor, extending, . vij^{li} vij^{s}

Thurisday.

Item, to ane man that careit the rest of the stains fre the Fische marcat, xvj^{d}

Fryday, Setterday.

Item, to the stane men, as said is, . . vij^{li} iij^{s}
Item, for walking the kirk, . . xij^{s}
[161] Item, for watter, sklattis and schellis this oulk, . xij^{s}
Item, for xv dosone sand, ... iiij^{li} x^{s}

Summa of this oulk precedent the xxvj day of Apryl, xx^{li} xiiij^{s} iiij^{d}

Sonnday, xxvij April: Monunday.

Item, for ane barrow, ... ij^{s}
Item, for iiij pypis, vij^{s} the pece; summa, . . xxvij^{s}

Tysday, Weddinsday, Thurisday, Fryday, Setterday.

Item, to Johnne Inglis, . xij^{li}
Item, for xij dosone sand, ... iij^{li} xij^{s}
Item, to Jok and his marrow for watter, sklattis and schellis, xx^{s}

JAMES WATSOUN, Dean of Guild. 1560-61.

Item, for walking the kirk, x^{s}
Item, for ij bussomes, . . iij^{d}
Item, for ij new creilis for schellis, . . . xij^{d}
Summa of this oulk precedent iiij of May, xix^{li} v^{s} iij^{d}

Sonnday, iiij Maij: Monunday, Tuysday, Weddnisday, Thurisday, Fryday, Setterday.

Item, to Johnne Inglis, ... xviij^{li}
Item, to Jok and his marrow for sklattis and schellis, xx^{s}
Item, for walking the kirk, . . . x^{s}
Summa of this oulk precedent xviij Maij, xix^{li} vj^{s}

Sonnday, xviij Maij: Monunday, Tuysday, Weddinsday, Thurisday.

Item, to vj men for bringing owpe of xlvj daillis fre David Symers howss, ilk man viij^{d}; summa, . . . iiij^{s}

Thurisday, Fryday, Setterday.

Item, to Johnne Inglis and Gilbert Cleuch in compleit peyment of iiij^{xx} lib, xiiij^{li}
Item, to Jok and his marrow for watter, sklattis and schellis, xx^{s}
Item, for walking the kirk, . x^{s}
Item, for xvj dosone sand this oulk, ... iiij^{li} xvj^{s}
Summa of this oulk precedent the first Junij, xxxiiij^{s}

Sonnday, primo Junij: Monunday, Tuysday, Weddnisday, Thurisday, Fryday, Setterday.

Item, to David Duncan for mending of the gret lok of the chartur howss, x^{s}
Item, to Johnne Cunnynghame for ordering the kirk for the communione, vj^{s}
Item, to iiij pynoris for carying tymmer, . iij^{s}
Item, for keiping the kirk, . . . x^{s}
Summa of this oulk precedent viij of Junij, xxix^{s}

[162] **Sonnday,** viij of Junij, the secund Communione ministret in Edinburgh be Johnne Knox.

Item, for iij^{xx} breid for vj^{d} the pece, . . . xxx^{s}
Item, for viij gallons of wyne, for xviij^{d} the pynt; summa, . iiij^{li} xvj^{s}

JAMES WATSOUN, Dean of Guild. 1560-61.

Memorand: that fre the viij day of Junij forsaid to the thrid communione, quhilk wes the vij of September, contenand xiiij oulkis, I hawe debursit no thing on the kirk, excepe for walking of the samyne, ilk oulk x^{s}; summa, ... vij^{li}

And alss the expenssis maid upon the poynting of Johnne Knox howss, the sklattis taking furth of the kirk, viz., to the sklatters, . xl^{s}

Item, for lyme, sand and watter, ... xvj^{s}

Item, for carying of certane tymmer fre the uer tron to the kirk efter the Queinis entress, . . . vj^{s} iiij^{d}

The thrid Communione haldine be Johnne Knox, the viij day of September, as befor.

Item, for xxiiij mane breid, xiiij^{d} the pece; summa, . . xxviij^{s}

Item, for vj gallons and ane halfe of wyne, xvj^{d} the pynt; summa, iij^{li} x^{s}

Item, for v greit candill quhilk day, . xx^{d}

Item, for foure candill at the durr and revestre, . viij^{d}

Item, to the wrichtis, vj^{s}

Item, to iiij pynoris, . iiij^{s}

Item, for j^{c} plancheor naillis, ... iij^{s} iij^{d}

Item, for keiping the kirk fre the viij day of September to the v of October, contenand iiij oulks; summa, ... xl^{s}

Summa of thir chargis abow vretine sene the viij of Junii to the v of October, (*blank*).

[163] Heir falowis the expenssis I hawe debursit upon Iron Vark, be my selfe and my servand, for the preparing of the kirk in Nouember:—

In primis, Johnne Bankis compt for xiij blak bottis and thare naillis, for the binding of the tymmer to the pillar, viij^{d} the pece; summa, . viij^{s} viij^{d}

Item, for viij quhyt crampettis for the loft, and ane cut bolt for the trevice dur, and ane stirrop and ane key for the lettron, with thar naillis all tynnit, . . . xvij^{s}

Item, ane trowche lok to the ouer wolt, vij^{s}

Item, for ij dosone small garrouns, . iij^{s}

Summa of this terat, . xxxv^{s} viij^{d}

JAMES WATSOUN, Dean of Guild. 1560-61.

Eod. die: followis Johnne Watsounis compt, blak smyth.

Item, delyuerit to the sklater vj^{c} dur naill for sklating the kirk, ij^{s} the hunder; summa, . xij^{s}

Item, for ij dosone small garounis, . . iij^{s}

Item, to him, iij^{c} braid hedit naills, pryce of the hunder iij^{s}; summa, . x^{s} [ix^{s}]

Item, delyuert to Johnne Cunnynghame j^{c} small garroun naill, pryce of the pece ij^{d}; summa, ... xx^{s} [xvj^{s} viij^{d}]

Item, ij^{c} dur naill, pryce of the hundereth xx^{d}; summa, . . iij^{s} iiij^{d} [iij^{s} iiij^{d}]

Item, delyueret to George Baxster j^{c} dur naill, pryce of the hunder xx^{d}; summa, ... viij [j^{s} viij^{d}]

Item, to him, iiij^{c} blynd plancheour naill, price of the hunder iij^{s} summa, ... xij^{s}

Item, to Jok, iij^{xx} plancheor naill, . . xx^{d}

Item, to Johnne Cunnynghame, xxiiij grytast garroun, iij^{d} the pece; summa, ... viij^{s} [vj]

Item, delyuerit to your awin servand, ij^{c} plancheor, vj viij^{d}

Summa of this terat, . . iij^{li} xiij^{s} viij^{d}

Primo Decembris: Johnne Watsoun, blak smythis compt.

Item, delyuerit to Johnne Cunnynghame xij dubill garrounis for the scaffat, iiij^{d} the pece; summa, . iiij^{s}

Item, to your servand, j^{c} garroun naill small, x^{s}

Item, ane band and ane bolt for the trevice, . . ij^{s}

Item, ane pare of bandis of ane stane wecht to ministers durre, xiij^{s}

Item, thre steppellis and ane slot to him, . ij^{s}

Item, ane pare of bandis and crowk to ane uther howss of his, of iiij lib wecht and ane halfe, and ane slot with stapellis tharto, wyth xviij plancheor naill; summa, ... vj^{s} viij^{d}

Item, for ane small pare of bandis to his awin chalmer dur, ij^{s}

Item, ane bot that beris togidder the pulpit fit, of v lib wecht, . . iiij^{s} ij^{d}

Item, to your selfe, xxiiij bottis for the pillars, vj^{d} the pece; summa, ... xiij^{s} [xij^{s}]

[164] Item, delyuerit to the glassinwricht in your presens vj stane of glass bandis to the south wyndois, xiij^{s} the stane; summa, . . iij^{li} xviij^{s}

JAMES WATSOUN, Dean of Guild. 1560-61.

Item, delyuerit to your selfe ane rewll and ane bot to the butrois of the pulpit, weyand ane stane and ane halfe, xiij^{s} the stane; summa, xx^{s}

Item, ane pare of bandis to the utter pulpit dur, ... ij^{s}

Item, vj dosone pykis for halding the men furth of the weymennis roundis, iij^{s} the dosone; summa, . . . xviij^{s}

Item, ij dosone plancheor naillis delyuerit to Johnne Cunynghame, . vj^{s} viij^{d}

Summa of this compt, . . . ix^{li} v^{s} vj^{d}

Heire followis Johnne Ahannayis compt and Johnne Bankis of the standaris, quhortis, bottis, glassbandis with sicce uther things pertening to thair craft for the ij windois:—

In primis, Johnne Bankis, viij thorttis to the eistmaist windo, weyand xxviij stane iij lib: Item, xij glass bandis to the sayme, weyand viij stane v lib halfe pund: Item, iiij quharttis to the westmaist wyndo, weyand iiij stane and ane halfe iij lib: Item, ij^{c} xx lwkit pinnis, weyand ij stane xij lib; summa, liij stane xv lib; ilk stane 13^{s};

Summa of money, . xxxiij^{li} xvij^{s} iij^{d}

Heire follows Jhonne Ahannayis compt of standartis, quhortis, glass bandis, bottis and sik uther things as requyrit to thair occupatioun:—

Item, iiij standers to the west wyndo and iiij bottis to tham, and ane quhort weyand xxij stane halfe; Item, viij glass bandis to the westmaist windo, weyand ix stane xj lib; Item, to the eistmaist wyndo iij standarts weyand xiij stane x pound; Item, in bottis to thame, weyand vij lib and ane halfe; Item, viij glass bandis to the eistmaist windo, weyand viij stane xiij pound; Item, eikit to the thre standartis viij pound; Item, j^{c} xx likit pynnis, weyand ane stane halfe stane; summa of Johnne Ahannayis compt is lvj stane ix pound halfe; summa of silver comptand xiij^{s} the stane is, . . . xxxvj^{li} xvj^{s}

[165] Heir followis the glassinwrychtis compt, ressavit and met be my self, of the hail new glass in the windois:—

Item, to Johnne Watsoun and his guid soun for viij^{c} iij^{xx} xij fute of glass, xviij^{d} the fute; summa, . . iij^{xx} v^{li} ix^{s} vj^{d}

JAMES WATSOUN, Dean of Guild. 1560-61.

Heir followis Johnne Watsouns compt, blak smyth, the xij day of Januar :—

Item, delyuerit to you, x of December, iiij^c^ plancheour naill, iij^s^ the hundereth ; summa,	xij^s^
Item, to iiij^c^ plancheour naill schank,	xij^s^
Item, iij^c^ blind naill, xx^d^ the hunder ; summa,	v^s^
Item, ane newe iron ladill,	vij^s^
Item, delyuerit your selfe, ij^c^ blind dur naill schank,	vj^s^
Item, j^c^ blind plancheour naill schank,	iij^s^
Item, xxx bottis, vj^d^ the pece,	xv^s^
Item, half ane hundereth blind naill,	v^s^
Item, to Johnne Cunnynghame, vj stirraps,	iiij^s^
Item, the xxj day of Januar, delyuerit to Johnne Cunnynghame, v stane xv pound wecht of glass bandis for the ij windois, xiij^s^ the stane ; summa,	iiij^li^ xj^s^
Item, therefter delyuerit vj greter bottis,	iij^s^
Item, the xxvij day of December, ij stane xv pound wecht of glass bandis, xiij^s^ the stane ; summa,	xxxvij^s^ iij^d^
Item, therefter, to your servand, j^c^ blind naill,	xx^d^
Item, the xxx day delyuerit your selfe, ij^c^ blind naill garroun schank, ij^d^ the pece ; summa,	xl^s^
Item, therefter, delyuerit xiiij pound wecht of glass bandis to the saidis wyndois ; summa,	xj^s^ vj^d^
Item, therefter, iiij bottis,	ij^s^
Item, the secund day of Februar, delyuerit to Johnne Cunnynghame ij plancheour naill schank,	vj^s^
Item, the x day, delyuerit x stane wecht of glass bandis,	vj^li^ x^s^
Summa of this compt,	xviij^li^ xv^s^ xj^d^

The xx day of Merche, ane uther compt geving be Jhonne Watsoun for furnishing of Iron Warkis to the kirk :—

Item, for iiij crewkis and iiij paire of gret bandis to the durris above the voltis, weyand iij stane xiiij lib, xiij^s^ the stane ; summa,	xlviij^s^ ix^d^
Item, delyuerit to your servand j^c^ plancheour naill,	iij^s^
Item, delyuerit to him iiij stane ane pound of glass bandis,	l^s^ x^d^

JAMES WATSOUN, Dean of Guild. 1560-61.

[166]

Item, to William Blak, xiij lib wecht of glass bandis, . . x^{s} viij^{d}

Item, the samyin day, therefter, delyuerit to him ane stane wecht of glass bandis, ... xiij^{s}

Item, ane parc of bandis to the turpyk dur, xiij^{s} of 1 stone wecht

Item, I browcht to the kirk ij^{c} planchcour naill, . vj^{s}

Item, delyuerit to yet xx bottis, . . x^{s}

Item, delyuerit to your self iij gret bottis, . . iij^{s}

Item, delyuerit to you ane meikill corss bot and xij nallis, pryce, xviij^{d}

Heir followis the expenssis and money that I have depursit upoun tymmer to the kirk, coft in Lieth be me:—

Item, the xiij day of October, coft in Lieth fre Patrik Bowman ij dosone Eistland burdis for viij^{s} the peice; summa, . ix^{li} xij^{s}

Item, for bringing oupe of thame, ... xij^{s}

Item, the tent day of December, coft fre Andro Sandis j dosone Eistland burdis for ix^{s} the pece; summa, . v^{li} viij^{s}

Item, for bringing oupe of thame on mennis bakkis, . . iij^{s}

Item, therefter, xj day of Maij, coft fre (*blank*) Hattmaker, j dosone Eistland burd for viij^{s} the pece; summa, . iiij^{li} xvj^{s}

Summa, ... xx^{li} xj^{s}

The distrubutioune of the Eistland burdis:—

In primis, ther wes stowin out of the kirk xij glewt pannellis, with certane standartis and intendens for the cistmaist trivice; Item, thar was put in wark in the iij pillaris, the pannaling of the cist trevice, the entres of the pulpit, with iij stageis on athersyd of the samyne, xxx Eistland burdis; Item, I haiffe delyuerit to Allexander Guthre xij glewit pannellis that suld heve beine put in the for face of the eist trevice and xiiij Eistland burdis; sic eque, ressat and delyuerance.

Heir followis the bing of daills that I coft in Lieth for scaffeting of the ij glass windois and doubill scaffeting of the west waill:—

In primis, the xvij of November, coft iij dosone daills fre Patrik Bowman for xl^{s} the dosone; summa, . vj^{li}

Item, for bringing owpe of thame, xij^{s}

JAMES WATSOUN, Dean of Guild. 1560-61.

Item, the xxvij of Appryle, coft x dosone of drest daillis reddy put in wark for xxxiiij^{s} the dosone ; summa, .	xvij^{li}
Item, for bringing oupe of thame, ...	xl^{s}
167] Item, coft vj lang Suadyn geistis for ane mark the pece for wall scaffeting fre G [George] Clarksoun ; summa,	iiij^{li}
Item, for bringing up of thame, ...	xviij^{s}
Item, therefter, coft v dosone daills for xl^{s} the dosone ; summa, .	x^{li}
Item, for bringing oupe of thame, . .	xxiiij^{s}
Item, xij garrouns for nedling for iij^{s} the pece ; summa, . .	xxxvj^{s}
Item, the iiij day of Maij, coft iij dosone ruf spar for v^{s} the pece ; summa, for neidling, . . .	ix^{li}
Item, for bringing upe of thame, ...	xviij^{s}
Item, to the warkmen that handlit this forsaid tymmer and helpit to cary it, . . .	xij^{s}
Summa of money, .	liiij^{li}

Followis the distributione of this tymmer forsaid :—

Item, of the x dosone of dressit daillis delyuerit to Allexander Guthre iiij^{xx}, David Symer tuk xxviij and xij to Johnne Knox study, quhilk makis the hail number of thai x dosone : sic eque.

Item, disponis of the uther daillis to Allexander Guthre, Deine of Gild, lyand in the kirk iij^{xx} vj, and xv in the revestre ; Item, to Johnne Knox study, xiij daillis ; Jamis Adamsoun tuk to the mylnis viij daillis ; summa of this distributione, xviij dosone and sax dales ; quhilk war of the iij^{xx} daillis that James Barroun left quhilk wer takin furth of the kirk with the rest of the akyn tymmer, for the Quenis entres, without estimatioun, I being commandit be the ballies to mak all patent to thame, I being occupyit with the preparatioune of the Cardinalis luging for the bankit.

Heire followis the leid I coft for yetting the bottis, standerts and quhortis of the ij windois, yetting of the botts of the iij pillars, the entres of the pulpet, the botting of the cist and south trevice, the clething of the bakis of the ij windois :—

JAMES WATSOUN, Dean of Guild. 1560-61.

In primis, coft fre David Froster iij stane of leid for vij^{s} vj^{d} the stane; summa, ... xxij^{s} vj^{d}

Item, fre David Wauce, x stane for vij^{s} vj^{d}; summa, iij^{li} xv^{s}

Item, for bringing oupe of it, ... xij^{d}

Item, coft fre Johnne Mowbray x stane for viij^{s} the stane; summa, iiij^{li}

Item, fre William Smyth, vj stane for x^{s} the stane, ... xlviij^{s}

Item, fre Jhonne Weir, iij wolbis of plet leid for the bakkis of the ij windois, weyand xxj stane, for x^{s} the stane; summa, . . x^{li} x^{s}

[168] Summa of money, . xxj^{li} xvj^{s} vj^{d}

Summa of leid l [fifty] stane, quhilk was al weyit upon the windois botting, the pillars, pulpet, and trevice, as I sawe meltit myself, and the wobit leid put on the bakis of the ij new windois: sic eque.

The burgeschipps givin be me to the provest, ballies, clarkis and utheris officiaris, conforme to the custome:—

In primis, to the provest in burgeschippis, x^{li}

Item, to the iiij ballies, . . . xx^{li}

Item, to Allexander [Guthre], commoun clark, v^{li}

Item, to his ij servandis, ... x^{li}

Item, to William Stewart for bynding of the boukis, v^{li}

Item, to my selfe, j burgess and j gildschippe, xv^{li}

Item, to my servandis, ... vj marks

Item, to the xij officiaris, ilk ane iij^{li} at Yule; summa, xxxv^{li}

Item, to Richard Trolhope, ... v^{li}

Item to Johnne Watsoun, for ane standing pensioun for mending of the hollis of the glass, ... iiij^{li}

Summa, . j^{c} xiiij^{li}

The answer of the preceptes direct to me be the provest, ballies and counsall:—

In primis, to the minister, ... ij$^{c\,li}$

Item, to Andro Lyndsay and thame haill javalloris, ... xl^{s}

Item, to William Libertoun for ane gret windo cleith was stowin out of the kirk, ... v^{li}

JAMES WATSOUN, Dean of Guild. 1560-61.

Item, for ij new wol pakis of new canness, contenand xxv elne, ij^{s} the elne; all borrouit to keipe the greine fre the spargeonris of the pillars, and war all stowin; summa, ... xl^{s}
Item, to Robe Drummond and Patrik, belman, gild officiaris, xvj^{li}
Item, to Johnne Fleming for being hurt in the Tolbuith, v^{li}
Lateris, . ij^{c} xxx^{li}

[169] Heire followis Adame Foulartonis dischargeis of the money that restit of the bellis and brassin wark :—

Item, for bringing of the bell and brassin work to the Trone, . . xxiiij^{s}
Item, for xxxvj capones of ake that wer in the brasine pillaris, weyand, as he tuke in his consience mare nor twa stane, dedusand therfor, . xxxvj^{s}
Item, for ane moudewall and ane lok to Johnne Knox study, xviij^{s}
Summa, ... iij^{li} xviij^{s}
Item, Jok allegis awin to him for ringing the bell to the Lordis conventioun, xx^{s}
Item, for ulie to the kirk, . xij^{s}
Summa, iiij^{li} ix^{s}

The xviij day of Julij, the yeire of God J^{m} v^{c} lxij yeiris :—
Watsone, Dene of Gild.

The xvij day of Julij, the yeire of God J^{m} v^{c} thre score and twa yeiris, the compt befor wreitin byand diligentlie red, examinat and understand be the auditouris underwretin, thai find the charge therof to extend to the soum of ane thousand twa hundereth nyntein pounds vij^{s} vij^{d}, and sue the said compter restis awand to the guid toun the soume of viij^{li} ix^{s} v^{d}, quhilk thai ordain to be delyuerit to Allexander Guthre, Deine of Gild, he to be chargit therwith in his nixt comptis.
Restis, viij^{li} ix^{s} v^{d}

Jamis Adamsoun.
Jamis Carmichell.
Maister Jamis Lindsay.
Allexander Park.
Maister Jhone Prestoun.
Thomas Udwart.

Jamis Curll.
Jhone Spotiswod.
Thomas Reidpeth, with my hand led be Allexander Guthre, noter:
ALEXANDER GUTHRE.

ALEXANDER GUTHRIE, Dean of Guild. 1561-62. [171]

THE CHARGE AND COMPT of ALEXANDER GUTHRE, Dene of Gild, and Commoun Clark of the burgh of Edinburgh, of all soumes intromettit with be him be wertew of the said office of Dene of Gildrie, the first yeire tharof, beginnis the (*blank*) day of October, the yeire of God Jm vc lxj yeiris, and endinge in October Jm vc lxij yeiris.

Item, the said Allexander Guthre chargeis him with the dewtie of the twa burgesschippis perteininge to Archebald Douglass, provest, and givin at his command to George Dury and Adam Murray, xli

Item, for Robert Harper, burgess, vli

Item, for James Gemmyll, burges, . vli

Item, xiije of October, Johnne Moffet, burges, . . . vli

Item, xv Octobris, William Lainge, cordinar, be rycht of Johnne Lainge, his father, . . vjs viijd

Item, to Archibald Skeldene, skinner, burges, . vli

Item, xxiiij Octobris, Patrik Murdo, swerd slipper, burges, . . vli

Item, penultimo Octobris, William Bryse, masser, keiper of the dur of the Secret Counsall, maid burges and gilde for service to be done to the guid toun; the dewitie tharof, ... xvli

Item, the same day, William Yorstoun, burges and gild be rycht of Johnne Yorstoun, his father, ... xxs

Item, the viij of Nouember, Johnne Quhitlaw, talyeour, and burges be rycht of Johnne Adamesoun, baillie; the dewitie therof, . vli

Item, xij Nouembris, Johnne Fynny, taverner, burgess and gild, . xvli

Item, the same day, James Cowper, tailyeor, maid burgess be Allexander Achesoun, baillie, ... vli

Item, the same day, Martene Davidsoun, swerdslipper, maid burgess, and efterwart dischargeit be the provest, baillies and counsell, . . vli

Item, xiije Novembris, Thome Blakburne, burges and gild be rycht off William Blakburne, his father, in presens of Maister Thomas Makalzeane, provest, and peyt therfor, ... xxs

Item, the samyn day, Allan McCartnay maid burgess be rycht of Agnes Broun, his spouss, daughter of umquhill Thomas Broun, and peyit, . xiijs iiijd

[172] Item, the samyn day, James Alexander maid gild, and peyit, . . x li
Item, xix, Alexander Crage, burgess be wrycht of Jonet Tindal, his wyffe, dochter of umquhill Henery Tindalle, and peyit, . . . xiij s iiij d
Item, the xxij Nouembris, the said Alane M'Cartnay, maid gild brother be ryt of the said Agnes Broun, his spouss, ... xx s
Item, x Decembris, Thomas Andersoun, baxter, burges, and peyit, . v li
Item, xij° Decembris, Johnne Robertsoun, burges be James Thomson, baillie, his maister, ... v li
Item, the same day, Allexander Hestie, burges, v li
Item, the same day, Patrik Thomsoun, burges, v li
Item, the same day, William Jhonstoun, burges, ... v li
Item, the same day, Johnne Huntar, burgess be rycht of Margret Aikman, his spous, dochter of umquhill Johnne Aikman, xiij s iiij d
Item, xvij Decembris, Johnne Aikman, burges, . . v li
Item, xviij Decembris, Johnne Girdwod, baxter, burgess, v li
Item, the same day, Johnne Blaire, cramer, burges, ... v li
Item, tertio Januarii, William Ury, goldsmyth, gild brother be rycht off Issobell Jhonstoun, his spouss, dochter of umquhill George Jhonstoun, xxxiij s iiij d
Item, the samyn day, Thomas Broun, maid gild be rycht of Thomas Broun, his father, ... xx s
Item, septimo Januarii, Richard Chankis, maid gild brother, and peyt, . x li
Item, the same day, William Chene, at the request of Maister James Makgill, ... xv li
Item, ix Januarii, Johnne Carebod, talzeour, maid gild be rycht of Marion Gray, his spouss, dochter of umquhill James Gray, flescheour, at the command of the provest, baillies and counsell for caussis moving thame, as the act in the gild buik beris tane fre me bot, v li
Item, xiij° Januarii, Thomas Bruse, gild brother, . . . x li
Item, xxiij° Januarii, James Michell, burgess, ... v li
Item, the same day, Henery Nisbet, burges and gild be rycht of Jonet Bannatyn, his wyfe, secound dochter of James Bannatyne, writter, xxxiij s iiij d
Item, xxix Januarii, Thomas Wallace, burges, ... v li
Item, the same day, Gilbert Lauder, eldest sone of umquhill Maister Henery Lauder, burgess and gild be his said fatheris rycht, xxxiij s iiij d

ALEXANDER GUTHRIE, Dean of Guild. 1561-62.

[173]

Item, the same day, Thomas Waik, burges, . v^li
Item, the same day, Robert Pursell, fleschour, ... v^li
Item, ultimo Januarij, James Dalgleche, burgess be rycht of Katharene Tindalle, his spouss, dochter to umquhill Henery Tindall, . . xiij^s iiij^d
Item, the same day, Adam Mauchane, second sone of umquhill Adam Mauchan, maid burges and gild be rycht of his said father, and peyit, ... xxxiij^s iiij^d
Item, this same day, James Chalmer, burgess be rycht of Helene Fergussoun, his spouss, dochter of Johnne Fergussoun, . . . xiij^s iiij^d
Item, quinto Februarij, Johnne Makcall, burges be rycht off Issobell Makmoran, his wyff, dochter of umquhill William Makmoran, . xx^s
Item, sexto Februarij, David Danielstoun, goldsmyth, burges, . v^li
Item, xij^o Februarii, Johnne Wemyis, chierurginar, burges and gild, . xv^li
Item, the same day, Cutbert Thomsoun, flescheour, burges be rycht of Johnne Thomsoun, his father, ... xiij^s iiij^d
Item, the same day, Patrik Wernour, eldest sone of Johnne Wernour, writter, burges be rycht of his said father, ... vj^s viij^d
Item, Johnne Inglis, masoun, gild, as ane act of the dait x^o Junij in the counsall buik beris, and givin him gratis for his service, . . x^li
Item, xxvj Februarij, Eduarde Jhonestoun, maltman, burges be rycht of Johnne Johnnestoun, his father, ... xiij^s iiij^d
Item, to Johne Skathuwie, burges and gild, and the dewite therof givin to Maister Thomas Makcalzeoun, provest, ... xv^li
Item, penultimo Februarij, Johnne Wischart, burges, in the presence of the Counsall and the request of the Lard of Pittarro, Comptroller, ... v^li
Item, the same day, Adam Newtoun, baxter, burges, v^li
Item, tertio Martii, Johnne Maxwell, baxter, burges, v^li
Item, xx Martii, Johnne Purdie, baxter, burges, ... v^li
Item, xxv Martii, William Scot, cutlare, burges be richt of Doratie Wat, his spouss, Johnne Wat, smythis dochter, ... xxxiij^s iiij^d
Item, penultimo Martii, David Moreiss, burges, merchand, v^li
Item, ultimo Martii, Johnne Makkie, cramer, burges, . v^li
Item, primo Apprilis, Gilbert Wat, fleschour, burges, v^li

ALEXANDER GUTHRIE, Dean of Guild. 1561-62.

Item, secundo Apprilis, Bathcat Baxter, burges, ... v li
Item, Henery Aytoun, writter, servand to the Justice Clark, maid burges and gild at the said Justice Clarkis requeist, ... xv li
[174] Item, septimo Apprilis, Adame Donaldsoun, flescheour, burges be rycht of Walter Donaldsoun, his father, . . xxxiij s iiij d
Item, xj Apprilis, George Wod, merchand, burges, . . v li
Item, xvij Apprilis, Johnne Reid, maltman, alis fat Johnne, burges, v li
Item, the same day, Thomas Somerveill, merchand, burgess, v li
Item, xxij Apprilis, Patrik Sandelandis, talzeour, burges, v li
Item, the same day, Johnne Philope, maltman, burges, ... v li
Item, xxiiij Apprilis, Alane Tindal, burges, be rycht of Henery Tindale, his father, ... xiij s iiij d
Item, vj Maii, Andro Wintoun, barbour, burgess, v li
Item, xxiij Maii, Robert Mure, steablare, burgess, v li
Item, xxvj Maii, Robert Stark, merchand, burgess, v li
Item, xiij Junii, Charlis Dischenetoun, saidlar, burges, v li
Item, Peter Mertene, merchand, gild, . . . x li
Item, xxv Junii, Allexander Calder, merchand, burges, be Maister James Marioribankis, baillie, . . . v li
Item, xxvij Junii, Thomas Widderspune, smyth, burgess, v li
Item, penultimo Junii, Gavin Quhippe, burgess, . . . v li
Item, vj Julii, Johnne Stalker, maltman, burgess, . . . v li
Item, viij of Julii, Richart Strange, be rycht of Mariorie Wigholme, his spouss, dochter of umquhill Andro Wigholme, . . . xxxiij s iiij d
Item, xiij Julii, Johnne Watsoun, skynner, burgess be rycht off William Watsoun, his father, ... xx s
Item, the same day, James Schawe, burgess be ryt of Allexander Schawe, his father, ... xx s
Item, septimo Julii, Thomas Younge, skynner, burgess, . v li
Item, xxiiij Julii, Gilbert Donaldsoun, merchand, burgess, . . v li
Item, George Rynd, goldsmyth, burgess be rycht of Thomas Rynd, his father, ... vj s viij d
Item, James Jhonestoun of the Coittis, gild, . . . x li
Item, George Heriot, goldsmyth, be rycht of his father burgess, . . vj s viij d

[175] Item, the same day, William Cokki, goldsmyth, secound sone of the said James, burgess, ... xiij^{s} iiij^{d}
Item, Mungo Brady, goldsmyth, be rycht of his father, goldsmyth, vj^{s} viij^{d}
Item, the same day, Adam Dennin, goldsmyth, be rycht of his father, . xiij^{s} iiij^{d}
Item, the same day, Nichol Sym, goldsmyth, burgess be richt of his father, xiij^{s} iiij^{d}
Item, Adam Allan, goldsmyth, burgess be richt of his father, . . vj^{s} viij^{d}
Item, William Watsoun, eldest sone of Thomas Watsoun, skynner, . vj^{s} viij^{d}
Item, quinto Augusti, Johnne Younge, merchand, gild be rycht of Marion Lowsoun, his wyffe, eldest dochter of umquhill William Lowsoun, xx^{s}
Item, x^{o} Augusti, William Hoyltoun, cutlar, burgess, . . . v^{li}
Item, the same day, Archibald Seinzeour, merchand, burgess and gild brother be rycht of Janet Craike, his wyffe, dochter of William Craik, xxxiij^{s} iiij^{d}
Item, xvij^{o} Augusti, William Smyth, browster, burgess, . v^{li}
Item, xix Augusti, Johnne Reid, wrycht and merchand, burges, . v^{li}
Item, the same day, James Brintoun, merchand, gild, . . . x^{li}
Item, xxv Augusti, Johnne Davidsoun, merchand, be rycht of Elspeth Stevinsoun, his wyffe, dochter of umquhill Archibald Stevinsoun, xxxiij^{s} iiij^{d}
Item, xxvij Augusti, Johnne Symsoun, talyeour, burges, . . . xiij^{s} iiij^{d}
Item, Allexander Weyland, smyth lorimer, maid gild for service done and to be done, ... x^{li}
Item, ultimo Augusti, David Beverage, merchand, burgess, . v^{li}
Item, the same day, the said David maid gild, . x^{li}
Item, the same day, Charlis Steidman, cuke, burgess, v^{li}
Item, the same day, Stewin Banantyne, litster, burgess, . v^{li}
Item, quinto Septembris, Rollie Menizeis, burges and gild, xv^{li}
Item, Johnne Sklatter, burgess at the requeist of the provest, . . v^{li}
Item, xv Septembris, Adam Craige, goldsmyth, burgess be rycht of his father, vj^{s} viij^{d}
Item, xxiij^{o} Septembris, William Broun, bonetmaker, burgess, . v^{li}
Item, James Jhonestoun, bonetmaker, burges, . . v^{li}
Item, the same day, Eduard Wylie, bonetmaker, burges, . v^{li}

[176] Item, the said compter chargeis him with the dewitie of the haill Scheppis frauchtit the said yeir of his office, extendinge in nummer iiij^{xx} viij^{o} scheppis, ... (*blank*)

ALEXANDER GUTHRIE, Dean of Guild. 1561-62.

Item, the compter chargeis him with the maillis of the Cordiner Schoppis the said yeir, ... xxj li

Item, maire, off the maillis of the goldsmythis buithis and in the first Adame Dannunis schope, . xxx s

Item, Johnne Gilbertis chope, . xxx s

Item, George Currouris chope, . xxx s

Item, the said George stand at the kirk dure, xl s

Item, Andro Heleis, stand thare, . xl s

Item, Cristall Galbraythis chope, . xxx s

Item, Robert Murrayis chope, xxx s

Item, maire, the said compter chargeis him with the fute and rest of Maister James Watsounnis compt, last Dene of Gild, . . viij li ix s v d

Summa of the haill charge of the compter is, vj c xxx li xj s v d

[177]

DISCHARGE.

Item, the said compter dischargeis him with twa burgesschippis gevin to Archebald Douglaiss, Provest, be the rycht of his office, x li

Item, the said Archibald Douglais being dischargeit, be the Quenis Grace, of his office, and Maister Thomas Makcalzeoun enterand Provest, to him twa burgesschippis, . x li

Item, the foure Baillies burgesschippis, . . xx li

Item, the Deine of Gild, ane burgesschippe and gildrie, . xv li

Item, Richart Trohop, ane burgesschippe, . v li

Item, the twalf servands, ewry one of thame iij li . xxxvj li

Item, Andro Lyndsay, javellor, ... xl s

Item, the Commoun Clark and his twa servandis, ewry one of thame ane burgesschipe, ... xv li

Item, to Watsoun, glassinwrycht, his pensioun, . . . iiij li

Item, to Patrik Gowane, belman, Robert Drummond and Jok Symsoun, keiperis of the kirk and knok, ilk one of thame for thar yeiris fee viij li; summa, ... xxiiij li

Item, the Dene of Gild, this yeir of his office, . . vj li xiij s iiij d

Item, the said compter dischargeis him with ane burgesschippe and gildrie

ALEXANDER GUTHRIE, Dean of Guild. 1561-62.

gevin at command [of] the proveist, baillies and counsall, to William Bryse, maisser and keiper of the houss and dur of the Secreit Counsall, for service to be done to the guid toun and utheris conditiouns conteinit in ane act of the dait the (*blank*) day (*blank*) the yeir of God J^m v^c lxj yeir, xv^{li}

Item, the said compter dischargeis him with the dewitie of ane burgess-chip gevin to Martene Davidsoun, sword slipper, quha wes slane and the said dewite dischargeit to the pure wyff and iiij barnis, as ane act of the dait (*blank*) beris, ... v^{li}

Item, the said compter dischargeis him with the dewite of ane burgeschip and gildrie gevin to William Chene, servand to the Clark of Register, at his requeist for his L [lordshipis] favoris in the townis affaris, . xv^{li}

Item, the said compter dischargeis him with the gildrie gevin to Johnne Inglis, masoun, conforme to ane act in the counsall buk of the dait the (*blank*) beris, ... x^{li}

Item, I ame to be dischargeit of the burgesschipe givin to Johnne Wischart, masoun, at the request of the Laird of Pittario, Comptrollour, for his favoris in court, ... v^{li}

[178] Item, the said compter dischargeis him with the burgesschipe and gildrie givin to Henery Aytoun, writer and servand to the Justice Clark, for his L [lordshipis] favouris in court, ... xv^{li}

Item, the said compter dischargeis him with the gildrie givin to Allexander Weyland, lorymer, at the command of the provest, baillies and counsell, as ane act of the dait the (*blank*) day of (*blank*) beris, . x^{li}

Item, the said compter dischargis him with the burgesschip gevin be command of the baillies and counsall to Johnne Sklatter, servand to the provest, for his service done to the guid toun, v^{li}

The necessar expenssis debursit be the compter upon the kirk, kirk-workis and utheris effaris of the guid toun, as efter followis :—

Item, the vj day of October 1561 yeiris, for ane patill with irne to patill the kirk flure, ... iij^s

Item, for ane rowe of walx to Johnne Cairnis to serve at the mornynge prayers, ... ij^s vj^d

Item, xxiiij Octobris, at the command of the provest, baillies and counsell,

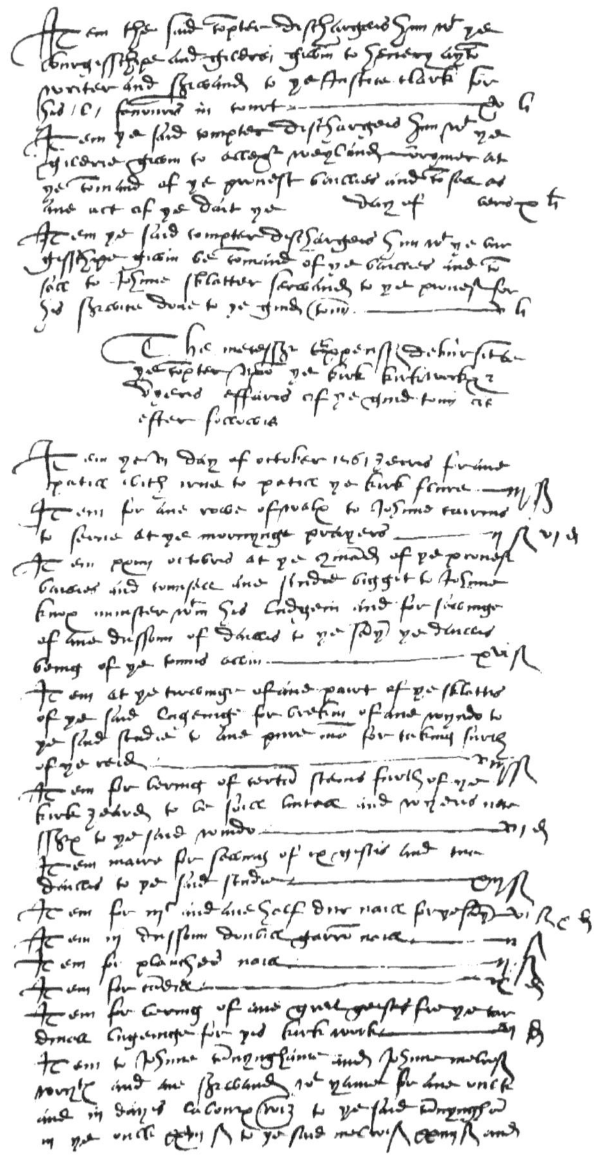

EDINBURGH ACCOUNTS:—Page 178 of old Accounts of Deans of Guild.

ALEXANDER GUTHRIE, Dean of Guild. 1561-62.

ane studie biggit to Johnne Knox, minister, within his ludgein, and for sawinge of ane dussain of daillis to the samyn, the daillis being of the tounis awin, ... xvj^{s}

Item, at the tirwinge of ane pairt of the sklattis of the said lugeinge for brekin of ane wyndo to the said studie, to ane pure man for taking furth of the reid, ... vij^{s}

Item, for bering of certane stanis furth of the kirk yeard to be soill, lintell and utheris necessaris to the said windo, . vj^{d}

Item, maire, for sawing of ix gestis and twa daillis to the said studie, xiij^{s}

Item, for iij^{c} and ane half dur naill for the samyn, vj^{s} x^{d}

Item, iij dossoun doubill garroun naill, ij^{s}

Item, for planchcour naill, ij^{s}

Item, for candill, ... ix^{d}

Item, for bering of ane greit geist fre the Cardinell lugeinge, for this kirk work, . . . vj^{d}

Item, to Johnne Cunnynghame and Johnne Melross, wrychtis, and ane servand with thame for ane oulk and iij dayis labouris, viz., to the said Cunnynghame in the oulk xxvij^{s}, to the said Melross xxiiij^{s} and thar

[179] servand xxij^{s}; summa togidder, ... iiij^{li} xvj^{s}

Item, to Johnne Inglis, masoun, for breiking of the wall and beigeinge of the said windo, ... xvj^{s}

Item, for careing of the sklattis fre the kirk for theiking of the wyndo, . iiij^{d}

Item, for lyme and sand to this wark, . . . iiij^{s}

Item, for ane peonardis wage for making of the mortour and bering of the tymmer fre the kirk to the said lugeing, ane day and ane halfe, and naillis to the loft of the wyndo, windo skewis, and necessaris tharof, ... iij^{s} vj^{d}

Item, to the sklatteris for thar laubouris and pointing of sume uther partis of the houss, ... xv^{s}

Item, for cat and clay to mend and fill certane hoillis of the awld mydwaill of the said study, ... ij^{s}

Item, mair, the said awld midde wall cuttit and the tymmer therof sawin for makinge entress fre the ministeris chalmer to the study, for naillis to the standartis, steppis, bilzeittis of the entre therto, . . vij^{s} iiij^{d}

ALEXANDER GUTHRIE, Dean of Guild. 1561-62.

Item, ane bot of irne to fessin ane of the standartis of the stanewall, and for leid and werkmanschip to the samyn, . . . xvj^{d}

Item, mair, for candill, ... ix^{d}

Item, for xxv futtis of new glass to the windo and windo skewis, the fute xviij^{d}; summa, ... xxxvij^{s} vj^{d}

Item, ane stane and ane quarter wecht bandis of irne to the windo and windo skewis, the stane therof xiij^{s} iiij^{d}; summa, . . . xvj^{s} viij^{d}

Item, for ane lok and key and snek within to the said study dur, . v^{s}

Item, for sawing of ane daill in lenthe and quarters to be molloures to the siloure of the said study, . . . xviij^{d}

Item, for blind naill to the molloures, . . iij^{s}

Item, xxv Octobris, to Mungo Hunter, for ane key to the dur of the Croce, ane gret key to the northeist dur of the kirk yard, ane lok with ane ke, ane rode of irne, ane cleik with ane hingand lok to the southe dur of the kirk, ... xx^{s}

Item, ane pannall of new glass, contenand iij fute and iij quarteris, to the windo above the loft, quhair the Lordis sittis, the fute xviij^{d}; summa, ... v^{s} vij^{d}

Item, for sex futtis of glass, auld, to the windo above the knok, . . iij^{s}

[180] Item, to Eduard, alias Sir Eduard Hendersoun, commandit be the counsall to oursie the workis of the kirk, for his service the tyme of the workis above writtin, . . . xiiij^{s}

Item, ane chopin of oill to the knok, . . . xiiij^{d}

Item, ultimo Octobris, to twa warkmen for sorting of the tymmer in the kirk at the ressait therof, fra Maister James Watsoun, the haill dayis waigis, ... iij^{s}

Item, for the signet to the Quenis lettres, dischargeing pakking and peling of fische above the Insche, ... v^{s}

Item, tertio Novembris, at the halding of the first Courte upon the Schoir of Leythe at the Quenis hame cuming, to the officiaris to thair denneris, vj^{s}

Item, thre nychtis candill in the kirk the tyme of the examinatioun, . xij^{d}

Item, v Novembris, fyve elnis Dornik to be ane burdclaythe for the Ambassator lugeit in Howeis lugeing in the Kowgait, the elne xx^{s}; summa, . . . v^{li}

Item, ij elnis Inglis greine for the burd in his chalmer; quhilk burd claithis ar heir present to be delyverit, ... xxxij^{s}

Item, at the provestis command, to thre peonaris that turst ane ledder to and fre the gallois for hinging of Wedder Craige, . . iij^{s}

Item, to Patrik Schange, wrycht, and twa servandis with him, for ane dayis labour in sorting of the beist tymmer fre the west, transporting of the samyn fre behind the hie havear and paking therof in the revestrie, . . . ix^{s}

Item, to ane warkman that helpit thame, xviij^{d}

The glass windo of the Blude Ile.

Item, for making of ane gret traist to the first skaffald of the windo of the blude Ile, . . . v^{s}

Item, mair, to Patrik Schang, wrycht, and his servand for making of the gret skaffald of foure skaffald heicht and foure skaffaldis outwith the windo, for dountaking of the auld glass and inputting of the new, xl^{s}

Item, for ij^{c} garroun naillis to the said skaffald, . xx^{s}

[181] Item, for plancheoure naillis, ... vij^{s} vj^{d}

Item, for beringe of certane glass fre the glassinwrychtis to the kirk, . vj^{d}

Item, to Thomas Watsoun and William Blak, glassinwrychtis, for xij^{xx} ix fut, and thre quarteris of ane fute new glass to the said windo, ilk fut xviij^{d}; summa, ... xviij^{li} xiiij^{s}

Item, to thame, for xij^{xx} xvij fute auld glass to the said windo, ilk fute vj^{d}; summa, ... vj^{li} viij^{s} vj^{d}

Item, to Johnne Watsoun, smyth, for xxj new bandis irne, contenand xxviij^{li} wecht, ... xxiij iiij^{d}

Item, for cuttinge of xvj auld bandis, xvj^{d}

Item, for makinge of xvj glass wegis, xiij^{d}

Item, for cuttinge and fassoning of new, and xxx auld bandis, iij^{s}

Item, mair, for new wagis, . v^{s} ix^{d}

Item, for leid, ... xxj^{d}

Item, to the said Patrik Schange and his servandis for taking done of the skaffaldin, ... xx^{s}

Item, for bering of the tymmer to the wark houss behind the hie altar, ij^{s}

ALEXANDER GUTHRIE, Dean of Guild. 1561-62.

The first tabill of the Communion, in the Compteris first yeir :—

Item, for beringe in and oute of thre dussoun of daillis fre the nether Tolbuith [to] be ane travess for haldin furth of the Non Communicantis, ij^s

Item, to foure warkmen, at the helpin oupe of the said travess, setting of the tabillis and taking done of the samyn, vj^s

Item, iij^c naillis to the said travess, ... ix^s ix^d

Item, to Patrik Schange and his twa servandis for his lauboris in divisinge and setting up of the said travess and donetaking of the samyn, xx^s

Item, for twa dussoun of breid, price of the pece xiiij^d, xxviij^s

Item, for vj gallouns twa pintis of wyne, . lvij^s vj^d

Item, for vj lib wecht of candill, the pund xv^d, vij^s vj^d

Item, ane row of walx to the minister, ij^s vj^d

Item, for wesching of the tabil claithis, ... xviij^d

Item, the thrie childeris disione that keipit the wyne and serwit tharwith, iij^s

Item, xvij Decembris, at the command of my Lord Provest, for castinge and beringe away of the haill red and stanis in the new laiche Tolbuith, efter the beiging of the new stane wall and leveling of the flure thairof for men to gange upon, ... lvij^s

Item, the saime nycht, to thre men that playit upon the suecheis for convening of the tounschipe for stancheing of the tumult betuix my Lord Deuke and the Erle Boithuileis servandis, and for playinge throw the toun all nycht, ... xv^s

[182] Item, for drink to thame at mydnycht, ... ij^s

Item, for beringe of ane dussoun of Eistland burdis of the townis furth of Maister James Watsounis to the revestrie, quhilk wer delyuerit to the maister of work, ... xij^d

Item, to Patrik Schange and his servandis, for makinge of lange skelffis and letteronis and saittis in the ministeris study, be the space of aucht dayis, xl^s

Item, to him for makinge of ane greit foure square lettrane to the ministeris, turneand upon ane wyce, and for troubling of his spreit in the inventing of that consait, ... xxx^s

Item, the glass windo above the horologe being blawin done, to the said Schange for making of ane case of tymmer for the said windok, and for mending and clewing of the haill windo skewis of the steipill, . viij^s

Alexander Guthrie, Dean of Guild. 1561-62.

Item, for lok and bandis to the greit lettrane, ... vj^{s}

Item, for candill and glew to the work of the skelffis, saittis and lettranis, iiij^{s} j$\frac{1}{2}^{d}$

Item, for plancheours and dur naill to all this wark, ... iiij^{s} vj^{d}

Item, the xij Januarii, it beinge commandit be the provest, baillies and counsall to prepare the revestrie for the Lordis of the Sessioun to sit in, for reddinge and takinge furth of the tymmer furth, . ij

Item, for sowpinge and cleingeinge of the revestrie and beringe of the filth furth of the kirk, . . . xij^{d}

Item, for candill thar and behind the hie alter, ... iiij^{d}

Item, for cleinging and bering furth of the stanis and red S. Johnnes Ile, ij^{s}

Item, for bussoimes, ... vj^{d}

Item, for thre laidis of sand ther, for lainge of the peyment of that Ile, . xviij^{d}

Item, for foure tubfull of watter, . . iiij^{d}

Item, to ane massoun for layinge of the peyment, . . viij^{s}

Item, for beiging upe of the windo in the revestrie with stane and lyme, ... iiij^{s} vj^{d}

Item, lyme and sand to this windo, iij^{s} x^{d}

Item, for watter, ... iiij^{d}

Item, to warkmen for making of the mortar and bringing of the stanis furth of the kirk yeard, . . . xviij^{d}

Item, for ane spar to the hainger in the revestrie, . . . xx^{d}

Item, for vij ruiddis of calsay before the cordinaris choppis, ilk rude xxxvj^{s}; summa, ... xj^{li} xij^{s}

[183] Item, at the provestis command, to support the calsay befor James Bannantyns waist land besyd the new well, ... xx^{s}

Item, at the counsalis command, to younge Wauchlop servand, beand dischargeit of his office, ... xx^{s}

Item, 3 Februarii, to George Small, saidlar, for new taggs and for hinginge and buklinge of the curfoir bell, ... x^{s}

Item, the minister, Johnne Knox, beinge chargeit be the haill kirk to pass in Anguss for chesinge of ane superintendit thair, the comptar beinge chargeit be the provest, baillies and counsall, as thair speceale ordinance beris, to pass with the said minister, and to deburss for his chargeis in all thingis necessar the space of his jornay, beinge xj

ALEXANDER GUTHRIE, Dean of Guild. 1561-62.

dayis, himself ij servandis and iij horss, quhais chargeis extendit be the said space, ... xx^li xv^s

Item, to Eduarde Hendersoun, for his laubors in a wating and attendence givin to the ordoringe of the revestrie, S. Johnnis Ile, Halieblude Ile and all the uther divissis maid for serving of the Lordis within the kirk be the space of xviij dayis, ... xxiiij^s

Item, the preistis preisoun abone the north kirk dur, for ane pare of bands and ane cruik to hinge ane dur upon the entrie of the said preisoun, . ij^s x^d

Item, ane lok and ane key to the samyn, ... ij^s iiij^d

Item, 3 Martii, for ane lok to the dur under the charterhouss, quhar the glassinwrychtis workis, ... iiij^s

Item, to ane masoun for leid to the cruik, making of the hoillis of the samyn, and sprent of the lok, ... ij^s iiij^d

Item, to the ministeris lugeing being falthie in diverss pairtis of the sklaittis tharof and the rane comand done abone his bed and buikis, for pointinge of the samin haill throche, xxiiij^s

Item, for lyme and sand, . xv^s

Item, for watter to the mortour, . viij^d

The secund Comunion.

Item, xiiij^o Martii, to the warkmen for upsetting and dountaking of the barrowis at the secound communion, . . v^s iiij^d

Item, for naillis, ... iij^s

Item, Patrik Schange, wrycht, and his servandis, . . . xx^s

Item, to the saids warkmen, for bering of the tablis and certane furmes furth of the Magdalen Chapell and carcing doun of thame agane, ij^s

[184] Item, for iij dussoun of breid, ... xlij^s

Item, twa barrellis wyne, contenand x gallounis, the pynt xvj^d, the gallon x^s viij^d; summa, . v^li xiiij^s iiij^d

Item, the childeris disione, ... iij^s

Item, for hinging of the tounge of the curfour bell for new taggis to ane parte of the uther bellis, and sewing and mending of sume uther taggis, x^s

Item, viij faddoum greit cordis to the paissis of the kirk, . x^s

ALEXANDER GUTHRIE, Dean of Guild. 1561-62.

Expenssis deburst be the compter upon the theiking, pointing and ordering of the rufe of the kirk, fre the stepill west, as followis:—

Item, the xvij of Aprile 1562, for thre laid of Eisthouss lyme, ilk laid iij^s; summa,	ix^s
Item, the samyn day, ane uther laid of the samyn,	ij^s vj^d
Item, xxiiij Aprilis, viij laids Coistland lyme, ilk laid iiij^s,	xxxij^s
Item, maire, ten laid Cowstland lyme,	xl^s
Item, maire, xxvij Apprilis, iiij laidis Cowstland lym,	xvj^s
Item, penultimo Aprilis, iiij laidis,	xvj^s
Item, ultimo Aprilis, twa laid of Eisthouss lyme,	iv^s vj^d
Item, x dussoun of sand,	iij^{li}
Item, twa puncheonis to put watter in,	x^s
Item, v dussoun watter,	iiij^s ij^d
Item, to Clany, candilmaker, for iij greit geistis, to be ane pairte of the new brandreth for uphaldin of the rufe of the volt abone S. Gabriellis Ile, and to be sillis to ane of the lange guteris of leid,	iij^{li} xij^s
Item, to Adame Purvess, wrycht, for making of this brandreth, prymeing and rasing of the haill rufe, and xxiiij garronis to the ruifle spar for lantlinge of the rufe, his laubors, and twa servandis, be the space of x dayis,	v^{li}
Item, to vj warkmen that he gat to raiss and pryme the said rufe, and for bering of the haill tymmer,	vij
Item, for sawing of the tymmer to the brandreth and garronis,	viij
Item, for garroun naill,	vj^s viij^d
Item, to Walter Scot, skletter, for theiking of the haill houss aboun the saids twa Ilis, contenand thre ruiddis xj naillis and ane halfe new wark,	x^{li}
[185] Item, maire, to the said Walter Scot, for pointinge, mending and theiking of new the maist partis of the ruffis of the twa lange voltis abone the new Tolbuith,	viij^{li}
Item, for xviij^c and ane half plancheour naill to him to his work,	xl^s j^d
Item, mair, for naillis,	vj^s
Item, to ane workman for bering of sklattis fre the ix of Maij to the xxj of the samyn,	xiiij^s j^d
Item, mair, for bering of iij^c sklattis,	ij^s

ALEXANDER GUTHRIE, Dean of Guild. 1561-62. Item, mair, xiiij tubfull of watter,	xij^{d}
Item, for cleinging of the spowtis, bering away of the red, and certane sklatts left of the wark, into the voltis,	xviij^{d}
Item, mair, to twa peonaris for rasing of the lange gutter of leid, being rewin, cuttit, and full of hoillis, and caryinge thereof to Johnne Weir, pudereris houss,	ij^{s} vj^{d}
Item, viij laiddis of sand to lay above the soill of the spout,	iiij^{s}
Item, the said lange gutter of leid being raisit and deliverit to Johnne Weir, contenit xxxvj stane xij lib wecht, inlakit in the newe casting foure stane iiij lib, and eikit therto of new leid viij stane and ane half, price of the stane xij^{s}; summa,	v^{li} ij^{s}
Item, for castinge of ilk stane xviij^{d}; summa,	xlviij^{s} ix^{d}
Item, to him for iij lib wecht tyn,	ix^{s}
Item, to him for laying of this gutter,	xij^{s}
Item, for bering of this leid fre Johnne Weiris to the kirk, quhare it was laid,	iij^{s}
Item, viij doubill garroun naill to the sawin gistis, quhilk is the soill of the said gutter,	xvj^{d}
Item, for vij dussoun leid naill,	xxj^{d}
Item, for coillis to be ane fyre to heit his irne with,	xxx^{d}
Item, mair, the first of Maij, anno 1563, enterit Adam Purvess, wrycht, to the making of the new brandrie for uphalding of the cuppill feit above the lange mid volt be west the steipill above the new Tolbuith, quhilk wer all consumit and rottin, and siklyk to mak bulyettis above the rufe spar of the haill syd of the said volt, for leveling of the said rufe, and furneist therto ij^{c} garron naillis,	xx
Item, mair, ij^{c} plancheour naill,	v^{s} iiij^{d}
Item, to the sawaris for iiij draucht of gistis to the brandereth,	x^{s}
Item, to Adame Purvess for his lauboris fre the first of Maij to the viij of the samyn, exclusive, upon the said brandear, by buleyettis, and laying of the soill of the said gutter of leid,	xxx^{s}
Item, to his ij servandis, the said space,	xl^{s}
[186] Item, for bering up of the tymmer,	xij^{d}
Item, for solding and mending of dyverss rystis in the uther gutteris,	iiij^{s}

Item, mair, vij Junij, to Walter Scot, sklatter, for pointing and mending of the large tufall above the Wobsteris, xl^s

Item, for viij laiddis of lyme, . xx^s

Item, for xviij laid of sand, ... ix^s

Item, mair, for theiking of the one syid of S. Johnns Ile, mending and pointing of the uther syd, xx^s

Item, for naillis, . . xviij^d

Item, for watter, ... ij^s

Item, to Jok Simsoun for beiring thair of sklattis, iiij^s ij^d

Item, for oyle to the kirk, ... xiiij^d

Item, for deichting and cleinging of the filth furth of the haill gutteris be eist the steipill fylit be the Wobsteris, . xviij^d

The Thrid Communion.

Item, the xviij Julij, to v workmen for upsetting, helping and dountaking of the barress, ilk man xviij^d; summa, . . vij^s vj^d

Item, for half ane hundereth planchcour naill, . . . xviij^d

Item, to Johnne Cunninghame, wrycht, for upsetting and donetaking of the saiddis barress and haill tablis, . x^s

Item, iij dussoun of breid, ... xlij^s

Item, x gallonis iij pyntis wyn, price of the pint xviij^d; summa, . vj^{li} iiij^s vj^d

Item, for weching of the tabill naprie, . xviij^d

Item, the childeris disione that servit, ... iij^s

Item, for casting furth of ij lyntillis abone the wobsteris, quhare thai wrocht, ... xij^d

Item, xix Julij, to David Graham, masoun, aud his servandis for beiging up of dyverss hoillis besyd the end of the stepill quhar the weit drafe in, and uther hoillis besyd the windo skewis for resisting of the drift, . vij^s

Item, for closing and bigging upe of the dur in the nether kirk yeard that enterit to Wate Chepmanis chapill, . . . vj^s

The Expenses deburst be the compter upon the beiging of the new thik wall in the ouer kirkyeard :—

187] Item, xj Augusti 1562, boucht xj laid of Coustland lyme, price of the laid iij^s; summa, ... xxxiij^s

ALEXANDER GUTHRIE, Dean of Guild. 1561-62.

Item, in drink silver to mak guid laidis, ... viij^d
Item, xiiij Augusti, vj laid Coustland lyme, ilk laid xxxij^d; summa, . xvj^s
Item, xv Augusti, vj laid, ... xij^s
Item, mair, the samyn day, ellevin laidis Coustland lyme, the laid xxxij^d; summa, ... xxix^s iiij^d
Item, to (*blank*) King, sande man, for lx laidis of sand, . . xxx^s
Item, xviij Augusti, xxxij laid Straton lyme, ilk laid xvj^d, . . xlij^s viij^d
Item, xxiij day of August, to William Straton for xxviij laiddis lyme, xxxvij^s iiij^d
Item, the same oulk, maire, foure dussoun of sand, . xxiiij^s
Item, xxij Augusti, xij laid Cowstland lyme, xxx^s
Item, xxvij Augusti, xx laid Cousland lyme, lj^s
Item, xxviij Augusti, ten laiddis lyme, . . xxx^s
Item, for drink silver, ... xij^d
Item, xxix Augusti, v dussoun sand, ... xxj^s
Item, Monunday, ultimo Augusti, nyne laid lyme, the laid xxviij^d; summa, xxj^s
Item, the same day, xij laidds lyme, price foirsaid, . . . xxviij^s
Item, primo Septembris, xiij laids lyme, the laid xxviij^d; summa, with the drink silver, ... xxix^s ix^d
Item, quinto Septembris, vj^{xx} xiij laidis sand, . . . iij^li vj^s vj^d
Item, for vj dussoun of watter brocht in befor the vij day of September, v^s
Item, mair, this oulk precedand the xiij of September, vj dussoun vj tubfull watter, ... v^s v^d
Item, the nixt oulk precedand the xx day of September, vj dussoun of watter, ... v^s

Workmen.

Item, to Jok Symsoun and Boyle, workmen, for ther wageis Furisday, the xiij of August, Fryday and Setterday nixt, in casting of the red and seiking of the ground of the said dike, ilk one of thame ij^s on the day; summa, ... xij^s
Item, for ij chaftis to pikis, and making of thame, ... xij^d
Item, to the saids Simsoun and Boyle, barromen, for their lauboris in bering of the red to the kirkyeard, and seiking of the said ground, the oulk precedand the xxij day of August, ... xxiiij^s
Item, the said xxij day, being Sonday, the tyme of the sermone efternone,

the said auld dike chot doune, and, upon Monunday therefter, enterit twa uther workmen to lay abak the stanis, quhilk wes to thame ane oulkis laubour, ... xxiiij^{s} ALEXANDER GUTHRIE, Dean of Guild. 1561-62.

[188] Item, to the said Symsoun and Boyle, besyd the uther twa workmen, being occupiit in bering of stanis fre the new Tolbuith to the said dike, the oulk precedand the xxix day of August, . . . xxxiiij^{s}

Item, to thame, the oulk precedand the fift of September, xxiiij^{s}

Item, to thame, the oulk precedand the xiij of September, . . xxiiij^{s}

Item, to Eduard Hendersoun, ordanet be the provest, baillies and counsall to await upon the tounis warkis, and for his service evry work day, sue be the space of iij oulks and ij dayis, . . . xl^{s}

Item, semeikle of the said dike as is bigit being compleit, and met in presence of the provest be Gilbert Cleutis, extendis to twa rude and ane halfe and sex elnis, ilk rude iij^{li}; summa, . viij^{li}

Item, ane ridill to this lyme, . xviij^{d}

Item, ane uther schule with the irne, ij^{s}

Item, ane barrell to be mortour tubbis, ... iiij^{s}

Item, ane key to the west dur of the kirk, and mending of the lok of the kirk yeard dur, the entrie of the key being fillit with stanis, . . iiij^{s}

The Expenses deburst be the compter upon the Gray frier dike :—

Item, secundo Septembris, boucht twa dussoun of lyme, the dussoun xxvij^{s}; summa, . . . liiij^{s}

Item, in drink silver to mak guid laiddis, ... xij^{d}

Item, the same day, xvij laiddis lyme, price forsaid; summa, with the drink silver, ... xxviij^{s} ix^{d}

Item, quarto et quinto Septembris, boucht foure dussoun ix laidds lyme at xxxvj^{s} the dussoun; summa, ... viij^{li} xj^{s}

Item, becauss the laiddis wer weill fillit, in drink silver, . . . ij^{s} vj^{d}

Item, viij Septembris, twa laiddis lyme, ... iiij^{s}

Item, mair, the same day, xxij laiddis lyme, xxvij^{s} the dussoun; summa, xlix^{s} vj^{d}

Item, ix Septembris, xiij laidds lyme, the laid ij^{s} vj^{d}; summa, xxxij^{s} vj^{d}

Item, in drink silver, ... vj^{d}

Item, xij laiddis Straton lyme, . . . xvj^{s}

ALEXANDER GUTHRIE, Dean of Guild. 1561-62.

[189]

Item, mair, betwix the sevint of September and the xiij of the samyn, to Richard Sym, sandeman, for vj^{xx} laid of sand, ... l^s vj^d

Item, to the said Sym for lxvj laid of sand in betuix the xiij and xxj September, ... xxxiij^s

Item, mair, to him for xxviij laidis sand betuix the xxj September and xxviij of the samyn, ... xiiij^s

Item, mair, to him for iij dussoun xj laid sand, laid in betuix the said xxviij September and the fift of October, ... xxiij^s vj^d

Item, mair, to the said Sym, for xxxv laidis sand, laid in betuix the xij of October and xvij of the samyn, ... xvij^s vj^d

Item, Wedinsday, secundo Septembris, enterit Mak Watter, quariour, for wynninge of stanis furth of the wallis within the Gray freris place, foure dayis wagis, ... viij^s

Item, to uther thre barromen that wrocht at the dikis of the freris, in casting bak of the muk and red, and seiking of the ground, be the space of v dayis precedand the xiij of September, ... xxx^s

Item, to twa of the saidis barromen for thar waigis, the oulk precedand the xxj September, ... xxiiij^s

Item, to Jok Symsoun for his wageis, the oulk, precedand the xxvj of September, ... xij^s

Item, to his marrow, twa dayis wageis, of the said oulk, and dischargeit the rest, ... iiij^s

Item, Monunday, the xxviij September, enterit agane with the said Symsoun, ane other barroman Boyle, and to thame for the oulk precedand the thrid of October, ... xxiiij^s

Item, to the samyn barromen for thair wageis, fre Monunday, quinto die Octobris, to Setterday, the thretene of the samyn, ... xxiiij^s

Item, mair, to the said barromen for thair wageis fre Monunday the xij of October to Setterday at evin, the xiij of the samyn, ... xxiiij^s

Item, to Eduard Hendersoun his waigis be the space of five oulkis five dayis, ilk oulk xij^s; summa, ... iij^{li} x^s

Item, be the said space, xxxv dussoun watter, ... xxix^s ij^d

Item, to the layaris for thar laubors in biggin of the wallis of the said freir kirkyeard dike, contenand foure rude and ane half of work, ilk rude l^s, xj^{li} v^s

ALEXANDER GUTHRIE, Dean of Guild. 1561-62.

Item, ane new schule, the auld being brokin, ... ij^{s}
Item, twa girthis to ane lyme tub, ... xij^{d}
Item, mair, sevin smaller girthis to ane uther tub, and barrell for the watter, ... xxj^{d}
Item, for crambis to ane stane barrell, . iij^{s}
Item, the making of this barrell and naillis to it, ... xij^{d}
[190] Item, the greit yet quhare the new Tolbuith is beigit tane doun and hounge upon the entress at the Gray freir kirkyeard dike, and for naillis to it, ... ij^{s}
Item, for ane bot of irne and ane lange catband to the said yet, . . xij^{s}
Item, ane laurge flaill of irne with ane staple to the samyn, twa plaittis of irne to the stane barrow, weyand all to gidder xix^{li} and ane half, and for walling of the pikis certane tymis, ... xviij^{s} iij$\frac{1}{2}^{d}$
Item, mair, twa stapillis to this yet, for making of the hoillis and leid to the yetting of thame, . xij^{s} vj^{d}
Item, ane ringe and ane snek, iij^{s}
Item, ane lok and ane key, ... iij^{s} viij^{d}
Item, mair, ane hundereth plancheour naill, iij^{c} dur naill for this yet, for naling on of the laith and garrouns of the west maist of the cordinaris choppis, quharof the rufe wes consumit, and new theikit with sklaittis, vij^{s} x^{d}
Item, to Adam Purvess, wrycht, for his laubors upon the yet and choppis, x^{s}
Item, for careing of sklaittis fre the kirk to this schope, . . iij^{s}
Item, for cariage of lyme and sand fre the freiris to this schope, . xviij^{d}
Item, for watter, ... vj^{d}
Item, twa pypis and ane puncheoun to be lath, . . xvij^{s}
Item, to Baxter, sklatter, for his laubors, . . . xx^{s}
Item, agane for girthing and mending of the watter puncheouns and mortar tubbis to lat thame fre falling doun, . . ij^{s}
Item, for laying to gidder of certane sklaitts in the kirk woltis, . . xij^{d}
Item, to Eduard Henrisoun for his wageis to thir workis be the space of viij dayis, ... xij^{s}
Item, for carcing away of ane hill and erd lyand befor the freir yeard, casting and bering away of the red within the yet, making of the passage mair esy for the buriall, ... x^{s}

ALEXANDER GUTHRIE, Dean of Guild. 1561-62.

Item, at the command of the provest, baillies and counsall, as the act in the counsall buik beris, to Maister James Watsoun, for certane expenssis laitlie deburst be him upon the ministeris lugeing as his particulare compt heir present to be schawin beris, . . . viij^{li} viij^{s} viij^{d}

[191] Item, the southmest lange gutter of leid being oure schort, to Johnne Weir, pulderar, for twa fute of leid eikit therto, contenand xviij li wecht, xiij^{s} vij^{d}

Item, ane pund and ane halfe of tyn, . iiij^{s} vj^{d}

Item, his lauboris, ... v^{s}

Item, for beiging up of all the stoppis in the lauche kirk yeard dike with stane and clay, and beichting of sum partes of the samyn, xx^{s}

Item, for renewing of the marking irne that birnis the firlottis, . iij^{s}

The aliwint day of Februarii, the yeir of God 1562 yeris, the compt of Alexander Guthrie, Dene of Gild, the first yeir of his office, viz., fra ye ix day of October, the yeir of God J^{m} v^{c} thre score ane yeris, to the ending in October J^{m} v^{c} thre score twa yeris, as is before writtin, quhais charge extendis to the sowme of vj^{c} xxxv^{li} xj^{s} v^{d}, and his discharge to the sowme of fyve hundereth xliij^{li} ij^{s} j½^{d}; and sua rests the compter awand to the toun the sowme of foure score sevintene pundis ix^{s} iij^{d} obolus.

Memorandum: Alexander Guthre charges him with this rest in his nixt comptis, and thare payit.

ALEXANDER GUTHRIE, Dean of Guild. 1562-63.

[193]

THE COMPT of ALEXANDER GUTHRE, Commoun Clerk and Dene of Gild of the burgh off Edinburgh, the secound yeir of his office, begynnand the (*blank*) day of October in the yeir of God J^{m} v^{c} thre score tua yeiris and endand the (*blank*) day of October, the yeir of God J^{m} v^{c} thre score thre; and first his charge.

CHARGE.

Item, the said Allexander chargeis him with the dewitie of the twa burgesschippis givin be Archebald Douglaiss, provest, the xix and xv dayis of November J^{m} v^{c} lxij yeiris be [to] William Dewar and Johnne Cok, talyoours, pertenand to his L[lordship] be rycht of his office, extending to, x^{li}

Item, the xviij of December, Thomas Aikinheid, burges be rycht of his father, ... xiij^{s} iiij^{d}

Item, the same day, Henerj Lowrj, burges be richt of his wyff, Margaret Broun, ... xiij^{s} iiij^{d}

Item, the xxj December, Johnne Peirsoun, merchand, burges and gild, . xv^{li}

Item, the penult of December, Johnne Gray, hering seller, burgess, v^{li}

Item, the same day, James Mowse, hering man, maid burges, v^{li}

Item, the same day, Johnne Bell, maid burges, . . v^{li}

Item, the samyn day, William Lyell, hering man, maid burges, . v^{li}

Item, the samyn day, Thomas Eistoun, hering man, burges, . v^{li}

Item, the same day, Stevin Inglis, maid burges and peyit, . v^{li}

Item, the samyn day, Patrik Mudie, cordiner, burges and peyit, . v^{li}

Item, the xx of Januar, George Howdane, loksmyth, maid burges, v^{li}

[194] Item, the compter charges him nocht with the burgesschippis grantit be the provest, baillies and counsall to William Adamsoun, talyeour, and givin him gratis at the request of the Counteis of Murray.

Item, the compter chargeis him with the burgesschippis of Nivene Hair, fische seller, ... v^{li}

Item, the secound of Februar, Allexander Weir, skynner, burges be richt of his father, Johnne Weir, customer, ... xiij^{s} iiij^{d}

Item, the xxviij of Januar, David Scot, travelour, burges, . . v^{li}

Item, the xvj of Februar, William Thomsone, merchand, burges and gild brother be richt of Mauss Moffet, his wyff, ... xxxiij^{s} iiij^{d}

Item, the same day, William Symsoun, merchand, burges and gild be richt of his father, William Symsoun, ... xxxiij^{s} iiij^{d}

Item, the xxiiij of Februar, Johnne Burne, merchand, burges be rycht of Alesoun Tod, his wyff, daughter of umquhill David Tod, . xiij^{s} iiij^{d}

Item, the secound of Marche, William Diksoun, flesher, burges, . . v^{li}

Item, the feird of Merche, Thomas Syefarid, merchand, burges, . . v^{li}

Item, the fyft of Marche, Archebald Duncane, merchand, burges, . v^{li}

Item, the compter chargeis him with the gildrie givin the same day be the provest, baillies and counsall to William Gray, barbour, at the request of my Lord of Morton, Chancellar.

Item, the xviij of Marche, Thomas Hoppringill, merchand, burges, v^{li}

ALEXANDER GUTHRIE, Dean of Guild. 1562-63.

Item, the vj of Apprile J^m v lxiij^o, Bartilemeo Symmerweill, merchand, burges, ... v^{li}

Item, the compter chargeis him with the twa burgesschippis givin gratis be the provest, baillies and counsall to Nicholl Andersoun and Robert Bell, masouns, for thair guid service in the Kirk work and new Tolbuith, (*blank*)

[195] Item, the tuelt of Aprile, Symond Johnnestoun, baxter, burges, . . v^{li}

Item, the first of Maij, Johnne Bell, seller of seidis, burges, . v^{li}

Item, the xiij of Maij, James Greinelaw, couper, burges, . . v^{li}

Item, the xxv of Maij, Johnne Craffurd, suerd slipper, burges, . . v^{li}

Item, the first of Junij, Johnne Farlie, broder to the Lard of Braid, burges, v^{li}

Item, the secound day of Junij, Allexander Wischart, bonetmaker, burges, v^{li}

Item, the v of Junij, Johnne Younge, merchand, burges, . . . v^{li}

Item, the tent of Junij, George Wilsoun, merchand, is maid burges be richt of his father, James Wilsoun, . . . vj^s $viij^d$

Item, the same day, Thomas Diksoun, furrour, burges, . . v^{li}

Item, the same day, George Duncan, talzeour, burges, . . . v^{li}

Item, the xiiij of Junij, the compter chargeis him nocht with the gildrie of William Kinkaid, givin him gratis be the provest, baillies and counsall for service done and to be done to the guid toun.

Item, the same day, the compter chargeis him with the burgesschip of the said William Kinkaid, ... v^{li}

Item, the xv of Junij, Johnne Spens, litstar, burges be rycht of rycht of his father, David Spens, littister, ... $xiij^s$ $iiij^d$

Item, the xxij Junij, Johnne Miller, merchand, burges, he peyit, . v^{li}

Item, the same day, Michell Sammill, merchand, burges, . . v^{li}

Item, the same day, Nicholl Reburne, merchand, burges, . . v^{li}

Item, the xxviij of Junij, Johnne Cunnynghame, merchand, burges, . v^{li}

[196] Item, the secound of Julij, J^m v^c lxiij, Johnne Jaksoun, merchand, burges, v^{li}

Item, the vj of Julij, Johnne Loch, merchand, burges, . . . v^{li}

Item, the samyn day, Thomas Cobburne, merchand, burges, . v^{li}

Item, the xv of Julij, James Miller, merchand, burges, . v^{li}

Item, the xx of Julij, Thomas Lowry, merchand, burges, . v^{li}

Item, the xxiiij of Julij, Johnne Johnnestoun, saidlar, burges, . v^{li}

Item, the compter chargeis him nocht with the burgesschip and gildrie grantit be the provest, baillies and counsall to Robert Hendersoun, chirrurgian, for his service done to the toun in curing of certane hurt personis at thair command, for the quhilkis he had the townis precept, conteinand the soume of twenty marks, and delyuerit thame the samyn agane for the said burgeschip and gildrie.

Item, the samin day, William Hendersoun, sumlier, servand to the Quenis Maiestie, maid burges and gild brother be rycht of his father and be rycht of his wyff, the douchter of James Fowlis, . . . xiij^s iiij^d

Item, the xvj of August, Mungo Fortoun, merchand, burges be rycht of Margaret Williamsoun, his wyff, . . . xiij^s iiij^d

Item, the xx of August, Johnne Lousoun, merchand, burges, . v^{li}

Item, the xj of September, Johnne Uddart, alias Capitan, gild broder be rycht of his father, ... xiij^s iiij^d

Item, the fourtene of September, Johnne Uddart, gild brother be rycht of his father, Thomas Uddart, ... xx^s

Item, the samyn day, Thomas Wilsoun, alias Tavernar, burges, . v^{li}

Item, the xv, Henerj Achesoun, gild, be his father, . . . xiij^s iiij^d

[197] Item, the xv of September, Patrik Rig, burges and gild be rycht of Elizabeth Houpe, his wyff, . . . xxxiij^s iiij^d

Item, Johnne Rig, burges and gild be rycht of Elizabeth Aikman, his wyffe, ... xxxiij^s iiij^d

Item, Archebald Forman, cuk, burges, ... v^{li}

Item, the xvj of September, Robert Scot, merchand, burges, v^{li}

Item, the xxiiij of September, Johnne Davidsoun, merchand, burges, v^{li}

Item, James Guthre, burges and gild broder, . . . xv^{li}

Item, the last of September, Archibald Kennedie, merchand, burges, v^{li}

Item, the first of October, Andro Murdesoun, merchand, burges, . . v^{li}

Item, the secound of October, Thomas Davidsoun, ypothecar, burges and gild be rycht of his father, ... xxxiij^s iiij^d

Item, Richart Blaklo, fysche seller, burges be rycht of his father, . xiij^s iiij^d

Item, James Marioribankis, gild brother be rycht of his father, . . xx^s

Item, David Lyle, merchand, gild broder be rycht of his wyff, Jonet Stevinsoun, ... xxxiij^s iiij^d

Item, the samyn day, Johnne Pacok, burges and gild, xv^{li}

ALEXANDER GUTHRIE, Dean of Guild. 1562-63.

Item, the viij of October, James Nicholl, merchand, maid gild broder be the ordinance of the provest, baillies and counsall, and hes peyit therfor allanerlie as thair act beris, ... v^{li}

[198] Item, the compter chargeis him with the dewitie of the haill Schippis arrivit at the port and hevin of Leiyth the said yeir, being in noumer iiij^{xx}, conforme to the schipp buik, ilk schipp xiiij^{s}, . . . lvj^{li}

Item, the compter chargeis him with the maillis of the Cordiner choppis the said yeir, ... xxj^{li}

Item, the compter chargeis him with the maillis of the Goldsmythis choppis following, viz., Adam Dennunis chop the said yeir, . . xxx^{s}

Item, the compter chargeis him with Robert Ryndis chop, xxx^{s}

Item, the maill of Andro Heleis stand on the south kirk dur, xl^{s}

Item, the maill of Christofer Galbrayth chop, xxx^{s}

Item, Allexander Gilbertis chop, ... xxx^{s}

Item, the compter chargeis him with the fut and rest of his last comptis, extending to the soume of, ... lxxxxvij^{li} ix^{s} iij^{d}

Item, the compter chargeis him nocht with the maillis of George Turnouris chop, and stand, quhilk was dischargeit him be the provest, baillies and counsall.

Item, the compter chargeis him nocht with the maillis of Robert Murrayis chop, quha hes not guidis to pey.

Item, the compter chargeis him nocht with the maillis of the twa new choppis at Oure Lady steppis, becauss thair is no yeirlie dewitie assignit to the occupyaris therof.

Lateris, . . . j^{c} lxxxij^{li} ix^{s} iij^{d} obolus.

Summa of this haill charge before writtin, extendis in the hale to, iiij^{c} lxxj^{li} ix^{s} iij^{d} obolus.

THE COMPTARIS DISCHARGE.

[199] Item, the compter dischargis him with the twa burgeschippis gevin to Archebald Douglaiss, Provest, be richt of his office, ... x^{li}

Item, to the foure Baillies, every ane of thame ane burgesschip; summa, xx^{li}

Item, to the Dene of Gild, ane burgesschip and gildrie; summa, . . xv^{li}

Item, to Richard Trohope, ane burgesschip, . . . v^{li}

Item, the xij servandis, everie ane of thame iiij^{li}; summa, xlviij^{li}

Item, to Andro Lyndsay, javellour, ... xl^s

Item, to the Commoun Clark and his twa servandis, every ane of thame ane burgeschip, ... xv^li

Item, to James Hunter, glassinwrycht, his ordiner pensioun for uphald of the glass wyndois in the kirk, ... iiij^li

Item, to Patrik Gowan, belman, Robert Drummond and Jok Symsoun, ordinar servandis in the kirk, for thair fies, ilk ane of thame viij^li; summa, xxiiij^li

Item, to the Dene of Gild for his fie the yeir of his office, . vj^li xiij^s iiij^d

Item, the compter chargeis him with the soume of thre ^li takin upoun him for the stand and chop maill in his last comptis, of George Turnour, quharof he gat no peyment, bot wes dischargeit of the samin be ane act of the counsall, in respect of the said Turnouris povertie, iij^li

[200] The Comptaris discharge off the necessar expensses debursit be him upon the kirk warkis and the uther effearis of the toun, as followis:—

Item, the xv day of November, the yeir off God J^m v^c lxij yeiris, to Adam Purvess, wrycht, for his lauboris in the upsetting of ane skaffald in Wat Chepmannis Ile, for bigging of the glass windo therof, himself and twa servandis, . . . x^s

Item, twa puncheouns to the said skaffald, . . viij^s

Item, the uther tymmer borrowit of the maister of wark and delyuerit agane.

Item, twa laid lyme to big up the half of the said wyndo in stane wark, . v^s

Item, foure laid sand, . . ij^s

Item, for watter to mak the morter, ix^d

Item, for garroun naill to the skaffald, . . ij^s

Item, to Arthur Hamyltoun, masoun, for his laubouris upon the said windo, ane oulk, ... xxx^s

Item, twa warkmen that servit him in making of the morter and bringing of stanis fre the nether kirk yeard, ... xviij^s

Item, to the glassinwrycht for lauboring and setting of iiij^xx xiiij fute and ane half auld glass to the said windo, ilk fute vj^d; summa, . xlvij^s iij^d

Item, to him for fiftie ane fute of new glass to the said windo, ilk fute xx^d; summa, ... iiij^li v^s x^d

*

ALEXANDER GUTHRIE, Dean of Guild. 1562-63.

Item, to the said glassinwrycht for mending of the windo above the Lordis heidis quhair thai sit at the preching, setting latheating and for ane pannell of new glass to the said windo, contenand thre futis, . . xvj^s viij^d

Item, the xxiij of November, aggreit with twa warkmen to beir away ane greit hill of red lyand outwith and inwith the buriall yet at the Gray Freris, and to thame for thair lauboris, . . . x^s

[201] Item, for ane lok to the dur that passes to the umast leidis of the steipill, with the key, ... vj^s viij^d

Item, the haill glass windo above the revestrie being brokin and blowin done be the wehemence of the north west wind, and to mak up the samyn agane, xxxj futtis and ane half new glass, price of the fute xx^d; summa, lij^s vj^d

Item, at the command of the provest, baillies and counsall, to Maister James Watsoun quhilk he debursit at thair command upon the windois and the ordoring of the ministeris new studies, as the particular comptis heir to schow beris, . . . viij^li xviij^s viij^d

Item, upon Sonnday the xx of December, and Sonnday the xxvij of the samyn, for xij gallownns thre quartis wyne to the Communioun, price of the pint ij^s; summa, ... x^li iiij^s

Item, thre dowsoun foure breid, price of the pece xiiij^d; summa, xv^s

Item, twa dousoun torcheis, . . . iij^li

Item, ane hundereth plancheour naill to the barress, iij^s

Item, for plancheour naill for the torcheis, . . . vj^d

Item, to foure warkmen for bering of the taiblis and fourmis and tymmer that was the barress baith the dayis, ... viij^s

Item, to Johnne Cunnynghame, wrycht, and his servandis for upsetting and dountaking of the taiblis and barress baith the dayis, . . x^s

Item, the servandis disiounis that servit the taiblis baith the Sonndayis, and keipit the kirk, ... vj^s

[202] Item, for wesching of the tabill claithis, ... xviij^d

Item, for bering of certane furrmis fre the Maitland Chapell and Tolbuith to the kirk, and fre thin to the Maitland Chapell and Tolbuith agane, ij^s vj^d

Item, the xviij of December, the tyme of the Wobstaris wirking in the woultis above the kirk, the leid guttars of the kirk being cuttit and stowin, for tirwing of the sklattis quhare the guttars wer cuttit, . iij^s

ALEXANDER GUTHRIE, Dean of Guild. 1562-63.

Item, to Johnne Weir, pouderar, for sax stane ane pund wecht new claith leid for mending of the saidis gutters, ilk stane xij^{s}; summa, . iij^{li} xiij^{s} ix^{d}
Item, to the said Johnne Weir for the change of thre stane auld leid, . v^{s}
. Item, to him for ane pund of tyn, . . . iij^{s}
Item, to him for laying of this leid and his uther lauboris, v^{s}
Item, for coillis to melt this tyn and heit the sowding irne, xviij^{d}
Item, for bering of this leid fre Johnne Weiris houss to the kirk rigging, xviij^{d}
Item, to Johnne Weiris servand in drink silver, . . xviij^{d}
Item, to Walter Scot, sklatter, for theiking of the houssis quhare the leid was stowin, and mending of the faltis of the uther houssis, xx^{s}
Item, for naillis to him for fessying on the serking agane, . . xviij^{d}
Item, efter this leid was stowin, for ane new lok to the stepill dur and twa keyis, the wobstaris being put furth, ... xij^{s}
Item, the xxvj Februar, to Robert Droummound, at the provest, baillies and counsallis command, for candill furneist be him the tyme of winter to the kirk cessioun, and generall conventiounis, . . xxviij^{s}
[203] Item, the xxvj Merche, the Baillies, Dene of Gild and certane nychtbouris, craftismen, send to Leith for strikking up of the sellar durris of Patrik Cokburne, Thomas Lyndsay and Johnne Broun, indwellaris of Leyth, quhare thai had sellerit certane wynis unenterit to the toun, quhilk durris wes strikkin up and the saidis wynis transportet to utheris sellaris to the tounis behouff, givin to David Spens, messinger, for intimeing of certane charges to the saidis personis of Leyth, and summoning of witnessis diverss tymes to prufe the tounis action intentit aganis thame, . x^{s}
Item, the last of Merche, for careinge of certane taibillis fre the Kirk to the Hie Scule, and fre thin to the kirk agane the tyme of the Assemblie befor the Communioun, ... v^{s}

The Expensis upon the theiking and tirwing of the heill Queir :—

Item, the last day of Merche, the haill queir being tirwit at the provest, baillies and counsallis command, for sex thousand sklattis to the theiking of the samyn agane, ilk thousand vj^{li}; summa, . . . xxxvj^{li}
Item, twa hundereth greit sklettis, ... iij^{li} xij^{s}
Item, becauss horss culd not be gottin to cary thir sklattis, the samyn

ALEXANDER GUTHRIE, Dean of Guild, 1562-63.

beand in the Queinis service, the saidis sklattis wer walkit five dayis and nychtis upon the Schor, ilk day and nycht iij^{s}: summa, . . . xv^{s}

Item, it being statut and ordanit be the provest, baillies and counsall that Eduard Hendersoun, als Sir Eduard, suld wait upon the kirk workis and owrse thame, for his lauboris in numring and ressawing of the saidis sklattis and delyuering agane, ... xvj^{s} viij^{d}

[204] Item, to twa warkmen that ressavit the saidis sklattis, tuk thame of the horss bakis, and sortit thame in the Halie Bluid Ile, quhar thai wer drest, be the space of foure dayis, . xij^{s}

The Secound Communion.

Item, the xv day of Aprile, for foure dowsoun thre breid to the Communion, ... iij^{li} xvj^{s} vj^{d}

Item, xij gallounis and ane half wyne bayth the dayis, price of the pint ij^{s}, x^{li}

Item, for candill bayth the dayis, ... xviij^{d}

Item, to foure warkmen that helpit to set the taiblis and barress baith the dayis, viij^{s}

Item, for naillis, ... ij^{s}

Item, to the wrychts that set up and tuk doun the barress baith the dayis, x^{s}

Item, the childeris and servandis disiounis baith the dayis, vj^{s}

Item, for wesching of the tabill claithis, . . xviij^{d}

The remanent expenses upon the Queir :—

Item, for bering up of ane thousand of thir sklattis above wreittin, thai beand drest, fre the Halie Blude Ile to the rigginis of the Queir, xxiiij^{s}

Item, for bering up of xiiij^{c} of the samyn sklattis, . . . vij^{s}

Item, ane boy that keipit the sklattis in the Halie Blud Ile, the tyme of the bering up of thame, . . . xij^{d}

Item, the sklatteris and thair boyis in drink, . xx^{d}

Item, Eduard Hendersounis wagie, the oulk precedand, . xij^{s}

Item, mair, ane thousand sklattis, vj^{li}

Item, the cariage of thame, . . xx^{s}

[205 Item, bering of thame to the steipill, ... vj^{s}

Item, xviij day of Julij, ix laid of lyme, price of the laid xxviij^{d}; summa, xxj^{s}

Item, mair, twa laid lyme, . . . v^{s}
Item, mair, v laidis lyme, the laid xxviij^{d}, . . . xj^{s} viij^{d}
Item, the xxv day of Julij, xj laid lyme, the laid xxviij^{d}; summa, . xxv^{s} viij^{d}
Item, the xxij day of Julij, twa laids lyme, . . . v^{s}
Item, xxv day of Julij, xj laidis lyme, . . . xxv^{s} viij^{d}
Item, iiij^{xx} laidis sand, . . xl
Item, xvj dosone of watter, . xiij^{s} iiij^{d}
Item, ane schule to mak the morter, ... xvj^{d}
Item, to Jok for ane oulkis laubouris, for bering of samony of the auld sklattis of the queir as wer haill to the woltis to be drest, . xij^{s}
Item, ane greit part of the serking of the queir being rottin and consumit, boucht vj daillis to helpe the samyn agane, price, . . xx^{s}
Item, for bering of thame furth of Leyth, . ij^{s}
Item, for sawing of thame, ... v^{s} iiij^{d}
Item, mair, boucht j dosone of daillis to the samin effect, price, l^{s}
Item, for bering of thame furth of Leyth, iiij^{s}
Item, sawing of thre of thame, . . iij^{s}
Item, sawing of viij of thame upon the edge, ... x^{s} viij^{d}
Item, to Adam Purves, wrycht, for mending of the haill sarking of the queir bow stringe, and mending of the samin in sindrie places with tymmer of his awin, givin him therfor, . xxvj^{s} viij^{d}
Item, for garroun naillis to the bow string, iij^{s}
Item, mair, to the sklatter, vj^{c} plancheour naill, . xiiij^{s}
Item, mair, to him, iiij^{c} plancheour naill, . x^{s}
Item, the xvj of August, to him, ij^{c} plancheour naill, . vj^{s}
[206] Item, mair, to him, ix^{c} plancheour naill, the hundereth xxxij^{d}; summa, . xxiiij^{s}
Item, the vj day of September, to him, viij^{c} plancheour naill, the hundereth xxxiiij^{d}, ... xxij^{s}
Item, mair, for bering of ij^{m} sklattis fre the Halie Blude Ile to the Queir ruffe, to Jok Symsoun, . . . vj^{s}
Item, mair, to him, for bering of ij^{c} sklattis, xij^{d}
Item, for twa rud of rigging stane, . iij^{li} x^{s}
Item, for bering of thame to the sklatters, ... xij^{d}
Item, for xiij puncheounis to be pynnes, price of the pece iiij^{s} vj^{d}; summa, lviij^{s} vj^{d}

ALEXANDER GUTHRIE, Dean of Guild. 1562-63.

Item, to William Robesoun and Walter Scot, sklatters, for theiking of the said Queir, the samin contenand xj rud and ane half of wark, price of the rud iij[li], ... xxxj[li] x[s]

Item, to thair childer in drink silver, ... x[s]

Item, for drink to thame selfis at the compleiting of the said wark upon the rigging of the houss, ... v[s]

Item, beand removit out of the Clarkis chalmer, quhilk was in David Forsteris, to ane littill houss of Michaell Gilbertis, for taking doun of the tymmer wark in the said auld chalmer and transporting of the samyn, ... iiij[s] vj[d]

Item, for foure daillis to be skalffis and benkis in the new chalmer, the pece xl[d]; summa, . . . xiij[s] iiij[d]

Item, for glew and naillis thair, xviij[d]

Item, the wrychtis lauboris, ... x[s]

Item, the bandis beand stowin of the pulpet dur, for ane pare of new bandis, iiij[s]

The Expenssis debursit be the compter upon the bigging of the Clarkis Chalmer, quhilk sumtyme wes the Revestrie, as followis :—

[207] Item, the (*blank*) of Maij, to Gilbert Cleuch, masoun, be command of the provest, baillies and counsall, beand enterit to wark of the said Revestrie, begynnand to brek the eist wall, quhar now is the entrie of the Clarkis Chalmer, for his wageis the oulk precedand the viij of Maij in anno lxiij, ... xxxv[s]

Item, to Nicholl Hendersoun, the masoun, the samyn oulk, . xxxj[s] vj[d]

Item, to James Cok, masoun, . . . xxxj[s] vj[d]

Item, to Robert Bell, masoun, the samyn oulk, ... xxxj[s] vj[d]

Item, the samyn oulk, to Johnne Symsoun and Hew Maklauchlane, barromen, quhilk wer occupeit in bringing of gret stanis fre the nether kirkyeard to be lyntellis, soillis, etc., to the dur and windok of the clarkis chalmer, ... xxiiij[s]

Item, to Johnne Boyil and Punnye, barromen, for redding of the revestrie, twa dayis, ... vj[s]

Item, for twa dousoun of daillis, to be ane part of the fluring of the ouer chalmeris, ... iiij[li]

Item, to Adam Purves, wrycht, for thre dayis wageis and ane half, this oulk,	xxj^{s}
Item, to Eduard Hendersoun, the said oulk,	xij^{s}
Item, for bering of the daillis furth of Leyth,	iiij^{s}
Item, ane dousoun of sand,	vj^{s}
Item, Monunday, x^{mo} Maij, to Gilbert Cleuch, for his oulkis wageis to Setterday, the xv of the samyn,	xxxvj^{s}
Item, his thre men, the said oulk,	iij^{li} xiiij^{s} vj^{d}
Item, twa barromen, the said oulk,	xxiiij^{s}
Item, to Adam Purvess, wrycht, the said oulk in laboring upon durris, [208] windokis, breddis, jiestis, the fluring of baith the chalmeris, the tymmer of the turnepik binkis and saittis, and uther necessaris of the chalmeris, etc.,	xxxvj^{s}
Item, his servand, the said oulk,	xxiiij^{s}
Item, for bering of xxxiij gret stanis fre the nether kirkyeard to the revestrie,	v^{s}
Item, for x laid of lyme, the laid iij^{s},	xxx^{s}
Item, xx laid of sand,	x^{s}
Item, iij dosone and ane halfe of watter,	iiij^{s} vij^{d}
Item, for ane schule,	xij^{d}
Item, to Eduard Hendersoun, for the oulk above wreittin,	xij^{s}
Item, foure Eistland burd to be ane dur to the clarkis chalmer,	xl^{s}
Item, for bering of thame fre Leyth,	ij^{s}
Item, mair, twa laid lyme,	viij^{s} vj^{d}
Item, to Johnne Wallace, wryter, at the presenting of the Commissioun of Parliament,	vj^{s} viij^{d}
Item, for bering of ane table fre the Tolbuith to the Magdalene Chapell, the Kirk being convenit thair,	viij^{d}
Item, the tyme of the said parliament, becauss of the braulinge of certane of Leyth, burroit be the Dene of Gild furth of the Castell upon his obligatioun of ij^{c} lange pikis, and for bering of thame to the Tolbuith,	xij^{s}
Item, the oulk precedand the xxij of Maij, for vij Eistland burdis to cleyth the turnepike to be broddis almeris,	iij^{li} x^{s}
Item, Adam Purves, wrycht, this oulk,	xxxvj^{s}

ALEXANDER GUTHRIE, Dean of Guild, 1562-63.

Item, to Adam Purves sonn, the said oulk, xxxj^{s}

Item, his servand, the samyn oulk, ... xxiiij^{s}

Item, the endis of twa jestis in the under houss of the clarkis chalmer

[209] being rottin and consumit in the waill, boucht uther twa jestis, price, . xxviij^{s}

Item, uther fyve jiestis to the ovir chalmer, ... iij^{li} x^{s}

Item, for certane lange tymmer to be bandis and standertis to the turnepik, xxx^{s}

Item, James Mosman, goldsmyth, havand in his possessioun the staff and steppis of the turnepik quhilk wes the Blak freris, and gevin him therfor, ... xl^{s}

Item, to the sawaris for sawing ix draucht of Eistland burd and lange tymmer, ... xix^{s} iiij^{d}

Item, Jok Symsoun, barroman, his wageis this oulk, . . . xij^{s}

Item, at the upbiggin of the revestrie dur that past in to the kirk, ane laid of lyme, . iij^{s} viij^{d}

Item, for twa laid of sand, xij^{d}

Item, for watter, . . . iiij^{d}

Item, to ane masoun that biggit this dur, ... vj^{s}

Item, to Mungo Hunter, smyth, for ane greit lok and ane key to the new dur of the clarkis chalmer, ... xvj^{s}

Item, to Johnne Achanny, smyth, for viij stane xiiij^{li} irne wark, eikit to the gret windok of the clarkis chalmer, ilk stane maid wark xvj^{s}, . vij^{li} ij^{s}

[210] Item, xxvj^{li} wecht of leid to the said windok and creukis of the new dur, xvj^{s} iiij^{d}

Item, for mending of certane glass bandis, . iij^{s}

Item, for mending of the pykis and schul irnis, xviij^{d}

Item, to the dur, ane hundereth quernall naillis, . . . xiiij^{s}

Item, iij^{c} doubill plancheour naill to the said dur and uther wark, x^{s}

Item, mair, ij^{c} plancheour naill, . v^{s}

Item, mair, iij^{c} naillis, . iiij^{s} vj^{d}

Item, mair, twa dosoun garroun naill, ... ij^{s}

Item, the irne creukis and bandis of the new dur (*blank*) weyand; summa, xx^{s}

Item, mair, foure boittis off irne to the fessinying of the standertis of the turnepik, the rest of the boittis maid of auld irne I had of the tounis awing, ... v^{s}

Item, mair, half ane stane of leid, . v^{s}

Item, the oulk precedand the xxix of Maij, Adam Purves, wrycht, for that oulkis wageis, . . . xxxvj^s

Item, to his sonn that oulk, . xxxj^s vj^d

Item, to his servand, ... xxiiij^s

Item, to the sawer for sawing of certane cuttis of treis, iiij^s vj^d

Item, to Eduard Hendersoun for his oulkis wageis, ... xij^s

Item, for bering of ane gryt almri with the tounis wreitingis furth of the Clarkis chalmer in Michaell Gilbertis land to the new chalmer, . vij^d

Item, the Parliament being endit, for careing of the lange pyks agane to the Castell, . xij

[211] Item, to the porter of the castell, ... v^s

Item, to the gunnaris, ordinaris and keiperis of the monitioun houss at the ressaving of the saidis pikis, ... x^s

Item, to Thomas Pettegrew, wrycht, for ane lok to the turnepik dur in the clarkis chalmer havand twa keyis, . ix^s

Item, for ane new byrning irne to the firlottis, ... vj^s viij^d

Item, mair, to Adam Purves, wrycht, his wageis the oulk precedand the v day of Junij, . xxxvj^s vj^d

Item, his servand, ... xxxj^s vj^d

Item, to ane uther servand, wrycht, freman, enterit this oulk for mair expeditioun of the wark, . . xxx^s

Item, to his uther servandis of auld, ... xxiiij

Item, to thame on Setterday at evin, in drink becauss I held thame besy all the oulk, ... v^s

Item, to ane masoun for laying of the hart of the chymnay in the ouir chalmer, ... xij^s vj^d

Item, to Jok for serving him with stanis and morter to the said hart and fylling of the hoillis at the endis of the jestis, twa dayis and ane halfe, v^s

Item, Eduard Hendersoun, the said oulk, ... xij^s vj^d

Item, mair, to Adam Purves, for his wageis, the oulk precedand the xij of Junij, ... xxxvj^s

Item, his sonn, . . xxxj^s vj^d

[212] Item, his servand, ... xxiiij^s

Item, to ane uther wrycht, callit William Kellemure, iiij dayis wageis, . xx^s

ALEXANDER GUTHRIE, Dean of Guild. 1562-63.

Item, the xv of Junij, boucht, mair, foure Eistland burdis, makand in the haill xvj to compleit the said turnepik windo broddis and lyddis of almries,	xl[s]
Item, twa ruffe spar to bind the portell of the mid chalmer, . .	x[s]
Item, mair, twa jestis quhareupon the endis of the jestis of unmeist chalmer rystis, ...	xxiiij[s]
Item, mair, xij daillis to end the forsaid portell, and to compleit the fluring of baith the chalmeris aboune, quhilk in the haill makis iij dosone; summa of thir dozone, ...	xlviij[s]
Item, for carrege of this ruff spar, wanescot and daillis furth of Leyth, .	ix[s]
Item, to the sawaris for twa draucht of thir daillis, .	xxxij[d]
Item, aucht draucht of wanescot, . .	iiij[s]
Item, twa draucht of ruff spar, ...	xxx[d]
Item, twa schort draucht of wanescot to the windo skewis,	vj[d]
Item, mair, vij draucht wanescot, . .	iij[s] vj[d]
Item, mair, twa quarter draucht to the windois, ...	vj[d]
Item, to Jok for bering of this haill tymmer to and fra the sawaris, .	ij[s] vj[d]
Item, Johnne Robesoun, twa dayis and ane half upon the fluring of the mid chalmer, ...	x[s]
[213] Item, mair, ane stane of leid to compleit the haill warkis,	xv[s]
Item, twa laidis lyme to big up certane windoks and bewellis,	v[s]
Item, for v laidis sand, ...	ij vj[d]
Item, for watter to mak this morter and to watter the haill thre houssis cleinging, ...	iij[s]
Item, to ane masoun for biggin up of thir windois, bewellis, hoillis, and laying of the nether hart, iij dayis, ...	xv[s]
Item, the warkmen that servit him and broucht stanis fre the nether kirkyeard, ...	iiij[s] vj[d]
Item, to Adam Purvess for ane pund of glew, .	ij[s] iiij[d]
Item, mair, for sawing of thre cuttis of treis, .	xviij[d]
Item, ane pare of bandis to the nether almery, ...	xviij[d]
Item, Adam Purves, for his last oulkis wageis, precedand the xix day of Junij, ...	xxxvj[s]
Item, his sonn, . .	xxxj[s] vj[d]
Item, his twa servands,	xliiij[s]

Item, to Eduard Hendersoun, ... xij^{s}

Item, for candill and thre pintis of aile to the warkmen, ... ij^{s} iiij^{d}

Item, Johnne Achanny, smyth, for aucht small wegeis of irne, contenand ij^{li} wecht, ... ij^{s}

Item, to the compleiting of the haill warkis, and nalling of the flure of baith the houssis, boucht iiij^{c} ½ doubill plancheour naill, xviij^{s}

Item, ane j^{c} singill plancheour naill, xxxij^{d}

[214] Item, mar, iij^{c} dur naill, . iiij^{s} vj^{d}

Item, ij^{c} windo naill, . . xxxij^{d}

Item, mair, vj boitts to the almareis, . . . iij^{s}

Item, iiij pannells glass in the nether chalmer, contenand xxv fute new glass, ilk fute xxij^{d}; summa, . xlv^{s} vj^{d}

Item, vj fute auld glass, ilk fute viij^{d}, . iiij^{s}

Item, ix fute new glass to the owir chalmer, xvj^{s} vj^{d}

Item, ij^{c} takattis, ... xx^{d}

Item, xviij pund wecht bandis to the windois, . . xviij^{s}

Item, for xj fute of tyrliss for utouth the nether windok quhar the clark wreittis, ilk fute viij^{d}, . . vij^{s} iiij^{d}

Item, vj boittis to it, ... xviij^{d}

Item, to Mungow Hunter for xx foure pair of bandis to the durris, windois, almeris, with rungis, naillis and snekis, . . iiij^{li} xij^{s}

Item, for ane key to the transs dur quhair the barnis ar babtist, iij^{s}

Item, ane new key to the yet of the buriall at the Gray freris, . . iij^{s}

Item, ane key to the box of the Common Seill, the Provestis key beane tynt, ...

Item, Johnne Bell, burges, beinge charget be the tounis decreit to remove him self fre the merchant buit occupiit be him and contemptouslie refusit be absenting him self, at the command of the baillies for fesching of four hammeris to braik of the box, ... xij^{d}

[215] Item, at the command of the provest, baillies and counsall for the charge and expenssis of ane wodman callit Keyth the space of xvj dayis, and for ane sark and ane pair of boyis of irne to him quhan he was lattin to libertie, ... xv^{s}

Item, at the command of the Provest, baillies and counsall to William

ALEXANDER GUTHRIE, Dean of Guild. 1562-63.

Stewart, writter in the clarkis chalmer, for wreiting of the tounis comptis and stent rollis, ... v^li

Item, William Douglass, servand, being dischargeit of his office, to ane pure woman callit Jonet Dunmure, quhais dettis he had uplift and noucht peyit agane, . . xl^s

Last Communione.

Item, ix Augusti, the thrid Communion, for xij gallounis thre quartes of wyne, bayth the dayis, price of the pint xx^d, ... viij^li x^s

Item, iiij dosone foure mane breid, the pece xviij^d; summa, . iij^li xviij^s

Item, the servandis and servandis disionis baith the dayis, viij^s

For candill at the settin of the table and barress, . . . iiij^d

Item, to the warkmen that bure the dayillis quhilk wes the barress, being borrowit in the toun, bering of the furmes and taiblis, and bering him of the daillis agane, ... viij^s

Item, to the wrychts that naillit the barres, set up the tabillis and tuk the samyn doun agane, bayth the dayis, x^s

Item, for naillis to thame, ... iij^s

Item, to the baxteris servandis in drink silver, bayth for this and the last yeir, v^s

Item, wesching of the claithis, ... xviij^d

[216] Item, at the counsallis command, to Douglass, servand, efter his deprivatioun, he being extreme pure, for his last reward, ... xl^s

Item, for bringing of certane greit furneyis furth of the Tolbuith to the kirk, viij^d

Item, for ane greit doubill plank to be ane spout abone the clarkis chalmer, and to Adam Purves for pik and uthers necessaris to it, and for his lauboris in makin of the samyn, . . xxx^s

Item, to Patrik, belman, for viij faddomis cord to the knok, x^s

Item, to him for ule de olyve to the knok the haill yeir, . . xij^s

Particule, . . iiij^li xij^s viij^d

Summa totalis exhonerationis befor this extendis in the hale to the soume of, ... iiij^c lxxiiij^li vj^s iiij^d

Summa of the Compteris charge extendis to, . iiij^c lxxj^li ix^s iij^d obolus

And sua, first compt and reknying haid, the compter is superexpendit, ... lvij^s obolus

[217] THE COMPT off ALLEXANDER GUTHRE, Commoun Clark and Dene of Gild of the burgh of Edinburgh, of the thrid yeir of his office, viz., fre the viij of October, in anno J^m v^c lxiij to the (*blank*) day of October in anno 1564.

ALEXANDER GUTHRIE, Dean of Guild. 1563-64.

ITEM, THE COMPTER CHARGEIS HIM with the burgeschip and gildrie of Andro Williamsoun, be rycht of his father, Archibald Williamesoun, sometyme baillie of this burgh, and that at the command of the counsall, notwithstanding his name wes not found in the lokit buik, and haiss peyit for his dewitie, ... v^l

Item, the secound day of November 1563, Robert Thomsoun, skynner, burgess, be the provest, ... v^li

Item, the xj of November, Johnne Birne, merchand, burgess, v^li

Item, the samyn day, George Welsche, barbour, burges, . v^li

Item, the xvj day of November, Arthur Fischer, draper, burgess, . v^li

Item, the xxvij day of November, Patrik Crafurd, tailzeour, burges be rycht of his wyff, Mariore Robesoun, dochter of umquhill Allexander Robesoun, tailzeour, and haiss peyit, ... xiij^s iiij^d

Item, the first December, Robert Galbrayth, merchand, is maid burges be richt of his father, Thomas Galbraith, . . vj^s viiij^d

Item, the xxiiij December, the compter charges him with the burgeschip and gildrie off William Abercrummie, at the command of the provest, baillies and counsall, at the request of my Lord of Sanct Colmes Inche.

Item, the samyn day, Thomas Johnnestoun, merchand, burges, . . v^li

Item, the viij of Januar, William Foular is maid burges and gild broder, and that in respect that his father wes diverss tymes, and therfor the counsall ordanit him to be ressavit for the dewite only, v^li

Item, William Cokburne, merchand, burges, ... v^li

[218] Item, the same day, George Rynd, sone and air of umquhill Thomas Rynd, is maid burges and gild broder, ... xxxiij^s iiij^d

Item, the first of Februar, How Glen, fische seller, is maid burges, v^li

Item, the fourt of Februar, Hencri Stalker, goldsmyth, burges, . . v^li

Item, the same day, Patrik Mertone, cordiner, is maid burges be rycht of his wyff, Issobell Gottray, ... xiij^s iiij^d

Item, the xviij of Februar, Patrik Tennend, merchand, burges, . v^li

ALEXANDER GUTHRIE, Dean of Guild. 1563-64.

Item, the xix of Februar, Thomas Hoppringill, litister, burges, . . v[li]
Item, the fourt of Marche, Michaell Rynd, goldsmyth, burges and gild broder be rycht of his father, ... xxxiij[s] iiij[d]
Item, the vij of Merche, Andro Abernethe, saidlar, burges, . . v[li]
Item, the viij of Merche, the compter charges him with the burgesschip of Heneri Smyth, cutlar, be the provest, givin be richt off his office, . v[li]
Item, the samin day, Adam Reid, sone and air to umquhill David Reid, burges be richt of his father, ... xiij[s] iiij[d]
Item, the tent of Merche, William Menteith, bower, is maid burges, . v[li]
Item, the xiij of Merche, Thomas Dougall, secound sone to Johnne Dougall, is maid burges, ... xx[s]
Item, the samin, the compter chargeis him not with the dewitie of the burgeschipp and gildrie of Maister George Strange, advocat, givin at command of the provest, baillies and counsall.
Item, the xviiij of Merche, George Thomsoun, lorymer, burges, . v[li]
[219] Item, the samin day, Johnne Blair, cramer, burges, . v[li]
Item, the xxij day of Merche, Jhonne Blyth, cramer, burgess, . v[li]
Item, the xxvij of Merche 1564, Robert Nisbet, merchant, burges, . v[li]
Item, the xij of Merche, Patrik Loutfute, litister, is maid burges be rycht of his wyff, Margaret Blak, dauchter of Allexander Blak, baxter, xxxiij[s] iiij[d]
Item, the samin day, Patrik Gray, soun of William Gray, burges, skinner, xiij[s] iiij[d]
Item, the xx day of Aprile, Robert Patersoun, merchant, burges, v[li]
Item, the xij of Maii lxiiij[o], Archebald Mathue, bonet maker, burges, . v[li]
Item, the samin day, Walter Huchesoun, merchand, is maid burges be rycht of his wyff, Katherene Lyell, eldest dochter of Allexander Lyall, xiij[s] iiij[d]
Item, the xv of Maij, Matho Broun, walker, burges, . v[li]
Item, the samin day, Johnne Lempetlaw, tailyeour, burges, v[li]
Item, the xxv of Maij, Thomas Reidpeth, merchand, burges, v[li]
Item, the samin day, Johnne Gibsoun, younger, bower, burges, . v[li]
Item, the thrid of Junij, Adam Wallace, merchand, burges, . v[li]
Item, the samin day, Roger Hereiss, burges be rycht of his wyffe, Mawss Diksoun, eldest douchter of Thomas Diksoun, and haiss peyit, . xiij[s] iiij[d]
Item, the tent off Junij, James Mure, saidlar, maid gild broder and hes peyit, ... x[li]

[220] Item, the xvj of Junij, James Robesoun, loksmyth, burges, hes peyit, . v^{li}

Item, the xx of Junij, the compter chargeit him not with the gildrie givin gratis to Michaell Merioribanks, sonn of umquhill James Marioribanks, quhilk wes bot, ... xiij^{s} iiij^{d}

Item, the xxviij of Junij, Allexander Auchterlone, baxter, burges, and hes peyit, ... v^{li}

Item, the penult day of Junij, the compter chargeis him not with the burgischipp and gildrie givin gratis be the provest, baillies and counsall at the request of the Bischop of Roiss to Johnne Aiton, writter, his servand.

Item, the vj of Julij, William Adamsoun, sone and air to umquhill William Adamsoun, younger, burges and gild, . . . xiij^{s} iiij^{d}

Item, the sevint of Julij, William Knox, merchand, burges, v^{li}

Item, the samin day, George Melroiss, burges and gild, . . . xv^{li}

Item, the samin day, Richart Fleming is maid burges be rycht of his father, Robert Fleming, burges and gild, . xx^{s}

Item, the tent of Julij, James Craige, merchand, burges, . v^{li}

Item, the same day, Johnne Broun, merchand, burges and gild, . xv^{li}

Item, the same day, George Smyth, younger, tailyeour, maid gild broder, and hais peyit, ... x^{li}

Item, the secound of August, Thomas Russall, eldest sone of Andro Russall, maid burges by rycht of his father, and hais peyit, . xiij^{s} iiij^{d}

Item, the samin day, Johnne Mitchell, merchand, burges, . v^{li}

Item, the viij of August, George Sandersoun, maid burges, and peyit, v^{li}

[221] Item, the compter chargeis him not with the gildschip givin to Johnne Patersoun, deikin of the masouns, at the command of the provest, baillies and counsall, in reward of his service at the new Tolbuith.

Item, the samin day, William Clark, tailyeour, burges, and hes peyit, . v^{li}

Item, the xxiij of August, Thomas Courtas, skynner, burges, and hes peyit, v^{li}

Item, the xxiiij of August, William Purvess, barbour, burges, peyit, . v^{li}

Item, the samin day, Johnne Wilsoun, cramer, burges, . . . v^{li}

Item, the xxvj of August, Gilbert Quhite, merchand, burges be rycht of his father, ... vj^{s} viij^{d}

Item, the samin day, Eduard Galbraith, burges be rycht of his father, vj^{s} viij^{d}

ALEXANDER GUTHRIE, Dean of Guild. 1563-64.

Item, the secound of September, Johnne Quhite, litster, burges, . v^{li}

Item, xviij of September, William Hoppringill, tailyeour, burges be rycht of Margrat Robesoun, his wyff, douchter of umquhill William Robesoun, flescheour, and hes peyit, ... xx^{s}

Item, the xxij of September, Johnne Mosman, goldsmyth, burges, . v^{li}

Item, the compter chargeis him not with the burgesschip givin to William Robesoun, sklatter, at the command of the provest, baillies and counsall, in reward of his service in theiking of the new Tolbuith, the Queir, Sanct Thomas Ile, Sanct Gabriellis Ile, pointing and mending of the haill remanent Kirk.

Item, George Hendersoun, goldsmyth, burges be richt of William Hendersoun, his father, ... $xiij^{s}$ $iiij^{d}$

Item, the penult of September, William Fairbarne, merchand, burges, v^{li}

Item, the samin day, Nicholl Couper, litster, burges, . . v^{li}

Item, the samyn day, William Stevinsoun, cramer, maid burges, . v^{li}

[222] Item, the compter chargeis him with the dewitie of the Schippis the said yeir, being in noumer $iiij^{xx}$ v, ilk schipe $xiiij^{s}$, ... lix^{li} x^{s}

Item, the compter chargeis him with the maillis of the Cordiner choppis the said yeir, ... xxj^{li}

Item, the compter chargeis him with the Goldsmythis choppis, and first with David Dinnholmes chop, . . xxx^{s}

Item, Robert Ryndis chop, . xxx^{s}

Item, Adam Allanis chope, . . xxx^{s}

Item, Andro Heleis stand in the kirk dur, xl^{s}

Item, Christall Galbraythis chop, . xxx^{s}

Item, Allexander Gilbertis chop, ... xxx^{s}

Item, the compter is to be chargeit with the maillis of the twa new choppis occupiit be David Dannelstoun and Johnne Gilbert, ilk ane of thame, foure merks ; summa, . . v^{li} vj^{s} $viij^{d}$

Particule, ... lxxxxv^{li} vj^{s} $viij^{d}$

Item, the compter chargeis him not with the mail of George Turnouris chope and stand in respect the samyn is dischargeit be the provest, baillies and counsall becauss of his povertie, and ordanit to be removit ther fre at Mertymes nixt.

ALEXANDER GUTHRIE, Dean of Guild. 1563-64.

Item, the compter chargeis him not with the maill of Robert Murrayis chop, quha was keipit in ward xv dayis, and lattin to libertie becauss he haid nocht to pey.

Item, the compter chargeis him not with the maill of Mychaell Bassindenis chop becauss he biggit, sklattit, furneist tymmer and all necessaris to the samyn himself, and therfor the first yearis maill dischargeit.

Summa of the hale charge before writtin extendis to, iij^c lxx^li vj^s viij^d

Item, mair, the compter is to be chargit for the gyrss of the buriale yaird, ... iiij^li vj^s viij^d

Summa of the hale charge, iij^c lxxiiij^li xiij^s iiij^d

[223] 1564.

The Comptaris discharge the said yeir of his office as followis :—

DISCHARGE.

Item, the comptaris discharges him with the dewitie of the twa burgessis grantit to Archebald Douglaiss, provest, be rycht of his office, extending to, ... x^li

Item, the said compter discharges with the dewitie of the foure burgisschippis pertening to the foure Baillies, . . . xx^li

Item, to the Dene of Gild, ane burgesschip and gildrie, . . xv^li

Item, to the xij seriandis, evry one of thame iiij^li ; summa, xlviij^li

Item, Richert Trowop, Edinburgh masser, ane burgisschip, v^li

Item, to Andro Lyndsay, jawellour, ... xl^s

Item, to Commoun Clark and his twa servandis, evry ane of thame ane burgisschip, ... xv^li

Item, Jame Huntar, glassinwrycht, for his pension and uphaldin of the glass windois, ... iiij^li

Item, to Patrik Gowan, belman, Johnne Symsoun and Robert Drummond, keipers of the kirk, and gild servandis, and for rewling of the knok, . xxiiij^li

Item, the Dene of Gild, his fe the yeir of his office, . v^li xiij^s iiij^d

[224] The Expenssis maid upon the new theiking and reparaling of Sanct Thomas Ile, being haill tirwit and theikit of new, at command of the provest, baillies and counsall as followis, to gidder with the uther necessaris expenssis upon the Kirk :—

ALEXANDER GUTHRIE, Dean of Guild. 1563-64.

Item, in primis, to Walter Scot, sclater, for j^{m} j^{c} sklattis,	x^{li}
Item, ij^{c} greit braid sklattis,	iij^{li} xij^{s}
Item, for cariage of the haill sklattis out of Leyth to the kirk,	xxxv^{s}
Item, foure laid of lyme,	viij^{s}
Item, twa dussoun of sand,	xij^{s}
Item, foure dussoun of sparris to be lath, price of the pece iij^{s}; summa,	vij^{li} iiij^{s}
Item, for cariage of thame fre Leyth,	iiij^{s}
Item, the suaris for sawing of thre dussoun of thir sparris in foure clift, ilk clift iij^{d},	xxxvj^{s}
Item, the uther dousoun sawing in thre clift, price forsaid,	ix^{s}
Item, for bering of thir same sparris to the kirk riggin,	viij^{d}
Item, twa thousand naillis to this lath, the hundereth ij^{s} v^{d}; summa,	lviij^{s} iiij^{d}
Item, mair, viij laid of lyme, price of the laid xxx^{d}; summa,	xx^{s}
Item, xx laid of sand, price,	x^{s}
Item, iij dusoun of watter, price,	ij^{s} vj^{d}
Item, becauss of the winter last of all for ther laubouring upon this Ile to the xviij day of Julij nixt, and boucht thame x laid of lyme, price of the laid xx^{d}; summa,	xvj^{s} viij^{d}
Item, to the fallowis that aucht the lyme in drink silver to fill guid laidis,	vj^{d}
Item, mair, for viij^{c} sklattis,	iiij^{li} xvj^{s}
Item, for cariage of thir sklattis from Leyth,	xxiiij^{s} iiij^{d}
Item, for taking of thame of the horss bakis and careing of thame to the woltis,	iiij^{s}
[225] Item, mair, boucht iiij laid lyme, price of the laid xix^{d}; summa,	vj^{s} iiij^{d}
Item, the laist of Julij, for vj^{c} sklattis,	iij^{li} xij^{s}
Item, for cariage of thame fre Leyth,	xxiiij^{s}
Item, for taking of thame of the horss bakis and bering of thame to the woltis,	iij^{s} iiij^{d}
Item, xv Augusti, vj^{c} naillis, price of the hundereth ij^{s} vj^{d}; summa,	xv^{s}
Item, mair, ij^{c} greit sklattis, price,	iij^{li} xij^{s}
Item, for cariage of thir frome Leyth,	vj^{s}
Item, the cariage of thame to the kirk rigging,	iiij^{s}
Item, for xv greit sparris to compleit the rest of the lath, ne utheris to be gottin in Leyth, price of the pece iij^{s} vj^{d}; summa,	lij^{s} vj^{d}

Item, for cariage of thame fre Leyth, . . ij^{s}

Item, xxxvj draucht of thir sparris, ... ix^{s}

Item, ane wricht that sought thir sparris in Leyth in syndrie dayis, the tymmer beand skant, . . . iij^{s}

Item, for vj^{c} naillis, . . xv^{s}

Item, the xxvj Augusti, iiij laid lyme, . x^{s}

Item, for sand to all the lyme above writtin, xxxvj^{s}

Item, mair, iiij dosone of watter, . . . iij^{s} iiij^{d}

Item, to Eduard Hendersoun, for the twa oulkis wageis past, xxiiij^{s}

Item, vj puncheonis to be pynnis, the pece iiij^{s} vj^{d}; summa, . . xxvij^{s}

Item, this Ile beand compleitlie theikit, the samin extendis to fyve rud and ane half of wark, price of the rud iij^{li}; summa, . . . xvj^{li} x^{s}

Item, to the said Walter Scot and William Robesoun, sklatters, for mending of the haill remanent howssis of the haill brok, the being givin thame in cash be the awyss of dyverss of the counsall, haveing the provestis, baillies and counsallis command therto, . x^{li}

[226] Item, to the samin, ij dosone vj laid lyme, the laid ij^{s}; summa, iij^{li}

Item, iiij^{xx} laidis sand, . . . xl^{s}

Item, to the sklatters childer in drink silver, . . . v^{s}

Item, this Ile being endit, upon the uther common effearis of the kirk as followis:

Thomas Pettegrew, for certane irne wark to curfur bell, it being almaist fallin doun, ... iij^{s}

Item, to ane saidlar for greit new taggis to the said bell, fessyning and hinging of it of new, ... x^{s}

Item, the xj day of November, for ane roll of walx to Johnne Cairnis, . ij^{s} vj^{d}

Item, the vj of December J^{m} v^{c} lxiij, for rasing and heichting and mending of the haill calsay betwix the Clarkis chalmer and Oure Lady Steppis, quhilk wes full of hoillis and stude with watter, . . . xv^{s}

Item, foure elnis blak to be ane mortclaith, price of the elne xxviij^{s}; summa, ... v^{li} xij^{s}

The First Communion.

Item, on Sonnday the xij of December, and Sounday the xix of the samin,

ALEXANDER GUTHRIE, Dean of Guild. 1563-64.

being the dayis of the first communion, the nobilitie being in the toun, for xiiij gallounis twa quartes of wyne, price of the pint xx^{d}, . ix^{li} xiij^{s} iiij^{d}

Item, iiij dosone and ane half breid, price of the dosone xviij^{s}; summa, . iiij^{li} xij^{d}

Item, xij^{li} wecht of candill, price of the pund xv^{d}; summa, . . xv^{s}

Item, to the pyonaris that bure the tymmer of the barress, furneiss and taiblis, helpit to pit up and tak doun the samyn baith the dayis, . viij^{s}

Item, for small candill to the setting of the barress, covering of the taiblis baith the dayis and morinyngis, ... xij^{d}

Item, to the wrychts that maid the barress and set the tabillis baith the dayis, ... x^{s}

Item, for naillis baith the dayis, ... v^{s}

[227] Item, twa dosone and ane half torcheis, price of the pece iij^{s}; summa, iiij^{li} x^{s}

Item, for wesching of the taibill claithis, . . xviij^{d}

Item, the officiaris and childers disionis baith the dayis, . . . vj^{s}

Item, the samyn tyme, at the command of the provest, baillies and counsall, quhar the bairnyis sat fornent the pulpet, and in the place therof biggit ane sait, the bak therof couvrit with Eistland burd, quhilk wer furneist be Johnne Cunnyngham, wrycht, and be appoint before the said counsale, efter lange pley, givin to him for the tymmer, glew, sawaris lauboris, his awin, and thre servandis lauboris upon the said deske, be the space of ane moneth, ... xxvj^{li}

Item, for thre daillis to the samyn, boucht at the maister of wark to the samyn, ... xv^{s}

Item, to twa masonnis quhilk for heist, be the space of twa nychts and ane day, war in wirking and in dressing of the pillar at the bak of the said desk and making of boit hoillis, ... xiij^{s} iiij^{d}

Item, for dur naill, . . . xviij^{d}

Item, xv lib leid to festin thir bottis, . ix^{s} iiij^{d}

Item, coillis to melt this leid, viij^{d}

Item, mair, iij^{c} band naill, xij^{s}

Item, for plancheour naill, . . v^{s} iiij^{d}

Item, xvj boittis of irne and naillis to thame, ... iij^{s}

Item, twa pare lange bandis, doubill gemmellit for the durris of the saidis deskis and for twa lokis with dyverss keyis therto, . . . xxij^{s}

Item, mair, ane corsstaile band, doubill, . iij^s ALEXANDER GUTHRIE, Dean of Guild. 1563-64.
Item, drink to the warkmen syndrie tymis, iiij^s vj^d
Item, for candill to thame all the tymis, ... iiij^s ix^d
[228] Item, the tyme of the greit Assemblie of the Kirk, for bering of furmes furth of the Kirk to the Tolbuith, and frome the Tolbuith to the Kirk agane, ... ij^s
Item, (*blank*) of Februar, becauss of the resort of the assassoris to the clarkis chalmer for awysing of the proceiss, boucht ane irne chymnay, weyand iiij stane xj^{li} wecht, iij^{li} iiij^s j^d obolus
Item, ane pare of taingis, ... v^s
Item, the baillies and assassoris being lait in the Abbay before the Secreit Counsale in the actioun betwix the Toun and the Abbot of Halierud-houss, to ane boy that careit torches before thame, quhilk lest ouer the Communion, ... iiij^d
Item, thre wynding schetis to thre pure bodies found deid in auld wallis, xv^s
Item, the key of the north eist kirk dur being brokin, for twa new keyis to the samyn, ... vj^s
Item, to Mungow Hunter, smyth, for ane lange flaill of irne with ane hingand lok to the bak of the buriall dur, xvj^s

Secound Communione.

Item, (*blank*) of Aprile 1564, xiij gallounis and ane half, baith the day of the Communion, price of the galloun xiij^s iiij^d, . ix^{li}
Item, iiij dosone of breid, ... iij^{li} xij^s
Item, the wrychtis for setting of the barres and taiblis baith the dayis, x^s
Item, the pynoris for bering of the furmes, taiblis and tymmer of the barres, viij^s
[229] Item, for naillis baith the dayis, . . iij^s
Item, the servandis servandis disiounis, vj^s
Item, for candill baith the mornyngis, viij^d
Item, for wesching of the taibill claithis, ... xviij^d
Item, to Robert Drummond that he debursit for the carrege of furmes and taiblis frome the Kirk to the Magdalen Chapell, at the Conventioun of the Generall Kirk, ... vj^s viij^d
Item, for gilting of the hand of the horologe, xxxvj^s vj^d

ALEXANDER GUTHRIE, Dean of Guild. 1563-64.

Item, xv Augusti, the Queinis Maiesties Lettres being proclamit in Leyth, Newhavin and utheris pairttis langis the Coist concernyng the Peist in the schippis laitlie cumin furth of Danskyn, to the officiaris proclamaris of the saidis lettres, ... ix^{s}

Item, at command of the counsall, to Robert Drummond for candill furneist to the Sessioun and Conventionis all the winter past, . . . xxxvj^{s}

Item, to him that he debursit for setting of the taiblis and furmes at the tyme of the ellecting of the elderis, ... xviij^{d}

Item, becauss of the Conventioun of the Counsale and Assisoris syndrie tymis in the clarkis chalmer, it was commandit the samin to be spargeonit all ouer, and to that effect boucht (*blank*) ladyis lyme, . . . vj^{s} viij^{d}

Item, the haill rest of the lyme, sand, glew, watter furneist be the said pergionar and givin to him with his twa servandis for pergionyinge baith the chalmeris, . . vj^{li}

Item, his servandis in drink silver, ... iij^{s}

[230] Item, efter the pergionar had endit his wark, for dichting of the chalmer, ij^{s}

Item, to ane officiar that past to Leyth with the Baillies and Dene of Gild, charginge the marinarris quhilk come on land furth of the infected schippis to pass to thair schippis agane, . v^{s}

Thrid Communioun.

Item, the xxv of August, at the thrid Communioun, for bering of furmes furth of the Kirk to the Tolbuith at the Conventioun of the brithering communicanttis for reconsiliatioun, ... xij^{d}

Item, xij gallounnis ane quart of wyne baith the dayis, price of the pint xvj^{d}; summa, ... vj^{li} x^{s} viij^{d}

Item, iij dosone and ane half of breid, the pece xvj^{d}; summa, . . lvj^{s}

Item, pyonaris for bering of the tymmer, furmes and taiblis, baith the dayis, ... viij^{s}

Item, to the saidis pyonaris for beringe xiiij daillis hame and a feild, borrowit fre Maister Robert Grahamis wark to be the said barres, . ij^{s} iiij^{d}

Item, for naillis, ... xxxij^{d}

Item, to the wrychtis for setting of the barress, taiblis, etc., x^{s}

Item, wosching of the taibill claithis, . . ij^{s}

Item, the servandis and servandis disiouns, ... vj^s
Item, the xxviij of August, boucht xvj laid of lyme for theiking and mending of the cordinarris choppis, the laid ij^s ij^d, xxxiiij^s viij^d
Item, xl laid sand, ... xx^s
[231] Item, hyrit ane auld stabill to lay the lyme and sand in for steling quhill sklattis and uther necessaris wer providit, and peyit therfor, be the space of xxx dayis. . . . . xl^d
Item, the last day of August, at the command of the provest, baillie and counsale, the haill gutters of stane quhilks were abone the new Tolbuith and set in the weit abone the Lordis, being riwin and brokine, the samin ordanit to be removit and new gutteris maid efter the dyvyss and counsal of Gilbert Cleuth, send ane servand to Ravelstoun to waill twa lange stanis, ilk ane xvj fute lenth the pece, and givin him to his disioune, ... ij^s
Item, the saidis twa stanis and cart hyr, ... xxxij^s
Item, to William Bikertoun and George Gude, masonnis, for thair lauboris in hewing, dressing and holking of the saidis guttaris, and to George Tailyefeir, masoun, being with thame twa dayis ½; summa to gidder, . xlij^s
Item, at the rasing of thir auld guttaris, the halfe of the sklate houss nixt unto thame tirwit for rasing of the sydwallis therof, and for this purpose to ane pyoner callit Maxwell, iiij dayis wagis preceidinge the feird of September, ilk day ij^s, . . . viij^s
Item, to Crechttoun, pyoner, iij dayis wageis, vj^s
[232] Item, to Aikman, pyonar, half ane day, ... xij^d
Item, to Jok Symsoun, fyve [dayis] precedand the said feird day of September, alltogidder occupiit in bering of stanis fre the kirkyeard, x^s
Item, ane uther pyoner callit Makwatt, ... ij^s
Item, for the beiging of the waillis and heichting of thame agane, boucht ix laid of lyme, the laid iij^s; summa, ... xxviij^s
Item, for xviij laid of sand; price, ix^s
Item, for iiij dosone watter, iij^s ix^d
Item, for ane mathok schaft, viij^d
Item, for ane schule, . . . ij^s
Item, Eduard Hendersounis wage this last oulk, . xij^s

ALEXANDER GUTHRIE, Dean of Guild, 1563-64.

Item, mair, fyve laid lyme to the theiking agane of the houssis quhilk wer tirwit, and to the laying of the guttaris and biggin the reist of the wallis, the laid ij^{s}, ... x^{s}

Item, mair, xxx laid of sand, . xv^{s}

Item, mair, ij dosone half watter, ... ij^{s} j^{d}

Item, iiij sparris to mend the lath of the houssis that wer tirwit, the pece iij^{s} vj^{d}, . . xiiij^{s}

Item, bering of thame fre Leyth, . xij^{d}

Item, for aucht draucht of thir sparris, ... ij^{s}

Item, thir lange stane gutteris being reddie to the laying, to thre pyonaris that helpit to the bering of thame to the kirk rigging, . . . xviij^{d}

Item, Monunday, quarto Septembris, efter the heichting of the saidis voltis xxiiij of the cupill feit being cuttit, quhilk wer rottin, joynit [233] agane and mendit, and for laying of ane lange jeist to be ane soile to the said cuppill feit langis the heid of the said wall, being him self and iij servandis twa dayis, ... xxx^{s}

Memorandum: This jeist ressavit of Maister Robert Glen, and givin him the auld rivin gutteris stanis therfor.

Item, Jok Symsoun and Makwatt, pyonaris, ane dayis wage in helping Adam Purves and his servandis, ... iiij^{s}

Item, vj^{c} naillis to Adam Purves and to the sklatteris at nailling on of the lath, ... xij^{s} vj^{d}

Item, xxj September, to twa pyonaris that helpit to drawe the lange gutteris through the houssis, ... xij^{d}

Item, Maxwellis wageis, the samin day at the carrige of the gutteris, ij^{s}

Item, Gilbert Cleuchis awin wageis be the space of foure dayis, . . xxiiij^{s}

Item, careing away of the red at the wirking of the saidis gutteris, . xvj^{d}

Item, Adame Hendersouns wage the twa oulkis precedand the xxij of September, ... xxiiij^{s}

Memorandum: The sclatters feis in theiking agane of the tua tirwit howssis comptit, x^{li} gevin of befor, for pointing of the howssis of the kirk.

Item, xxiiij^{o} Septembris 1564, for ane suachin burd to be ane cloiss spout, to resist the dynt of the wynd that draife bak the watter under the

[234] cisingis of the sklattis, and wes the occasioun of the greit weit that ran doun the south pillaris of the steipill, ... viij^s

ALEXANDER GUTHRIE, Dean of Guild, 1563-64.

Item, to Adam Purvess, for making of it and for symount, pik, naillis and uther necessaris, ... vj^s

The Expenses upon the Littill Schop at the clarkis chalmer :—

Item, the roume that wes laist unbiggit betwix Michaell Bassendenis chope and the clarkis chalmer being continewalie fylit with filth, it wes commandit be the provest, baillies and counsall to be beigit and theikit, and first for ane lange tre, xviij^s

Item, for ij daillis, viij^s

Item, iiij sparres, ... x^s

Item, the saweris for twa draucht of daillis, . iiij^s viij^d

Item, thre draucht of the lang tre, iij^s

Item, ij^c planchcour naill, . . v^s

Item, ij^c ½ dur naill, iiij^s ij^d

Item, xiiij garroun naill, . ij^s viij^d

Item, ij laid of lyme, v^s

Item, foure laid of sand, . ij^s

Item, for watter, . . x^d

Item, ane puntioun to be lath, . . . v^s vj^d

Item, the sklattis of this chope furneist of the tounis auld sklattis, and to Jok for bering sa mony fre the woltis as servit for this chope, . xij^d

Item, ane lok and twa keyis to the dur of this chope, the one of thame for Michaell Bassindenis, the uther for the clarkis chalmer, viij

[235] Item, for bandis and creukis to thir dur, . . iiij^s vj^d

Item, Adam Purvess and his servandis for thair lauboris, xx^s

Item, the sklatteris for thair lauboris, . . x^s

Item, Eduard Hendersoun, this last oulkis wageis, . . . xij^s

Item, the last of September, as of before being commandit to thik and mend the cordinier choppis, bocht v^c sklattis, price of the hunder xij^s ; summa, iij^{li}

Item, efter the losing of thame in Leith, the hale wark horss being in the Quenis Maiesties service, for bering of thir sklattis to ane yard quhill horss mycht be gottin, ... xxxij^d

ALEXANDER GUTHRIE, Dean of Guild. 1563-64.

Item, yeard maile tua nychtts, ... iiij^{d}

Item, careage of thame fre Leyth to the Cowgait, quhar thai wer laid in the stabill besyd the lyme, ... x^{s}

Item, becauss the winter approchit, causit Johnne Weir, pouderar, to wesy and mend the haill falthis and ryftis in the leid gutters of the kirk, and in first for ane burding of coillis to melt his tyn, . xxj^{d}

Item, for candill to him, ... j^{d}

Item, to him for his panyis and lauboris, and for his tyn, . . x^{s}

Item, mair, to Eduard Hendersoun for this laist oulkis wageis for his service in bying of the sclattis, awaiting upon the lading of the careage horss that broucht thame fre Leyth, and for awating upon Johnne Weir, xij^{s}

[236] Item, ane servand of Gilbert Cleuthis, for the hewing and dressing of ane greit braid flag and indenting of the samin in the stepill wal above the pulpet for resisting of the greit weit that fell doun thair, half ane dayis lauboris, ... ij^{s} vj^{d}

Item, to twa men that brocht the said stane fre the nether kirkyeard to the kirk rigging, helpit to lay the samin and to serve the masoun with morter, ij^{s}

Item, the minister, Johnne Knox, being direct be the kirk in Merss, Tauiodale, Nethisdale and uther pairttis for preching of the Word, and the provest, baillies and counsal being informit he was not to returne schortlie agane, ordanis Johnne Chalmer, servand to the said minister, to be sent to the kirk of Sanct Andrewis, with thair wreittingis requeisting thame to suffer Maister Guidmane to remaine in this toun to the returne of our said minister, his expenssis, . . . iij^{li}

Item, v^{to} Octobris J^{m} v^{c} lxiiij^{o}, boucht vj daillis to be fluring under the clarkis feit, above the cauld eird, in the clarkis chalmer, . xxx^{s}

Item, iij greit fyr sparris, ... vj^{s}

Item, upbringing of thir daillis and sparris, . ij^{s} viij^{d}

Item, for nales, ... vj^{s} iiij^{d}

Item, Adam Purvess and his servandis for thair lauboris, . . xx^{s}

Item, for lynning of ane almory in the ower chalmer, quhar money wreittingis wer spilt be the weit fallin doun the wall:

Item, to Gibesoun and Jok, warkmen, for bering of clay the haill day and sadding and rammaing of it under the daillis, ... iiij^{s}

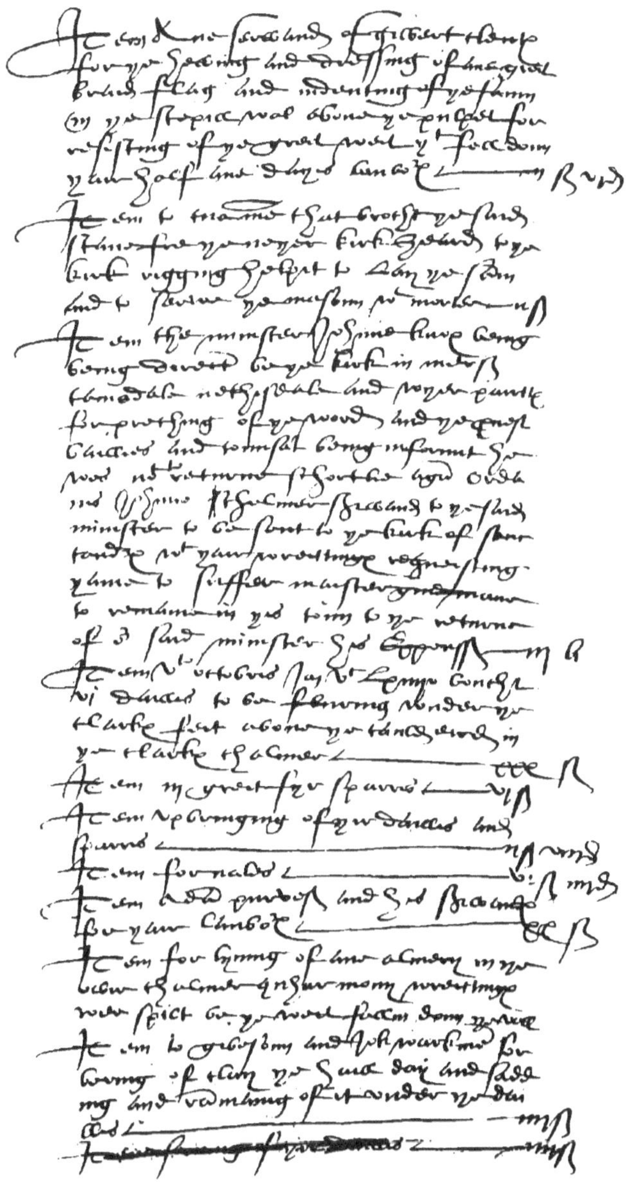

EDINBURGH ACCOUNTS:—Page 236 of old Accounts of Deans of Guild.

[237] Item, for sawing of thir daillis, ... iiij^{s} ALEXANDER GUTHRIE, Dean of Guild. 1563-64.

Item, the compter discharges him with the soume of xxvij^{s} vj^{d} debursit be James Young, cutler, upon the wark of the clarkis chalmer, xxvij^{s} vj^{d}

Item, the said compter is to be dischairgit of the rest of the fute of his last compt as the samyn beris, ... lvij^{s} obolo

Summa of the compteris hale dischairge, iij^{c} lxxix^{li} ij^{s} viij^{d} obolo

Summa of his charge of this last yeir, viz., fra the ix of October 1564 [1563] is, ... iij^{c} lxxiiij^{li} xij^{s} iiij^{d}

And sua is the compter superexpendit of the tua yeris compttis before writtin, viz., fra October in anno 1562 to October in anno 1564, as the charges and discharges before writtin treulie examinat be the Auditoris under writtin beris, futtit and hard be thame and subscrivit xxv^{to} Januarii J^{m} v^{c} lxiiij^{to} iiij^{li} x^{s}

---

[241] THE COMPTE of ALEXANDER PARK, Dene of Gyld of the burgh of Edinburgh, of the yeir of his office, viz., fra the ix day of October in anno 1564 to the (*blank*) day of October anno 1565. ALEXANDER PARK, Dean of Guild. 1564-65.

ITEM, THE COMPTAR CHARGIS him with the burgeschip of Patrik Cochrane, merchant, and he hes payitt to the Dene of Gyld, . v^{li}

Item, the xviij day of October 1564, Ilarie Smyth is maid burges and gyld be rycht of Margarett Wilsoun, his spous, eldest dochter of Patrik Wilsoun, burges and gyld, and hes payitt, . xxxiij^{s} iiij^{d}

Item, the xxvj day of October 1564, Jhonn Giffartt, merchand, is maid burges and hes payitt for his dewtie, ... v^{li}

Item, the thrid day of November 1564, George Wauchop, merchand, is maid burges, and hes payitt for his dewtie, ... v^{li}

Item, the iiij day of November 1564, Jhonn Carrutheris, tailyour, is Non onerand. maid burges be rychtt of Jhonn Sym, bailye, and gevin him gratis, the quhilk the comptar charges him nocht with.

Item, the auchtt day of November 1564, the comptar chargis him nochtt Non onerand. with the burgeschip of William Weir, cordoner, the quhilk is gevin gratis be Archebald Douglass, proveist, be rycht of his office.

Non onerand. Item, the samyn day, Jhonn Michelsoun, cordonar, is maid burges be

ALEXANDER PARK, Dean of Guild. 1564-65.

rycht of Richartt Trolhop, Edinburgh maissar, and the comptar charges him nochtt with.

Item, the x day of November 1564, Jhonn Duncane, tailyour, is maid burges and hes payitt to the Dene of Gyld for his dewtie, . . . v^li

Item, the samyn [day] Andrew Wilsoun, tailyour, is maid burges and

Non onerand. gevin him gratis be the rycht of Archibald Douglass, provest, the quhilk the comptar chargis him nocht therwith.

Item, the xvj day of November 1564, Jhonn Arnott, merchand, is maid burges be rycht of Jonett Symervaill, his spous, dochter to umquhill Jhonn Somervaill, hir father, burgis, and hes payitt, . . . xx^s

Item, the xxj day of November 1564, Alexander Quhyntene is maid burges, and hes payitt for his dewtie, ... xx^s

Item, the xxij day of November, Androw Libbertoun, fourrour, is maid burges be rychtt of William Libbertoun, elder, and hes payitt, . xiij^s iiij^d

Item, the samyn day, James Nicholsoun, wrytar is maid burges and gyld be rychtt of Alishan Houp, his spous, dochter of umquhill Jhonn Houp, and hes payitt for his dewtie, ... xxxiij^s iiij^d

[242^b] Item, the first day of Januar, Mathow Smyth, pryntcis to William Smyth, is maid burges and hes payitt for his dewtie, ... v^li

Item, the samyn day, Thomas Jhonnstoun, cordonar, servand to William Falsyde, is maid burges and hes payitt for his dewtie, ... v^li

Item, the thrid day of Januar 1564, James Lowrie, eldest sone of umquhill James Lowrie, is maid burges and gyld be rychtt of his father, and hes payitt, ... xxj^s

Item, the samyn day, Jhonn Dinysoun of Wingstoun is maid burges and

Non onerand. gyld brother, and hes payitt for his dewtie, xv^li; quhilk was assynitt to Alexander Guthre.

Item, the samyn day, Alexander Clark is maid burges and gyld brother,

Non onerand. and thatt be the requeist of my Lord of Murray and giffin him gratis.

Item, the xiiij day of Februar, Jhonn Richesoun, sadelar, is maid burges be rychtt of Jhonn Richesoun, merchand, his father, and hes payitt, . vj^s viij^d

Item, the samyn day, David Widderspone, wrycht, prenteis to Robert Widderspone, his brother, is maid burges be rychtt of Issobell Symsoun, his spous, eldest dochter to Thomas Symsoun, wrycht, and payitt, . xiij^s iiij^d

ALEXANDER PARK, Dean of Guild. 1564-65.

Item, the samyn day, Patrik Murray, wrycht, prenteis to George Tod, is maid burges and hes payitt, ... v^li

Item, the samyn day, Lourence Curroor, cordoner, prenteis to Thomas Merreleis, is maid burges, and hes payitt, ... v^li

Item, xvij day of Februar, Robert Weir, saidlar, prenteis to William Harlay, is maid burges, and hes payitt, ... v^li

Item, the xxij day of Februar 1564, Tymothie Carginok, is maid burges and gyld be rychtt of Janett Curll, his spous, eldest dochter to James Curll, and hes payitt for his dewtie, ... xx^s

Item, the second day of Merche 1564, William Walker, bonnett maker, prenteis to Henrie (*blank*), bonnett maker, is maid burges, and hes payitt, v^li

Item, the ix day of Merche 1564, Jhonn Borthuik, baxter, prenteis to William Fiddes, baxter, is maid burges, and hes payitt, . v^li

Item, the samyn day, James Laing, tailyour, is maid burges, and hes payitt for his dewtie, ... v^li

Item, the xxj day of Marche 1564, William Courroir, skynner, prenteis to Andrew Robesoun, skynner, is maid burges, and payitt, . . v^li

Item, the samyn day, James Dobie, flescheour, prenteis to Thomas Dobie, flescheour, is maid burges, and payitt, ... v^li

Item, the penult day of Marche 1565, Robert Patersoun, flescheour, prenteis to Rolland Gairdner, flescheour, is maid burges, and payitt, . v^li

Item, the xj day of Aprylc 1565, Nenian Arneill, prenteis to Mathew Kenwod, flescheour, is maid burges, and payitt, . . . v^li

Item, the xiij day of Aprylc 1565, Johnn Gardener, listar, prenteis to David Gardner, is maid burges, and payitt, ... v^li

[242²] Item, the xvj day of Maij 1565, Alane Skynner, prenteis to umquhill Andrew Alane, is maid burges, and payitt, ... v^li

Item, the samyn day, Maister Michaell Chisholme, is maid burges and gyld brother, and hes payitt, ... xv^li

Item, the second day of Junij 1565, David Patersoun, tailyeour, is maid burges be rycht of Katherine Park, his spous, and dochter to umquhill William Park, bakster, payitt, ... xiij^s iiij^d

Non onerand. Item, the xiiij day of July 1565, Alexander Craig is maid burges and givin him gratis be David Forester, bailye.

ALEXANDER PARK, Dean of Guild. 1564-65.

Item, the first day of August 1565, George Hyslop, armorar, is maid burges, and hes payitt for his dewtie, ... v^{li}

Item, the iiij day of August 1565, Alexander Arbouthneth, is maid burges and gyld, and hes payitt for his dewtie, xv^{li}; quhilk was assignitt to Alexander Park be wertu of his office. — Non onerand.

Item, the v day of September 1565, Robertt Tailzefeir, masson, is maid burges be rychtt of Margarett Ochyltrie, dochter to Jhonn Ochyltrie, maisson, and hes payitt for his dewtie, . . . xiij^{s} iiij^{d}

Item, the x day of September 1565, Robertt Scott, merchantt, is maid burges be rychtt of William Patersoun, baille. — Non onerand.

Item, the xij day of December [September], Jhonn Park, merchand, is maid burges be rychtt of Issobell Hendersoun, his spous, dochter to William Hendersoun, fleschour, and hes payitt for his dewtie, . . xiij^{s} iiij^{d}

Item, the samyn day, Archebald Prestoun, merchand, is maid burges be rychtt of Sir Symoun Prestoun, proveist. — Non onerand.

Item, the first day of October, Robertt Andersoun, merchand, is maid burges be rychtt of Alane Dixesoun, baille. — Non onerand.

Summa of the Burges and gyldschippis, bye the proveist and bailles, clarkis and troupis, is sex scoir ane pond.

Item, the compter chairgis him with the deutie of the entres of the Schippis in the yeir of the comptaris office, being in nomber lxix schippis, ilk schip xiiij^{s}; summa, ... xviij^{li} vj^{s}

Item, the comptar chairges him with the mailles of the Cordonaris Choppis;

in the first Thomas Mirleis, . xxvj^{s} viij^{d}

William Harperfeild, xxvj^{s} viij^{d}

Jhonn Broderstanis, ... xxvj^{s} viij^{d}

Jhonn Bynnyne, Laird Gibsoun, and William Falsyde, Androw Wilsoun, Michaell Haistie, Jhonn Newlandis, Jhonn Cunnynghame, ilk man xx^{s}; summa, ... vij^{li}

Jhonn Forress, tua choppis, ... xl^{s}

The comptar is nochtt to be chairgitt with Issobell Rutherfurdes chop, becaus itt is gevin gratis to hir for keping of sklaittis.

Item, Jhonn Reid, Alexander Andersoun, Robert Mure, and George Cowanis choppis, ilk man xx^{s}; summa, ... iiij^{li}

Jhonn Smyth, tua choppis, pryce, ... xl^{s}

Summa of the cordonnaris choppis above specefeitt, by Rutherfurdis chop gevin gratis, is, . . . xix^{li}

[243] Item, the comptar chairges him with the Goldsmythis Choppis; the first Alexander Gilbertt, . . . xxx^{s}

Robertt Murray, . . xxx^{s}

Item, Henrie Stalker, xxx^{s}

Androw Heleis, xl^{s}

Michaell Rynde, . xxx^{s}

Adame Alane, . xxx^{s}

David Donaldsoun, ... xxx^{s}

Item, ane half yeiris maill of David Donaldsounis chop, xxvij^{s} viij^{d}

Somme of the choppis above specefeitt is, . . xij^{li} vj^{s} viij^{d}

Summa of the haill chairge is tua $^{c\ li}$ twelf schillingis, auchtt penneis.

THE COMPTARIS DISCHARGE, as followis:—

Item, the comptar discharges him with the dewtie of tua burgeschippis grantitt to Archibald Douglas, Proveist, be vertu of his office, . . x^{li}

Item, the comptar discharges him with four burgeschippis grantitt to the four Bailles, ... xx^{li}

Item, to the Dene of Gilde, ane burgeschip and gildrie, . xv^{li}

Item, to xij officiares, ilk ane of thame iiij li, . . xlviij^{li}

Item, to Richard Trolhop, Edinburgh masser, ane burgeschip, v^{li}

Item, to Androw Lyndesay, janelour, ... xl^{s}

Item, to the Commoun Clerk and his tua servandis, ilk ane of thame ane burgeschip, ... xv^{li}

Item, to Patrik Gowane, bellman, Jhonn Symsoun, Robertt Drummond, keparis of the kirk and gyld servandis, ilk ane of thame viij^{li}; summa, xxiiij^{li}

Item, to the Dene of Gild, for his fie, ... vj^{li} xiij^{s} iiij^{d}

Item, to Sir Symoun Prestoun, Proveist, tua burgeschipis, . x^{li}

James Hunter, glassinwrycht, his pentioun, ... iiij^{li}

Item, the xx day of Maij 1565, resavitt ane preceptt to answer Alexander Guthre, Dene of Gilde, the yeir precedand the comptaris office, quhilk he was superexpenditt in his comptes, . . . iiij^{li} x^{s}

ALEXANDER PARK, Dean of Guild. 1564-65.

Mair, gevin him, be the samyn preceptt, ane burgeschip to Maister Thomas Makcalzoun, ... v[li]

The First Communioun.

Item, upoun Sonday the xiij day of December and upoun the Sonday the xx day of the samyn moneth, being the dayis of the first communion the nobilitie being in the toun, for four dosoun ane half of breid, the dosane xiij[s]; summa is, ... iij[li] iij[s]

Item, for xv gallonnis of wyne, the pinte xx[d]; summa, . x[li]

Item, for tua dosane of torches and half, the dosane, xxx[s], iij[li] xv[s]

Item, for ane stane of candill, ... xx[s]

[244] Item, for careing of ane dosane of dailes furth of Leith to the kirk to putt above the pillaris, ... iiij[s] vj[d]

Item, for tua hundreth planchour naill to naill the dailes on the pillaris, the pryce of thame, ... vj[s] viij[d]

Item, for takketis to naill the torches to the stallis, ... vj[d]

Item, for careing of thre fourmes furth of the Maidlane Chaipell, . . xij[d]

Item, for bering of the fournes and dailles and helping to putt thame up and take thame doun, to four men for thair laubour, ... viij[s]

Item, gevin to the wrychtis for thair laubour baith the dayis, . x[s]

Item, gevin for the servandis jeunis thatt waititt on the taibles, . vj[s]

Item, gevin for wesching of the claithis baith the dayis, . x[s]

Item, for ane roll of wax to Jhonn Carnis to reid the prayeris, . . iiij[s]

Item, for ane new stok lok to the south kirk dur with tua new keyis, the pryce thairof, ... xiiij[s]

Item, for careing of the furmes outt of the Tolbuith to the Kirk, iiij[d]

The expenssis maid upoun the Lettroun of the exerceis and commoun prayeris :—

Item, in the first, for ane Eistland burde and half, the price of the burd xvj[s]; summa, ... xxiiij[s]

Item, for sawing of thame, ... ij[s]

Item, for ane aikin garroun to be stoupis thairto, . vj[s] viij[d]

Item, for ane hunder and half of planchour naill, v[s]

Item, for ane hunder blind naill, . . . xx[d]

Item, for ane dosonn singill garrow naill, . xviij^{d}

Item, for four yrne boittis and tua cleikis, iij^{s} iiij^{d}

Item, gevin for four pond of leid to yett thame, . iij^{s}

Item, gevin to Thomas Wod, wrychtt, for his laubour; somme, . . xvj^{s}

Item, gevin for careing of the garroun and Eistland burdis furth of Leyth to the kirk, . . . xij^{d}

The expenssis of the leid quhilk was cuttitt furth of the gutteris of the kirk, the xiiij day of Januar, be Alexander Thomsoun and Jhonn Grahame:—

Item, in the first, gevin to Androw Somer, glasinwrycht, thatt coft this leid fra Alexander Thomsonn and Jhonn Grahame, . . . xv^{s}

Item, for clainging of vj stane wechtt of leid, to Jhonn Weir, ilk stane xviij^{d}; summa, ... ix^{s}

[245] Item, to Jhonn Weir for iij stane and xiij^{li} of new leid, the stane xiij^{s}; summa, xlix^{s} vj^{d}

Item, to Jhonn Weir for tua pund of tyn to be soldin, . viij^{s}

Item, to Jhonn Weir for laying of the guitteris, . vj^{s}

Item, for ane buirding of cullis to sowd thame, . xxij^{d}

Item, for nailis to naill thame with, . . . x^{d}

Item, for tua laid of lyme for the sklaitting aboutt thame, vij^{s}

Item, for four laid of sand, . . ij^{s}

Item, for walter to mak the morter with, ... viij^{d}

Item, for the bering ane hunder sklaitis outt of the Cougaitt to the kirk gutteris, ... xij^{d}

Item, for ane hunder planchour naill to naill the sklaittis, iij^{s}

Item, to William Robesoun, sclaitter, for his laubour, . . . xx^{s}

Item, for dichting of thir gutteris and bering away of the red quhen thay war done, . . xvj^{d}

Item, for sklaitt pynnis, . xij^{d}

The expenssis of the syling of the pillar of the loft, quhair the Lordis sittis:—

Item, in the first, bochtt auchtt Eistland buirdis, the pece xvj^{s}, . . vj^{li} vj^{s}

Item, for v garronnis to naill the Eistland buirdis upoun, the pryce of the pece vj^{s} viij^{d}, ... xxxiij^{s}

ALEXANDER PARK, Dean of Guild. 1564-65.

Item, to the saweris for xij drauchtt of Eistland burdis, ilk draucht viij^{d}; summa, ... viij^{s}
Item, to the saweris for v drauchtt of garronnis, ilk drauchtt x^{d}: summa, iiij^{s} ij^{d}
Item, for ane mannis waige for waiting on this laubour, . . xij^{s}
Item, for xiij bottis to the samyn pillar, ilk fute vj^{d}; summa, vj^{s} vj^{d}
Item, for naillis to the same bottis, ilk bott iij naillis; summa, . xij^{d}
Item, for ane stane of leid to yett thir bottis, xiij^{s}
Item, for coillis to melt the leid with, ... viij^{d}
Item, for xiij pikis to putt the knoppis upoun the heidis of the pannellis, ij^{s} ij^{d}
Item, for ane hunder and half planchour naill, . . v^{s}
Item, for ij hunder blind naill, . iij^{s} iij^{d}
Item, for xxx blind garrow naill, . . ij^{s} vj^{d}
Item, to Thomas Wod, wrychtt, for his laubour, . v^{s}
Item, to ane maisson for making of the bottis hoilis, vj^{s}

The Secound Communioun.

Item, the (*blank*) day of Apryle 1565, beand the dayis of the second communioun, for four dosane of breid, the dosane xiiij^{s}; summa, . lvj^{s}
[246] Item, for xiiij gallonnis of wyne and ane quartt, the gallonn xij^{s}; summa, viij^{li} xj^{s}
Item, for candill to sett the taibles and keip the kirk durris in the mornyng, ... ij^{s}
Item, for naillis to naill the dailes aboutt the pillaris; somme, . v^{s}
Item, to four men thatt helpitt to sett the taibles, viij^{s}
Item, for saip and wesching of the buird claythis, . . . iij^{s}
Item, to the wrychts for thair laubours to putt up the dailles aboutt the pillaris and setting of the taibles, . . x^{s}

The expenses maid upoun the Cordonarris Choppis, 1565:—

Item, for tua dailles to be eising buirds under the sklaittis, the pece v^{s} vj^{d}; summa, ... xj^{s}
Item, for bringing of thame outt of Leyth, ... viij^{d}
Item, for vj garronnis to be angleris to the choppis, the pryce of the pece iiij^{s}; summa, ... xxiiij^{s}
Item, for careying of thame outt of Leyth, . . xvj^{d}
Item, for mending of ane band to Thomas Andersonnis chop, xij^{d}

ALEXANDER PARK, Dean of Guild. 1564-65.

Item, for ane thousand sklaittis bochtt to the chopis be Sir Eduard Hendersonn, the pryce of thame,	vj^{li}
Item, for careing of thame outt of Leyth,	xx^{s}
Item, for tua ^{c} naillis to the sklaitter,	vj^{s} viij^{d}
Item, four punitionn to be sklaitt pinnis,	vj^{s}
Item, to the sklaitter for his laubour,	iij^{li} x^{s}
Item, to Thomas Wod, wrycht, for his laubour,	xvj^{s}
Item, for ane stok lok to Jhonn Bynnyns buith,	v^{s}
Item, for ane new band to William Herperfeildis chop dur, weyand iiij^{l} wechtt; summa,	iiij^{s}

The expenses maid upoun the Dyke in the Kirk yaird and making of ane yaird thairin:—

Item, in the first, for wynnyng of stanis in the Grayfreirs, to four warkmen ane oulkis waige, ilk man xij^{s}, is,	xlviij^{s}
Item, for ane pik schaft,	viij^{d}
Item, for schairping of the piks att syndrie tymes,	xvj^{d}
Item, to sax men that buir the stanis furth of the Grayfreris yaird to the kirk yaird ane oulk and thre dayis, ilk man on the day ij^{s},	v^{li} viij^{s}
Item, for viij laid of lyme, the laid iij^{s} iij^{d}; summa,	xxvj^{s} viij^{d}
Item, xvj laid of sand, ilk laid vj^{d}; summa,	viij^{s}
Item, for ane oylye barrell to be morter tubbis,	iiij^{s}
Item, for making of ane mear to beir the morter in; summa,	viij^{d}
Item, for half ane daill to be the mear,	ij^{s} vj^{d}
Item, to four men thatt red the ground, ane oulkis wage, ilk man in the oulk xij^{s}; summa,	xlviij^{s}
Item, for four laid of lyme, the laid iij^{s} iiij^{d}; summa,	xiij^{s} iiij^{d}
Item, for tua laid of lyme, the laid xxx^{d}; summa,	v^{s}
[247] Item, for xv laid of lyme, the laid iij^{s},	xlv^{s}
Item, for vij laid of lyme, the laid iij^{s},	xxj^{s}
Item, for ix laid of lyme, the laid ij^{s} viij^{d}; summa,	xxiiij^{s}
Item, for ane hunder sand,	iij^{li}
Item, to Gilbertt Gordoun, maisson,	xxij^{s}
Item, to William Barrie, maisson,	xxij^{s}
Item, to David Grahame, maisson,	xviij^{s}

ALEXANDER PARK, Dean of Guild. 1564-65.

Item, to vj warkmen ane oulkis waige, ilk man xij^{s}, is . iij^{li} xij^{s}

Item, for iij laid of lyme, the laid ij^{s} viij^{d}; summa, . viij^{s}

Item, to Gilbertt Gordonn, maisson, ... xxij^{s}

Item, to William Barrie, maisson, ... xxij^{s}

Item, to David Grahame, maisson, ... xviij^{s}

Item, to thre men thatt servitt the maissonis, ane oulkis wage, ilk man in the oulk xij^{s}; summa, . . . xxxvj^{s}

Item, vij laid of lyme, the laid ij^{s} viij^{d}, xviij^{s} viij^{d}

Item, for half ane hundreth sand, . . . xxx^{s}

Item, to William Barrie and Gilbertt Gordon, maissonis, xliiij^{s}

Item, to tua warkmen thatt servitt thame j oulk, . . . xxiiij^{s}

Item, to Richartt Sym for xvj dosone of eird led be him to the gairding, the pryce of the dosone ij^{s}; summa, ... xxxij^{s}

Item, to tua warkmen iij oulkis and ane day, and lauboring into the gairding, ilk man on the day xviij^{d}, lvij^{s}

Item, to the gairdnar for his laubouris, . xxxv^{s}

Item, for tua skainze of threid to be lynis, xij^{d}

Item, for ane mattow schaft, . . viij^{d}

Item, for ane riddill to riddill the eird with, . xvj^{d}

Item, for tua pounschons to be pinnis to the bankis, xiiij^{s}

Item, for vij hunder ½ of faill, the ^{c}, iiij^{s}; summa, xxx^{s}

Item, for ane spaid and ane yrne to itt, v^{s}

Item, for v dosone of scheirettis, ... v^{s}

Item, for water to the lyme, and watering of the yeard, . . . x^{s}

Item, gevin ane mannis wage quhilk waittitt on the wark for four oulkis, ilk oulk xij^{s}; summa, ... lvij^{s}

The Thrid Communioun.

Item, the xxj day of August 1565, for iiij dosane breid, the pece xiiij^{d}, . lvj^{s}

Item, for xiiij gallonnis and thre quartis of wyne, the galloun xij^{s}; summa, ... viij^{li} xvij^{s}

Item, for candill, to cover the taibles and keip the kirk dur with, . ij^{s}

Item, for naillis to naill the daillis aboutt the pillar, baith the dayis, . vj^{s} viij^{d}

Item, to foure men thatt helpitt to sett the tablis and lift the fourmes, . viij^{s}

Item, to the wrychtt for his laubour, . x^{s}

Item, for wesching of the buird claiss baith the dayis, .	iij^{s}
[248] Item, for the servandis disiunes thatt waititt on the taibles,	vj^{s}
Item, for careing of four fournes outt of the Maidland Chaipell, .	xvj^{d}
Item, for clanging of the filth thatt lay above the kirk and att the Tolbuith dur, and syndrie tymes,	iij^{s}

The expenses maid upoun the Kingis Grace saitt making, anno 1565 :—

Item, the xxiij day of July 1565, for twa lang geistis of xxviij fute lang, of the pece xxxvj^{s}; summa, . .	iij^{li} xij^{s}
Item, for careing of thame outt of Leith, . .	iiij^{s}
Item, for ij greitt corbellis to be pilleris, the pece xx^{s}, is, .	xl
Item, for careing of thame furth of Leyth, .	ij^{s} viij^{d}
Item, for ane geist of xxiiij fute lang to be fute gang,	xxxij^{s}
Item, for careing outt of Leyth of thir tua treis, . .	iiij^{s}
Item, for ij dosone Eistland burdis, the pece xvj^{s}; summa,	xx^{li}
Item, for the careing of thame furth of Leyth, . .	viij^{s}
Item, for ij dosone of knappell, the dosone xvj^{s}; summa,	v^{li}
Item, for careing of thame furth of Leyth,	vij^{s}
Item, for xvj dailes, the pece xvj^{s}; summa, .	iiij^{li} xvj^{s}
Item, for ane dosone and thre of quarter clift, the pece v^{s}, is,	iiij^{li} x^{s}
Item, for ane geist to be the ravill of the stair, .	xxx^{s}

The Sawaris.

Item, gevin for sawing of xij draucht of Eistland buirds, the pryce of the draucht of thame viij^{d}; summa, . .	viij^{s}
Item, for sawing of vij draucht of Eistland buird, .	iiij^{s} viij^{d}
Item, for sawing of iij draucht in ane geist, ilk draucht xx^{d}, .	v^{s}
Item, for sawing of ane draucht in ane geist to be the fute gang, .	xx^{d}
Item, for sawing of ij draucht in ane geist to be soill and lyntell to the loft, the draucht xx^{d}; summa, ...	iij^{s} iiij^{d}
Item, for ij draucht sawing in ane corbell, the draucht xiiij^{d},	ij^{s} iiij^{d}
Item, for tua draucht of daillis, the draucht xvj^{d}; summa, . .	ij^{s} viij^{d}
Item, for xij draucht in four Eistland burdis, the draucht auchtt ^{d}; summa,	viij^{s}
Item, for ane draucht in ane geist to be the revill, . . .	xx^{d}
Item, for sawing of nyne draucht of Eistland buirdis, the draucht viij^{d}, .	vj^{s}

ALEXANDER PARK, Dean of Guild. 1564-65.

[249]

Item, for ane draucht in ane lang trie, . . xvj^{d}
Item, for vj draucht of cuttis, ilk draucht viij^{d}, is, . iiij^{s}
Item, for vj scoir draucht Eistland buird, the draucht iiij^{d}, is, ij^{s}
Item, for four scoir draucht, ... xvj^{d}
Item, for ix drauchtt in quarter clift, the draucht viij^{d}; summa, . vj^{s}
Item, for ane drauchtt in ane ald trie, xvj^{d}
Item, for iij scoir drauchtt, xij^{d}
Item, for vj draucht in buirds, ... iiij^{s}
Item, for bering of the tymmer to the sawaris and fra thame, x^{s}
Item, for careing ane dosane ½ of dailes outt of Leyth, v^{s} iiij^{d}
Item, gevin for turnyng of the thre greitt pilleris, . xviij^{s}
Item, for careing of thame to the tournour and fra thame, iij^{s}
Item, for ij draucht sawing in ane ½ geist, xx^{d}
Item, for sawing of tua draucht in ane ald trie, . . . ij^{s} viij^{d}
Item, gevin for inbringing to the kirk of all the tymmer fra the cairtis, . iij^{s}

The wrychtis viij dayis expenssis precedand the xxiiij day of Julij 1565:—

Item, in the first oulk, to Thomas Wod, . . xxxiiij^{s}
Item, William Stevinsoun, . xxiiij^{s}
Item, Jhonn Fender, . xxj^{s} viij^{d}
Item, to George Tod, . xxj^{s} viij^{d}
Item, to Adam Schang, xx^{s}
Item, to Patrik Bowman, . . xxj viij^{d}
Item, to Thomas Lyndesay, xx^{s}
Item, to Cuthbertt Wallace, ... xx^{s}

This auchtt dayis expenssis precedand the first of August 1565:—

Item, to Thomas Wod, . . xxxiiij^{s}
Item, to William Stevinsoun, . xxiiij^{s}
Item, to George Tod, . xxj^{s} viij^{d}
Item, to Patrik Bowman, . . xxj^{s} viij^{d}
Item, to Thomas Lyndesay, xx^{s}
Item, to Cuthbertt Wallace, xx^{s}
Item, to Adam Schang, xx^{s}
Item, to Jhonn Fendar, . xxj^{s}

Alexander Park, Dean of Guild. 1564-65.

This viij dayis expenssis precedand the viij day of August 1565 :—

Item, to Thomas Wod,	xxxiiij s
Item, to William Stevinsoun,	xxviij s
Item, to Jhonn Stewartt,	xxv s
Item, to George Tod,	xxvj s
Item, to Jhonn Fyndar,	xxviij s
Item, to Thomas Lyndesay,	xxiiij s
Item, to Patrik Bowman,	xxvj s
Item, to Adam Schang,	xxiiij s
Item, to Cuthbertt Wallace,	xxiiij s
Item, for auchtt pound of glew,	xij s

[250] The auchtt dayis expenssis precedand the xv day of August 1565 :—

Item, in the first, to Thomas Wod,	xxxiiij s
Item, to William Stevinsoun,	xxviij s
Item, to Jhonn Stewartt,	xxx s
Item, to George Tod,	xxvj s
Item, to Thomas Lyndesay,	xxiiij s
Item, to Patrik Bowman,	xxvj s
Item, to Cuthbertt Wallace,	xxiiij s

This auchtt dayis expenssis precedand the xxij day of August 1565 :—

Item, first, to Thomas Wod,	xxxiiij s
Item, to William Stevinsoun,	xxviij s
Item, to Jhonn Stewartt,	xxx s
Item, to George Tod,	xxvj s
Item, Thomas Lyndesay,	xxiiij s

This auchtt dayis expenssis precedand the xxix of August 1565 :—

Item, in the first, to Thomas Wod,	xxxiiij s
Item, to William Stevinsoun,	xxviij s
Item, to Jhonn Stewartt,	xxx s
Item, to George Tod,	xxvj s

The auchtt dayis expenssis precedand the iiij day of September 1565 :—

Item, in the first, to Thomas Wod,	xxxiiij s
Item, to William Stevinsoun,	xxviij s

ALEXANDER PARK, Dean of Guild. 1564-65.

Item, to Jhonn Stewartt, ... xxv^s
Item, to Jhonn Bowman, ... xxiiij^s
Item, to Cuthbertt Wallace, ... xx^s

This auchtt dayis expenssis precedand the xj day of September 1565:—

Item, in the first, to Thomas Wod, . . . xxxiiij^s
Item, to Jhonn Stewartt, ... xxx^s
Item, to Jhonn Bowman, . . . xxiiij^s
Item, to Cuthbertt Wallace, ... xxiiij^s
Item, to Jhonn Inglische, servandis maison, for v dayis laubour in making of the bott hoills and hewin of the pillar, ... xxv^s

[251] This auchtt dayis expenssis precedand the xix day of September 1565:—

Item, in the first, to Thomas Wod, xxviij^s iiij^d
Item, to Jhonn Bowman, . . xvj^s
Item, to Cuthbertt Wallace, . . xvj^s

The compte of the nailles.

Item, in the first, viij^c planchour naill, the hunder iij^s iiij^d, xxvj^s viij^d
Item, for iiij^c blind naill, dur naill schank, the ^c xx^d, vj^s viij^d
Item, for ane hunder singill garroun naill, blind, . v^s
Item, for vj^c dur naill, blind, the hunder xx^d, . . . x^s
Item, for iij^c planschour naill, blind, the hunder iij^s iiij^d; the somma, x^s
Item, for iij^c doubill garroun, the pece ij^d, is, . vj^s
Item, for vj^c planchour naill, blind, the hunder xx^d, . x^s
Item, for vij^c dur naill, heidit, the ^c xx^d, is, xj^s [xj^s viij^d]
Item, for ane hunder singill garrow naill, . . . v^s
Item, for iiij^c planchour naill, to naill on the crop, the hunder xl^d, x^s [xiij^s iiij^d]
Item, for ane hunder quhyte naillis, planchour naill schank, . . v^s
Item, for vj^c flurin naill, the ^c iiij^s, ... xxiiij^s
Item, for vj^c planchour naill and iiij^c dur naill and ane hunder quarter hunder naill, ... xxiiij^s
Item, to ane man thatt waititt on the work in the kirk the space of nyne oulkis, ilk oulk xiiij^s; summa, ... vj^li vj^s
Item, for tua new keyis to the dur thatt is in the Laich Tolbuith thatt gais up to the Chakker houss, ... iiij^s

ALEXANDER PARK, Dean of Guild. 1564-65.

Item, for ane key to the Freir yett and mending of the heinging lok thairof, ...	ij^s
Item, for ane new boiss lok to the stall quhair the Counsell sittis, .	viij^s
Item, for ij½ stane of bandis and cruikis to the south kirk dur, the pryce of the stane xvj^s; summa, . .	xl^s
Item, for ane new slott to the lok of the auld kirk dur, . .	xviij^d
Item, for ane greitt stok lok to the south kirk dur, . . .	x^s
Item, for ane stane ½ of bottis to the Kingis Grace saitt, the stane xvj^s; summa, ...	xxiiij^s
Item, for tynnyng of ane of the greitt bottis and four garroun nails,	xvj^d
Item, for xvij bottis to the Kingis saitt, sax of thame quhyte, the pryce of the pece vij^d, ...	xj^s iiij^d
Item, for ane stane x^li of leid to yett thir bottis, the stane xvj^s, .	xix^s vj^d
[252] Item, for xij pikis to sett the fyallis, ...	xviij^d
Item, for ane pare cors tallitt bandis doublitt gamett, with naillis all quhyte,	x^s
Item, for ane quhyte lok of plaitt to the Kingis saitt, . . .	viij^s
Item, for ane new kye to the stepill dur quhair the fidlar was putt, weyand v^li wecht, .	iiij^s iij^d
Item, for oile to the knok, . .	iij^s
Item, for ane string to the commoun bell,	ij^s
Item, for towis to putt up the Kingis paill, .	viij^s
Item, to the workmen thatt buir the greitt ledder, .	vj^s

Summa of the haill dischairge is thre hundreth thre scoir auchtt ^li fyventene schillingis nyne penneis.

Decimo quinto Augusti J^m v^c sexagesimo sexto.

The quhilk day the Auditouris of comptis underwritten hes sene and considеritt and laid this your compte of Alexander Park, Dene of Gyld, begynnand in October the yeir of God J^m v^c and thre scoir and foure yeiris, and chairge and dischairge being consideritt and laid, fyndis the comptar superexpenditt, quhilk the gude toun is restand awand to him, the somme of ane hundreth and thre scoir auchtt pounds thre schillingis ane pennye, and for verificatioun thairof hes subscryvitt the samyn as efter followis.

[The Account is not signed.]

JOHN PRESTOUN, Dean of Guild. 1565-66.

[254]

THE COMPTE of Maister JHONN PRESTOUN, Dene of Gild of Edinburgh, of the yeir of his office begynnand the feird day of October in the yeir of God J^{m} v^{c} thre scoir fyfe yeiris, and indurand quhill October in the yeir of God J^{m} v^{c} thre scoir sax yeiris.

THE COMPTARIS CHAIRGE.

Item, in the first, the comptar is to be chairgitt and chairgis him with the haill money of burgessis and gild brether maid in the yeir of the comptaris office foirsaid, as the lokkit buke proportis, to the quhilk the comptar referris him;

Non onerand. Item, the comptar is to be chairgitt with the money of James Prestoun, quha was maid burges the sevint day of November 1565, in presence of James Nicoll, baille, and the dewtie thairof gevin to the said James Prestoun gratis be Schir Symon Prestoun of Craigmillar, knycht, provest, be resson of the dewtie of his office.

Non onerand. Item, the comptar is to be chairgit with money of David Condyet, quha was maid burges the ix of November 1565, in presence of the provest, baillies and counsell, and the dewtie thairof gevin to Hectour Trolhop, Edinburgh maisser, be ressoun of his office.

Item, the comptar chairgis him with the dewtie of Androw Walker, webster, quha was maid burges the day and yeir above written, and payitt, ... v^{li}

Non onerand. Item, the comptar is to be chairgitt with the money of Mongo Ross, patescher, quha was maid burges the xvij day of November 1565, in presence of James Nycoll, baille, and the dewtie thairof gevin to the said Mongo gratis be the said provest be ressoun of his office.

The comptar chairgis him with the dewtie of Robert Stevinsoun, tailyour, quha was maid burges the day foirsaid, and payitt for his dewtie, . v^{li}

Item, the comptar chairgis him with the dewtie of Jhonn Alexander, tailyour, quha was maid burges in presence of James Nicoll, bailye, the xxj day of November 1565, and payitt, be ressoun of the privelege of his wyfe, Margaret Blak, dochter to umquhill Roger Blak, burges of this burgh, . . . $xiij^{s}$ $iiij^{d}$

[255] Item, the comptar chairgis him with the dewtie of Jhonn Makbaitht, skynner, quha was maid burges the xx day of December 1565, in presence of Jhonn Sym, baille, and payitt for his dewtie, . . v[li]

Non onerand. Item, the comptar is to be chairgitt with the dewtie of Androw Arneill, merchant, quha was maid burges the fyft of Januar 1565, in presence of James Nicoll, bailye, and payitt v[li] quhilk was gevin to Androw Stevinsoun, baille, be resson of the dewtie of his office.

Non onerand. Item, the comptar is to be chairgitt with the dewtie of Mongo Ross, pattescher, quha was maid gyld brother the fyft day of Januar 1565, and the dewtie thairof gevin to him gratis be the provest, baillies and counsell, and that for service to be done be him to the gude toun att sic tymes as itt salhappin thame to mak bankettis.

Non onerand. Item, the comptar is to be chairgitt with the dewtie of Jhonn Wodheill, draipper, quha was maid burges the first day of Februar 1565, and the dewtie thairof gevin gratis be the provest, baillies and counsell att the requeist of George Prestoun, bruther to the provest.

Non onerand. And with the dewtie of Mathow Mure, officiar, quha was maid burges the day foirsaid be rycht of his wyfe, Marionn Gray, dochter to umquhill Robert Gray, and the dewtie thairof gevin gratis.

Non onerand. Item, the comptar is to be chairgitt with the dewtie of Jhonn Fortoun, quha was maid burges the second day of Februar 1565, and payit v[li] quhilk was gevin to William Stewart, clark depute, be ressoun of the dewtie of his office.

Item, the comptar chairgis him with the dewtie of William Ellot, cordonar, quha was maid burges the day foirsaid, and payitt, . . v[li]

Non onerand. Item, the comptar chairgis him with the dewtie of Jhonn Gray, cowpar, quha was maid burges the feird day of Februar 1565, quha payitt v[li] quhilk was gevin to Alexander Carstairis for Alexander Guthre, commoun clark, be resson of the dewtie of his office.

Item, the comptar chairgis him with the dewtie of Nicolas Corboneir, quha was maid burges the saxt day of Februar, and payitt, . . v[li]

Non onerand. Item, the comptar is to be chairgitt with the dewtie of George Richartsonn, cowpar, quha was maid burges the day foirsaid, and payitt v[li] quhilk was gevin to James Roger, clark depute, be resson of his office.

JOHN PRESTOUN, Dean of Guild. 1565-66.

[256]

Item, the comptar chairgis him with the dewtie of Andro Richartsonn, fleschour, quha was maid burges the vij day of Februar, and payitt, . v^li^

Item, the dewtie of Androw Cuthbertsonn, drapper, quha wes maid burges the day foirsaid, and payitt, ... v^li^

Item, the comptar chairgis him with the dewtie of Robert Rig, skynner, quha was maid burges the xv of Februar 1565, and payitt, . . v^li^

Item, the comptar chairgis him with the dewtie of Gilbert Prymroiss, cyrurgeane, quha wes maid burges the xix day of Februar, and payitt, v^li^

Item, with the dewtie of Jhonn Gybsoun, merchantt, quha was maid burges the xxij day of Februar 1565, be the privelege of his wyfe, Alesoun Sclaiter, douchter to umquhill Patrik Sclater, burges of this burghe, and payitt, ... xiij^s^ iiij^d^

Item, with the dewtie of Jhonn Smyth, craymer, quha was maid burges the xxv day of Februar 1565, and payitt, ... v^li^

Item, with the dewtie of Thomas Trynche, fleschour, quha wes maid burges the first day of Marche 1565, and payitt, . . . v^li^

Item, with the dewtie of Adam Christesonn, fleschour, quha wes maid burges the day foirsaid, and payitt, ... v^li^

Item, with the dewtie of Robert Mathew, bonetmaker, quha wes maid burges the vj day of Aprile 1565 [1566], and payitt, . . . v^li^

Item, with the dewtie of Jhonn Barclay, tailyour, quha was maid burges the day foirsaid, and payitt, ... v^li^

Item, with the dewtie of Jhonn Cuthbertsonn, quha was maid burges the day foirsaid, and payitt, ... v^li^

Item, the comptar is to be chairgitt with the dewtie of James Olephantt, quha was maid burges and gyld brother the viij day of Aprile 1566, in presence of the provest, baillies and counsell, and payitt xv^li^ quhilk was allowit to the Dene of Gyld, comptar, be ressoun of the dewtie of his office. — Non onerand.

Item, the dewtie of Maister David Chalmer, quha was maid burges the day foirsaid, and the dewtie thairof gevin to him gratis be the provest, baillies and counsell. — Non onerand.

Item, with the dewtie of Jhonn Gibsoun, alias Capitane Gibsoun, goldsmyth, quha was maid burges and gyld be rycht of the privelege of his — Non onerand.

father, umquhill Thomas Gybsoun, quha was burges and gyld brother of this burgh, and the dewtie gevin to the said Jhonn gratis be the provest, baillies and counsale.

Item, the comptar chairgis him with the dewtie of Jhonn Patoun, tailyour, quha was maid burges the xxvij day of Aprile 1566, and payitt, . v^{li}

[257] And with the dewtie of Alane Young, marchantt, quha was maid burges the penult day of Aprylc 1566, and payitt, ... v^{li}

Item, the comptar chairgis him with the dewtie of William Roger, tailyour, and eldest sonn to James Roger, burges and merchantt of this burgh, and payitt be the ressoun of his said father, ... xiij^{s} iiij^{d}

Item, the comptar chairgis him with the dewtie of Jhonn Symsoun, wobster, quha was maid burges the tentt day of Maij 1566, and payitt, v^{li}

Item, the comptar chairgis him with the dewtie of Stevin Forrest, quha was maid burges the day foresaid, and payitt, ... v^{li}

Item, the comptar chairgis him with the deutie of Robert Coupar, tailyour, quha was maid burges the xxiiij day of Maij 1566, and payitt, . v^{li}

Item, the comptar chairgis him with the dewtie of George Cokburn, quha was maid burges the xxix day of Maij 1566, and payitt for his fredome, ... v^{li}

Item, the comptar is to be chairgitt with the dewtie of James Makcall,
Non onerand. servitour to Maister Alexander Sym, quha was maid burges the last day of Maij 1566, and the dewtie thairof gevin to him be Jhonn Sym, baille, be ressoun of the dewtie of his office.

Item, the comptar is to be chairgitt with the dewtie of James Aikman, quha was maid burges the day foirsaid, be ressoun of the privelege of his wyfe, Elizabeth Douglas, dochter to umquhill Alexander Douglas, burges and merchantt of this burgh, and payitt, . . . xiij^{s} iiij^{d}

Item, the comptar chairgis him the dewtie of Thomas Bell, skynner, quha was maid burges be ressoun of his fatheris privilege, Jhonn Bell, the xij day of Junij 1566, and payitt, ... xiij^{s} iiij^{d}

Item, the comptar is to be chairgitt with the dewtie of George Ramsay of
Non onerand. Dalhousy, quha was maid burges the xiiij day of Junij 1566, and the dewtie thairof gevin to him gratis be the provost, baillies and counsell.

Item, the comptar is to be chairgitt with dewtie of Jhonn Cathart,

JOHN PRESTOUN, Dean of Guild. 1565-66.

cuitlar, quha wes maid burges the xxj day of Junij 1566, and payitt for his fredome, ... v li

Non onerand.

Item, the comptar is to be chairgitt with the dewtie of James Nisbett, mairchantt, quha wes maid burges and gyld brother the thrid day of Julij 1566, and the dewtie of the burgeschip gevin to him be William Foular, baille, be ressoun of the dewtie of his office, and the dewtie of the gyld gevin to him gratis be the provost, baillies and counsell at the requeist of Maister Robert Richartsonn, Thesaurer to Our Soverane.

Item, the comptar is to be chairgitt with the dewtie of Alexander Uddart, [258] merichantt, secound sone to William Uddart, umquhill, quha was maid burges and gyld brother the day foirsaid and, be ressoune of the privelege of his father, payitt, ... xxxiij s iiij d

Item, the comptar is to be chairgitt with the dewtie of David Wemes, glassinwrycht, quha was maid burges the vj day of July 1566, and payitt, ... v li

Item, with the dewtie of Jhonn Ireland, marchant, quha was maid burges and gyld brother the tentt day of July 1566, be rycht of the privelege of his wyfe, Margrett Todrik, dochter to George Todrik, quha is burges and gyld of this burgh, and payitt, ... xxxiij s iiij d

Item, with the dewtie of Roger Steill, craymer, quha was maid burges the xj day of July 1566, and payitt, ... v li

Item, with the dewtie of Frances Bischop, skynner, secund sone to umquhill Thomas Bischop, skynner and burges, and payitt be the privelege of his said father, ... xiij s iiij d

Item, the comptar is to be chairgitt with the dewtie of Jhonn Halyday, marchantt and burges, quha was maid gyld brother be rycht of the privelege of Elene Dik, douchter to umquill William Dik, burges and gyld brother, and payitt, ... xx s

Item, the comptar chairgis him with the dewtie of James Daglesch, younger, merchant and burges, quha was maid gyld brother the last day of July, and payitt thairfor, ... x li

Item, the comptar chairgis him with the dewtie of Jhonn Farquhar, merchantt, quha was maid burges and gyld brother the thred day of August 1566, be the rycht of his wyfe, Issobell Galbraith, douchter to umquhill Thomas Galbraith, quha was burges and gyld brother, and payitt, ... xxxiij^{s} iiij^{d}

Item, the comptar chairgis him with the dewtie of Jhonn Watsoun, burges and merchantt, quha was maid gyld brother the iij day of August 1566, and payitt, ... x^{li}

Item, with the dewtie of Jhonn Eistoun, candilmaker, quha was maid burges the vij day of August 1566, and payitt, . . v^{li}

Item, with the dewtie of Alexander Mychell, quha was maid burges the xxj day of August 1566, and payitt, . v^{li}

Item, with the dewtie of Robertt Synclar, maisson, wes maid burges the xxj day of August, and payitt for his fredome, v^{li}

Item, with the dewtie of Hew Broun, masoun, quha wes maid burges the xxvij day of August, and payitt, . . v^{li}

Item, the comptar chairgis him with the dewtie of William Biccartoun, maisson, quha was maid burges the day foirsaid, and payitt for his fredome, ... v^{li}

Item, with the dewtie of Jhone Graihame, skynner, quha was maid burges the day foirsaid, and payitt thairfor, ... v^{li}

Item, the comptar is to be chairgitt with the dewtie of Jhonn Nicoll,
Non oneraud. skynner, quha was maid burges the xxvj day of September 1566, quha payitt v^{li} quhilk was gevin to James Nycholl, bailye, be ressoun of the dewtie of his office.

Soume of the money of all burgessis and gyldis maid in the yeir of the comptaris office with the quhilk he is to be chargitt, is,

Summa of thir Burgeschippis, ... j^{c} lxxx^{li}

[259] Item, the comptar chairgis him with the entres and frauchtin of all Schippis frauchtis in the yeir of the comptaris office, to the nomber of thre scoir xviij schippis, ilk schip att xiiij^{s}, as is contenit in the tounis entres buke, to the quhilk the comptar referris him ; soume, . . . liiij^{li} xij^{s}

Item, the comptar chairgis him with the mailles of the Cordonnaris Choppis in the yeir of the comptaris office, beand in nomber tuentie choppis as efter followis ; in the first, Thomas Mirreleis chop, . xxvj^{s} viij^{d}

Item, Harparfieldis chop, . xxvj^{s} viij^{d}

Item, Brouderstanis chop, . xxvj^{s} viij^{d}

JOHN PRESTOUN, Dean of Guild, 1565-66.	Jhonn Bynningis chop, .	xx^{s}
	Robert Gybsonis chop, . .	xx^{s}
	Item, Jhonn Forrest for twa choppis,	xl^{s}
	Item, for Forsythis chop, . .	xx^{s}
	Androw Wilsonis chop,	xx^{s}
	Laurens Cortis chop,	xx^{s}
	Robert Flemyngis chop,	xx^{s}
	Jhonn Chepmanis chop, .	xx^{s}
	Jhonn Cunynghames chop,	xx^{s}
	Margarett Rutherfuirds chop,	xx^{s}
	Jhonn Reidis chop, .	xx^{s}
	Alexander Andersonis chop,	xx^{s}
	Jhonn Neilsonis chop, .	xx^{s}
	George Cowan, .	xx^{s}
	Jhonn Smyth, tua choppis, ...	xl^{s}
	The haill soume of thir tuentie chopis maill in the yeir is, . .	xxj^{li}
	Item, the comptar chairgis him with the yeirlie mailles of the Goldsmythis Choppis and standis aboutt the kirk wall as efter followis; and, in the first, with the yeris maill of the comptaris office of Alexander Gilbertis chop, ...	xxx^{s}
Non onerand.	Item, with the maill of Robert Murrayis goldsmyth chop, quhilk is xxx^{s}, bot itt wes waist the yeir of the comptaris office, lykas itt standis yitt waist and na man will tak itt oure his heid, . . .	xxx^{s}
	Item, with the maill of Crystell Galbrayth goldsmythis chop, the yeir of the comptaris office, ...	xxx^{s}
	Item, with the yeris maill of Androw Heleis stand in the kirk dur, .	xl^{s}
Non onerand.	Item, with the yeris maill of Eduard Ryndes chop, quhilk in lyke maner stands waist, bott suld be, . . .	xxx^{s}
	Item, with the maill of Adam Alane goldsmythis chop, . . .	xxx^{s}
Non onerand.	Item, with the maill of Edward Bassendyne goldsmythis chop, quhilk suld be xxx^{s}, ...	xxx^{s}
	bot itt standis waist as is notourly knawin.	
	Item, with the maill of Jhonn Mosmanis chop, goldsmyth, .	xxx^{s}
[260]	Item, with the maill of Jhonn Gilbert goldsmythis chop, . .	liij^{s} iiij^{d}

Item, with the maill of David Denneistonnis chop in the yeir of the comptaris office, ... liij^{s} iiij^{d}

Soume of the yeris maill of the haill choppis and standis (*blank*).

Summa of the comptaris haill chairge, ij^{c} lxxiij^{li} viij^{s} viij^{d}

THE COMPTARIS DISCHAIRGE.

Item, the comptar is to be dischairgit with the money of the burgeschippis of the tuelf officiaris of this toun, with the jaillour, in the yeir of the comptaris office, viz., ilk officiar with the jaillour iij^{li}; soume, . . xxxix^{li}

Item, the comptar is to be dischairgit with the xx^{s} yeirlie gevin be the gude toun to everilk ane of the saidis officiaris with the said jaillour to thair support, and thatt for thatt they suld abstene fre ganging for money through the honest houssis of the tyme callitt Yule; soume of this is, ... xiij^{li}

Item, the comptar is to be dischairgit with the feis of Patrik Govvane, bellman, Jhonn Symson, ringer of the bellis, and Robert Drummond, gild servandis, everilk ane of thame thre, in the yeir of the comptaris office, viij^{li}; soume, ... xxiiij^{li}

Item, the comptar dischairgis him ij^{s} viij^{d} gevin be him, the xx day of October 1565, to David Duncane, smyth, for ane new key to the kirk dur in Sanct Jhonis Ile, to Jhonn Kairnis order, . . . ij^{s} viij^{d}

Item, the samyn day, for ane row of walx to Jhonn Kairnis for the mornyng prayeris, ... iiij^{s}

Item, the last day of October 1565, gevin to David Duncane, smyth, for four keyis quhilk he maid to the lok of the dur of the stall quhair the provest, baillies, counsell sittis att preching, ... vj^{s} viij^{d}

Item, the viij day of November 1565, for tua braid dailes quhilk I coft and gaif to Maister Jhonn Craig, minister, the quhilk he desyritt to mak skelfis and lettronis to his buikis, pryce of the pece v^{s} iiij^{d}; somme, x^{s} viij^{d}

Item, for bering of thame fra Leyth to the said Maister Jhonis hous, . viij^{d}

Item, the fyft day of November 1565, quhilk day Marionn Scott was bureit, I gaife to Jhonn Symsoun and his marrow to mak the uner stap of the buriall, ane quartt of aill, ... viij^{d}

[261] Item, the xxiij day of November 1565, for ane choppin of ulie to the greitt bell, . . . xviij^{d}

JOHN PRESTOUN, Dean of Guild. 1565-66.

Item, the xx day of December 1565, for fyve glassin bandis for the wyndow in the chairter houss, weyand ix lib v unces, pryce of the pund weicht xij d, ix s iij d ob

Item, to James Hunter, glassinwrycht, for ane new glassin wyndow to the said wyndow, contenand xx futes, pryce of the fute ij s; soume, xl s

Item, to the said James Hunteris servand in drink sylver, . . xviij d

Item, the xx day of December 1565, for mending of the lok and key of the said kirk dur in Sant Jhonis Yle, quhilk the laddis hald spilt be putting in of stanes in the said lok, . . . ij s viij d

Item, the samyn day, for ane uther roll of walx to Jhoun Cairnis for the reding of the mornyng prayaris, ... iiij s

Item, the tent day of Januar 1565, for ane fyne lok with sax keyes to the west dur of the stall quhair the provest, baillies and counsell sittis, to David Duncane, smyth, ... xvij s vj d

Item, gevin be me for furneissing of candill to the General Assemble for the kirk in wynter, quhilk lastitt vj nychtis, . . . vj s

Item, the xxiij day of Februar 1565, gevin to Robert Drummond be ane precept for furneissing of the candill in wynter in the yeir of the comptaris office to the sessioun of the kirk xxxvj s, quhairof I have ellis allowitt for the candill of the Generall Assembly vj s; sua gevin to him bot, ... xxx s

Item, the second day of Merche 1565, for mending of certane yrne work of the kirk, and for lokis to itt, ... viij s

Item, the xviij day of May 1565 [1566], gevin to Thomas Kennydie, wrycht, for making of ane interdise in the stall quhair the provest sittis att the sermond, and furneissing of the tymmer and warkmenschip, and with nailles to itt, ... vj s viij d

Item, the samyn day, gevin to Patrik, belman, to furneis ule olyve, for the yeir of the comptaris office, to the kirk, ... xij s

Item, for furneissing of the candill in the mornyng all the Sonndayis at the mornyng prayeris betwix Alhalonmes and Candilmes or thairby, extending to xij Sondays, ilk Sonday xij d; soume, . . . xij s

[262] Item, gevin to ane pure man, callit Auld Sandy, for dychting and halding cleine of the calsay and gutteris betwix the entres of the Stynkand Style and the New Counsalhous dure, ilk oulk vj d; soume in the yeir is, xxvj s

Item, for carcing of the formes furth of the kirk to the nether New Counsalhous and in bering of thame agane at bayth the Generall Assembleis, baitht in wynter and symmer, . . xvj^d

Item, for four faldome of ane greit cord to the belstring, pryce of the faldome [viij^d], ... ij^s viij^d

Item, for ane greit lok and ane key to the greit woult of the nether Tolbuith dur quhan I biggitt the Haly Blude Ile, . . x^s

Item, for ane small lok and ane key to the inner Tolbuith voult, pryce, . vj^s viij^d

Item, for the mending of the lok, key, and ane new stepill to the workhous dur in the kirk end, . . . ij^s

Item, the comptar dischairgis him with the soume of xxx^s gevin be him to William Robesoun, sclater, for the mending and poynting of ane part of the kirk above Sant Bastianis Ile, quhilk sclatter fand lyme, sand, sclait and warkmanschip, . xxx^s

The expenssis maid upon the thre Communions in the yeir of the comptaris office, with the quhilk expenssis he is to be dischairgit:—

Item, on Tuisday the feird day of December 1565, gevin for bering of formes furth of the kirk to the Tolbuyth to the Assembly of the Kirk, and fra the Tolbuyth to the kirk agane, ... viij^d

Item, on Setterday the viij day of December 1565, for the upbringing of xviij dailles quhilk I borrowitt fra Maister Robert Glen, thesaurer, fra Sant Paullis Wark to the kirk to mak the transis, . iij^s

Item, for ane hundreth planchour naill for baith the Sondayis, . iij^s

Item, to the workmen for bering and setting of the buirdis, fourmes and transis, the tua Sondayis, ... viij^s

Item, to the warkmen, ilk Setterday at evin, ane quart of aill, . . xvj^d

Item, to Thomas Kennedy, wrycht, for upputting and dountaking of the transis the tua Setterdayis at none, ... x^s

Item, for xxxij torches, pryce of the dosane xxx^s, to George Jhonstoun; soume, ... iiij^li

[263] Item, for ane stane and four pondis of candill to Jhonn Clavy, candilmaker, pryce of the stane, xviij^s viij^d, ... xxiij^s iiij^d

Item, for ane pounchoun of wyne, to James Nicoll, and bering of itt, . x^li j^s vj^d

JOHN PRESTOUN, Dean of Guild, 1565-66.

Item, for nyne quartis of mair wyne the last Sonday becaus the pounchoun wes very littill and servit not, pryce of the quart iij^{s}; soume, . . xxvij^{s}

Item, for foure dossoun communion breid for the tua Sondayis, fra William Fiddes, baxster, pryce of the dosane xiiij^{s}; soume, xlvj^{s}

Soume of the expenssis of the first Communion is, xx^{li} xiij^{s} x^{d}

The Second Communion.

Item, on Setterday the xxiij day of Merche 1565, for bering of the formes to the Kirk Assemblye to the Tolbuyth, and to the kirk agane, viij^{d}

Item, for ane hundreth planchour nailles to baith the Setterdayis, . iij^{s}

Item, to the werkmen for bering and setting of the formes, buirdis and tymmer for the transis bayth the Setterdayis and Sondayis, viij^{s}

Item, to thair drink the tua Setterdayis at evin, . . . xvj^{d}

Item, to Thomas Kennedye, wrycht, for his laubour in setting up and doun the transis on bayth the Setterdayis and Sondayis, . x^{s}

Item, the first Sonday in the mornyng for tua punds of candill, . ij^{s} iiij^{d}

Item, for ane pounchoun and wyne, to Andro Craigis wyfe, xv^{li} x^{s}

Item, for bering of it to my sellar, . . . xviij^{d}

Item, for four dosane of communion breid, to William Fiddes, . lvj^{s}

Item, for bering agane of the auchtene dailes, quhilk I borrowit fra Maister Robert Glen, to his awin werk, ... xviij^{d}

Soume of the expenssis of the second Communion, xix^{li} xiiij^{s} iiij^{d}

The Thrid Communioun.

Item, on Setterday the xxviij day of July 1566, for bering of the greitt formes furth of the kirk to the Tolbuyth for the Assemblye of the Kirk, and in agane, ... viij^{d}

[264] Item, for ane dosane of fyne dailles to remane in the kirk to be transsis, iij^{li} x^{s}

Item, for laying of thame of the bing quhair thai lay, . . iiij^{d}

Item, for upbringing of thame fra Leyth, . . iiij^{s}

Item, for bering thame into the kirk, . vj^{d}

Item, for ane hundreth planchour nailles, ... iij^{s}

Item, to the workmen to beir the tymmer, the fourmes, and sett the buirdis, the tua Setterday and Sondayis, . viij^{s}

Item, to thame in drink on the Setterdayis at evin, ilk Setterday ane quartane, ... xvj[d]
Item, to Thomas Kennedy, wrycht, for his laubour in upputting and doun taking of the transis ilk Setterdayis and Sondayis, ... x[s]
Item, for ane pounschoun of the wyne, to Maister Patrik Bissetis wyfe, . xix[li]
Item, for bering of itt to my cellar, ... xvj[d]
Item, for four dosane of breid, to William Fiddes, pryce of the dosane xiiij[s]; soume, ... xvj[s]

Soume of the expenssis of this thred Communioun is, xxvj[li] xv[s] ij[d]

Item, for wesching of the lynnenn naipre the haill yeir, . . vj

The expenssis maid upoun the steppis and entres att the Gray freris buriall :—

Item, gevin be Allane Dixesoun, ane of the Counsell of this burgh in the tyme of the comptaris office in the moneth of August in anno 1566, the comptar beand absent and furth of the realme, to the quariouris and cairtar, for the haill wynnyng, out laying and carcing of the haill stappis att the entres of the buriale, of the burgeschip of ane Alexander Michell quha was maid burges in the said tyme and the said Alane souertie for the payment thairof, ... v[li]
Item, for ten laidis of lyme to thait werk, pryce of the laid ij iiij[d]; soume, xiij[s] iiij[d]
Item, for tuentie laidis of sand, ... x[s]
Item, to ane werkman, ... xij[s]
Item, to Mourdow Walker, for the hewing and laying of all thay steppis and entreis, in task, . . . iiij[li] x[s]

The expenssis maid on the pairt of the kirk callit the Haly Blude Yle and reparaling thairof, begynnand the ix day of Junij 1566 :—

Item, for xxvj laidis of lyme, pryce of the laid ij[s] iiij[d]; soume, . iiij[li] iiij[s]
Item, for vj dosane of laidis of sand, pryce of the dosane vj[s]; soume, xxxvj[s]
Item, for riddeling of the lyme and sand, to Jhonn Symsoun, . . vj[s]
[265] Item, for leding of tua hundreth wall stanis and ane half furth of the Gray freris to the kirk, pryce of the hundreth leding xxv[s]; soume, iij[li] ij[s] vj[d]
Item, for the wynnyng of the said stanes, to Jhonn Symsoun and his marrow, ... xiiij[s]

JOHN PRESTOUN, Dean of Guild. 1565-66.

Item, to ane barrowman to cast the ground, to beir away the red thairof, and to serve the maisons all the tyme of the werk quhilk was to him iij oulks, xij^{s}; soume, ... xxxvj^{s}

Item, for x rabale stanes, with sole and lyntall to the dur, pryce of the pece at the querrall ix^{d}; soume, ... ix^{s}

Item, for cairt hyre fra the querrall, beand foure draucht, ilk draucht ij^{s} vj^{d}; soume, . . . x^{s}

Item, for bering of thame into the kirk, . xij^{d}

Item, for ane schule, . xij^{d}

Item, for ane yrne to the schule, . xij^{d}

Item, for ane riddell, . . x^{d}

Item, for walter to the baill wark, . . v^{s}

Item, for tua croukis, weyand iij punds ane half, pryce of the pound xij^{d}, iij^{s} vj^{d}

Item, for four pondis of leid to yett the croukis with, pryce of the pond x^{d}; soume, ... iij^{s} iiij^{d}

Item, to Mourdow Walker, maisson, for the hale massoun werk, be task, vj^{li}

Item, to his servandis in drink sylver, . . . iiij^{s}

Item, for thre laidis of lyme to be spairgein mortar, pryce of the laid ij^{s} ij^{d}, . . vj^{s} vj^{d}

Item, for sax laidis of sand to itt, iij^{s}

Item, for walter to itt, ... vj^{d}

Item, to the spargenar for his hale laubour within and without in spargein, xvj^{s}

Item, to Thomas Kennedy, wrycht, for the making of the dur to the Haly Blude Ile, . . . xij^{s}

Item, for tua greit bandis to the dur, weyand xiiij^{li} iiij unces, pryce of the pund xij^{d}, ... xiiij^{s} iij^{d}

Item, for ane lok and ane key to the said dur, vij^{s}

Item, for naillis to the bandis, ... iiij^{d}

Item, the xj day of July 1566, for ane dosane of dailles to mak the bynkis and burde within thatt houss, . . iij^{li}

Item, for laying of thame of the bing, iiij^{d}

Item, for cairt hyre of thame, . iij^{s} iiij^{d}

Item, for bering of thame into the kirk, ... iij^{d}

Item, for bering of certane ald tymmer furth of the nether wolt of the

Tolbuith to the Haly Blud Yle to be ane part of the traistis to the benkis of the said yle, ... vj^{d}

Item, for ane corbell trie in Leyth to be ane pairt of the creddill of the buird, ... xij^{s}

Item, for upbringing of it fra Leyth, xiiij^{d}

Item, for sawing of it, . . xij^{d}

Item, for sawing of pairt of auld tymmer, . xviij^{d}

Item, for tua fyre sparris in Leyth and upbringing of thame, . . iij^{s}

[266] Item, to Thomas Lyndesay, wrycht, for his laubouris on Thurisday the xj day of July 1566, Fryday and Setterday therefter, ilk day iiij^{s}; soume, xij^{s}

Item, on Mononday the xiiij day of July 1566 for sawing of fyve dales, . vj^{s} viij^{d}

Item, for sawing of the sydes of the said corbell, tua draucht, xvj^{d}

Item, for sawing of uther auld tymmer, ... iij^{s}

Item, for bering of the tymmer and dailles to the sawaris and fra the sawaris, and syndrie tymes, ... xvj^{s}

Item, for tua hundreth dur nailes, pryce of the hundreth xviij^{d}; soume, . iij^{s}

Item, for half ane hundreth planchour nallies, xviij^{d}

Item, for ane pond of glew for the burds, . . . ij^{s}

Item, on Setterday the xx day of July 1566, to Thomas Kennedy and Adam Schang, wrychtis, of their oulkis wagis, ilk ane of thame xxv^{s}; soume, ... l^{s}

Item, for thair Setterdayis supper at even, to thame bayth, ij^{s}

Item, for ane yrne slot and tua stappils of the yle dur, ij^{s}

Item, to ane maisson to mak ane slott hoill, ... vj^{d}

Item, gevin to Thomas Kennedy, wrycht, efter the ending of this wark for futting and mending of certane furmes thatt was brokin in the kirk, and mending of the saitis of the mariage place quhilk wer brokin, iiij^{s}

Item, for nailles to him, ... vj^{d}

Soume of the haill expenssis maid in biggin and reparing of the said Yle (*blank*).

The expenssis maid on the theking of ellevin of the Cordonaris Chopis of new, and the poynting and mending of the faltes of the rest that misterit, begynand the xxvij day of September 1566.

Item, in primis, gevin for ane houss male to lay and keip the lyme, sand

JOHN PRESTOUN, Dean of Guild. 1565-66.

and tymmer, and sclaits to the said wark during the tyme thairof quhilk wes (*blank*) oulkis, ... xij^{s}

Item, for xvj laidis of lyme, pryce of the laid ij^{s}, ... xxxij^{s}

Item, for iij dosane and foure laidis of sand, pryce of the laid vj^{d}, soume, xx^{s}

Item, for ane dosane of greit double sparris, to be lacht to the choppis, pryce thairof, ... xxiiij^{s}

Item, for bringing of the said sparris fra Leyth, . . iij^{s} viij^{d}

Item, for ane greit aik rufe spar to be garrons to the choppis, . vij^{s}

Item, for bering of itt fra Leyth, ... viij^{d}

Item, for tua thousand sclaitis fra Ker of Dundie, pryce of the hundreth xij^{s}; soume, ... xij^{li}

Item, for leding of ilk thousand fra Leyth, xx^{s}, ... xl^{s}

Item, to ane man to beir the sclaitis into the hous and setting of thame, iiij^{s}

Item, for ane uther thousand sclaitis, . vj^{li}

Item, for leding of thame fra Leyth, . . xx^{s}

Item, for bering and setting of thame in the hous, . ij^{s}

[267] Item, for xvj garroun nailles, pryce of the pece j^{d} obolus, . . ij^{s}

Item, for tua hundreth planchour nailles to the begynnyng burdis of the chopis; pryce of the hundreth iij^{s}, ... vj^{s}

Item, to ane wrycht, for ane dayis laubour, thatt putt in the corbellis and menditt sum tymmer werk, ... iiij^{s}

Item, to the sawaris for xlviij draucht of the double sparris to be lacht to the choppis, pryce of the draucht iiij^{d}; soume, ... xvj^{s}

Item, for tua draucht of the aikin rufe spar, pryce of the draucht ix^{d}; soume, xviij^{d}

Item, for bering of sax dosane of walter to the lyme and sand, pryce of the dosane viij^{d}; soume, ... iiij^{s}

Item, for xxvj^{c} lacht nailles, pryce of the hunder xx^{d}; soume, . . xliij^{s} iiij^{d}

Item, to the sclaiter for the theking of thre ruid and nyne elnes of new work, pryce of the rude liij^{s} iiij^{d}; soume, . . . viij^{li} xiij^{s} iiij^{d}

Item, for poynting of the rest of the choppis and was faltous, and mending thairof, ... xx^{s}

Item, for iij pounschonis to be pynnis to the said werk, viz. ilk rude ane pounschoun, ... xxiiij^{s}

Soume of this precedent work (*blank*).

JOHN PRESTOUN, Dean of Guild. 1565-66.

Item, the comptar is to be dischairgit with his fie in the yeir of his office, ... vj[li] xiij[s] 4[d]

Item, in lyke maner the comptar is to be dischairgit with the fie of ane servand oversear of the werkis in the yeir of the comptaris office, quhilk is saix merks, ... iiij[li]

Item, the comptar is to be dischairgit with fourtie[s] gevin be him to George Gourlay, officiar, in gathering of the males and dewties of the said office, ... xl[s]

Item, the comptar is to be dischairgit with the male of Robert Murray golksmythis chop in the yeir of the comptaris office, quhilk chop stude waist and na man wald tak the said chop oure his heid, . . xxx

Item, the comptar is to be dischairgit with the male of Eduard Ryndis chop quhilk in lyke maner standis waist, and the said Eduard beand ane pure boy unable be him selfe to occupye it he can haife male of na utheris thairfoir to pay sa mekle as is the yeirlie dewtie thairof, . . xxx[s]

Item, the comptar is to be dischairgit with the male of Eduard Bassendeinis chop quhilk standis waist lyke as itt standis yit as is notourly knawin, ... xxx[s]

Soume of the hale dischairge, . . ij[c] lvij[li] ix[s]

Sua restis the comptar awand the soume of, xv[li] xvij[s] vj[d] obolus

[268] The xxiiij day of Januar the yeir of God J[m] v[c] lxvij yeiris the compte of Maister Jhonn Prestoun, Dene of Gyld, the first yeir of his office begynnand the feird of October the yeir of God J[m] v[c] lxv yeris to October J[m] v[c] lxvj yeris; and efter examinatioun and consideratioun bayth of chairge and dischairge be the auditouris underwrittin, the comptar is found restand awand to the gude toun the soume of fyftene punds sevintene [s] vj[d].

[The Account is not signed.]

[THE

JOHN PRESTOUN, Dean of Guild. 1566-67.

[270]

THE COMPTE of Maister JHONN PRESTON, Dene of Gylde of Edinburgh, of the secound yeir of his office, begynand the feird day of October in the yeir of God J^m v^c thre scoir sax yeris, and indurand quhill October the yeir of God J^m v^c thre scoir sevin yeris.

THE COMPTARIS CHAIRGE.

Item, in the first, the comptar is to be chairgit and chairgis him with the money and fute of the rest of his compte quhilk he restis awand to the toun at the making on his compte of the said office in the yeir precedand quhilk wes first yeir of the comptaris office, extending to the soume of, ... xv^{li} $xvij^s$ ij^d obolus

Item, the comptar chairgis him with the haill money of the burgessis and gild brether maid in the yeir of the comptaris office foirsaid as the lokkit buke proportis, to the quhilk the comptar referris him, and in the first with the dewtie of Robert Bowdane quha was maid burges the xj day of October 1566, in presence of the provest, baillies and counsale and payit, ... v^{li}

Item, the comptar chairgis him with the dewtie of Patrik Campbell, tailyour, quha was made burges the xj day of October 1566 and the dewtie thairof gevin to him gratis be Sir Symon Prestoun of Craigmillar, knyght and provest, be ressoun of his office. — Non onerand.

Item, the dewtie of James Clark, tailyour, quha wes made burges the xxiij day of October 1566 and the dewtie thairof gevin to Maister Robert Glen, baille, be ressoun of the dewtie of his office. — Non onerand.

Item, with the dewtie of Jhonn Pillane, cordynar, quha wes maid burges the sevint day of November 1566 and the dewtie thairof gevin to Hectour Trolhop, Edinburgh maissar, be ressoun of the dewtie of his office. — Non onerand.

Item, with the dewtie of Clement Cor, merchant, quha was made burges and gild brother be vertu of the rycht of his father umquhill Andrew Cor, quha wes burges and gild brether, and the said Clement his eldest sone payit, ... xx^s

Item, with the dewtie of Robert Campbell, quha wes made burges the xj day of November 1566 be wertu of his fatheris rycht, Michaell Campbell quha was burges, and payit, ... $xiij^s$ $iiij^d$

JOHN PRESTOUN, Dean of Guild. 1566-67.

[271] Item, with the dewtie of Jhonn Ellot, cordynar, quha was made burges
Non onerand. the xvj day of November 1566 and his dewtie gevin to William Stewart, clark depute to Alexander Guthre, commoun clark, be resson of his office.

Item, with the dewtie of Jhonn Wrycht, cramer, quha was maid burges the xxiij of November 1566, and payit, ... v^{li}

Item, with the dewtie of Robert Patersoun, merchant, quha was maid burges the xxv of November 1566, be vertu of the rycht of Elizabeth Aikman in the Bow, quha is burges, and payit, . . . xiij^s iiij^d

Item, with the dewtie of Jhonn Eistoun, quha wes maid Burges the thred
Non onerand. day of December 1566, and the dewtie thairof gevin to Edward Littill, baille, be ressoun of the dewtie of his office.

Item, with the dewtie of Mathow Jamesoun quha was maid burges and gild brother be the privelege of Elizabeth Nicoll his spous, dochter to James Nicoll, eldar, quha is burges and gild brother, and payit, xxxiij^s iiij^d

Item, with the dewtie of Jhonn Dougell, marchant, quha wes maid burges and gild brother be the privelege of umquhill Jhoun Dougell his fader, quha was burges and gild brother, and payit, . . . xx^s

Item, with the dewtie of Patrik Hardye, cordynar, quha wes maid burges
Non onerand. the xiiij day of Januar 1566, and the dewtie thairof gevin to Maister David Chalmer, clark for the tyme.

Item, with the dewtie of Jhoun Hendersoun, tailyour, quha wes made burges the v day of Februar 1566, be ressoun of Margaret Hunter, his spous, dochter to Jhoun Huntar, quha is burges, and payit for his dewtie, xiij^s iiij^d

Item, with dewtie of Jhonn Barinsfather, tailyour, quha wes made burges the day foirsaid be the privelege of Sibilla Ballendene, his spous, dochter to Henry Ballendene quha is burges, and payit, . . xiij^s iiij^d

Item, with the dewtie of Thomas Cock, merchant, quha wes maid burges be rycht of the privelege of Elizabeth Nisbet, his spous, dochter to umquhill Adam Nisbet, the vj day of Februar 1566, and payit, . xiij^s iiij^d

Item, with the dewtie of Patrik Libertoun, tailyour, quha was made burges the xxvj of Februar 1566, be ressoun of the privelege of his father umquhyle William Libertoun, quha was burgess of this burgh, and payit for his friedome, ... xiij^s iiij^d

JOHN PRESTOUN, Dean of Guild. 1566-67.

Item, with the dewtie of James Ross, burges and merchant, quha was maid gyld brother the xj day of Aprylo 1567, and payit for his dewtie of gildry, ... x li

Item, with the dewtie of Thomas Aikinheid, burges and skynner, quha wes made gild brother the day foirsaid and payit for his gyldrie, . . x li

Item, with the dewtie of Walter Balcasky, cowper, sone to umquhel James Balcasky, quha was maid burges be the privelege of his said father the xiiij day of Aprile 1566, ... xiij iiij d

Item, with the dewtie of Robert Ker, younger, eldest sone to umquhill [272] Robert Ker quha wes burges and gild brother of this burgh, and be ressoun of his faderis privelege wes maid burges and gild brother the last day of Aprylo 1567, and payit for his dewtie, . . . xx s

Item, with the dewtie of Thomas Alexander, burges, quha wes made gild brother the day foirsaid, and for his gyldrie, ... x li

Item, with the dewtie of Lyonn Smailly, burges, quha wes made gild Non onerand. brother the second day of May 1567, and the dewtie thairof assignit to the comptar be ressoun of the dewtie of his office.

Item, with the dewtie of Barthilmo Meyne, quha wes maid burges the day foirsaid be the privelege of his spous Elizabeth Weir, douchter to Jhonn Weir, quha is burges, and payit, ... xiij s iiij d

Item, with the dewtie of Jhonn Matho, bonet makar, quha wes maid Non onerand. burges the fyfte day of May 1567, and the dewtie thairof assignit to the comptar as his burgeschip be ressoun of his office.

Item, with the dewtie of Jhonn Lausoun, barbour, quha wes maid burges the vij day of Maij 1566 [1567], and payit for his fredome, . v li

Item, with the dewtie of Jhonn Hepburn, ane of the portaris of the Non onerand. Castell, quha wes maid burges and gild brother the xxiij day of May 1566 [1567], and the dewtie thairof gevin to him gratis be the provest, bailles and counsale.

Item, with the dewtie of Jhonn Carrik, cordaner, quha wes made burges Non onerand. the xxix day of May 1566 [1567], and the dewtie thairof gevin to Alexander Clark, baille be ressoun of the dewtie of his office.

Item, with the dewtie of Mongo Loche, marchant, eldest sone to umquhill Mongo Loche, quha was made burges and gild brother the penult day of Maij 1566 [1567], be the privelege of Jonet Towris, dochter to David Towris, burges and gyld brother of this burgh, and payit, xxxiij^s iiij^d

Item, with the dewtie of William Murray, servautour to Maister James Balfour, quha wes maid burges the fyfte day of Junij 1566 [1567], and the dewtie thairof gevin to him gratis be the provest, bailles and counsell at the requeist of the said Maister James, his maister. Non onerand.

Item, with the dewtie of James Nicoll, younger, merchant, quha wes maid burges and gyld brother be the privelege of his fader, James Nicoll, quha is burges and gyld, and wes maid the day foirsaid and payit for his fredome, ... xxxiij^s iiij^d

Item, the comptar chairgis him with the dewtie of James Norowell, eldest sone to Jhonn Norowell, burges and gyld, and was maid burges and gyld brother the day foirsaid be the privelege of his said father, and payit for his fredome, ... xxxiij^s iiij^d

Item, the comptar is to be chairgit with the dewtie of Eduard Yair, quha was maid burges the xx day of Junij 1566 [1567], and the dewtie thairof gevin gratis be the provest, bailles and counsell at the requeist of Jonet Adamsoun, spous to Maister James Makgill, Clark of Oure Soveranis Registre. Non onerand. [273]

Item, with the dewtie of Henry Eistoun, candilmaker, quha was maid burges the feird day of Julij 1566 [1567], and payit, . . v^li

And with the dewtie of William Nisbet, second sone to umquhyle Adam Nisbet, quha was maid burges the ix day of July 1566 [1567], and payit for his fredome xx^s, and the rest gevin to him gratis be the provest, bailles and counsell for causis moving thame, . . . xx^s

Item, with the dewtie of William Richartsoun, skynnar, quha was maid burges the xxij day of July 1566 [1567], and payit for his dewtie, . v^li

Item, with the dewtie of Androw Lammye, alias Capitane Lamy, quha was made burges the day foirsaid, and the dewtie thairof gevin to him gratis be the provest, bailles and counsell. Non onerand.

Item, the comptar is to be chairgit with the dewtie of Sir James Balfour of Pettindreych, knyght, Clark of Oure Soveranes Registre and Capitane of the Castell of Edinburgh, quha was maid burges and gild brother, and the dewtie thairof gevin to him gratis be the provest, baillies and counsell.

JOHN PRESTOUN, Dean of Guild. 1566-67.

Non onerand. Item, with the dewtie of Henry Blythe, cyrurghane, quha was maid burges the first day of August 1567, and the dewtie thairof gevin to Alexander Guthre, commoun clark, be ressoun of the dewtie of his office.

Non onerand. Item, with the dewtie of Jhonn Gavelok, brouster, quha was maid burges the xxij day of August, and the dewtie thairof gevin to the provest be ressoun of the dewtie of his office.

Non onerand. Item, with the dewtie of James Sandelandis, merchant, quha was maid burges the xv day of September 1567, and the dewtie thairof gevin to Alexander Guthreis servand be ressoun of the dewtie of his office.

Non onerand. Item, with the dewtie of Jhonn Broun, quha was maid burges the xvij day of September 1567, and the dewtie thairof gevin to Alexander Uddart, bailye, be ressoun of the dewtie of his office.

Item, with the dewtie of Mathow Aikman, ypothicar, quha was maid burges and gyld brother be the privelege of umquhill William Aikman, his father, quha was burges and gyld bruther of this burgh, and the said Mathow wes maid the xvij day of September 1567, and payit, xxxiij^{s} iiij^{d}

Non onerand. Item, with the dewtie of Eduard Littill, eldest sone to umquhile Clement Little, quha was maid burges and gyld brother the xix day of September be ressoun of his fatheris privelege, of his father, and the dewtie thairof gevin to him gratis, be the provest, baillies and counsell, in consideratioun of his paynis and lauboris tane be him in the gude tounis affaires.

[274] Item, with the dewtie of William Littill, alsua sone to the said umquhill Clement, quha was maid burges and gild brother the xxvj day of September 1567, be the ressoun of the privelege of his said father, and payit for his dewtie, ... xxxiij^{s} iiij^{d}

Item, the comptar chairgis him with the frauchtin and entres of all the Schippis frauchtit and enterit in the yeir of the comptaris office to the noumer of four scoir sax schipis, and for ilk schip xiiij^{s} as is contenit in the entres buke of the toun, to the quhilk the comptar referris him; soume, ... lx^{li} iiij^{s}

Item, the comptar chairgis him with the males of the Cordonaris Choppis at the fute of the nether Kirk yaird in the yeir of the comptaris office, beand in noumer tuentie chopis as efter followis; in the first, in the yeir, Thomas Merellyis chop, ... xxvj^{s} viij^{d}

JOHN PRESTOUN, Dean of Guild. 1566-67.

Item, with the male of William Herperfeildis chop in the yeir,	xxvj^s viij^d
Item, with the male of Jhonn Broderstanis chop in the yeir,	xxvj^s viij^d
Item, with Jhonn Bynningis chop male, . .	xx^s
Item, with Robert Gibsonis chop male, .	xx^s
Item, with Jhonn Forrest tua chopis male,	xl^s
Item, with William Forsythis chop male, .	xx^s
Item, with Androw Wilsonis chop male, .	xx^s
Item, with Lourence Cor chopis male,	xx^s
Item, with Robert Flemyngis chop,	xx^s
Item, with Jhonn Chepmanis chop male, .	xx^s
Item, with Margaret Rutherfuirdis chop, .	xx^s
Item, with Jhonn Reidis chop male,	xx^s
Item, with Jhonn Neilsonis chop male,	xx^s
Item, with George Cowan chopis male,	xx^s
Item, with Jhonn Smythis tua chopis,	xl^s
Item, with Jhonn Cunnynghamis chop, . . .	xx^s
The hale soume of thir tuenty choppis male in the yeir is, . .	xxj^{li}
Item, the comptar chairgis him with the males of the Choppis and standis about the kirk in the yeir of the comptaris office ; and, in the first, with the yeiris male of Alexander Gilbertis chop, ...	xxx^s
Item, with the yeiris male of Robert Murrayis chop, quhilk is xxx^s, bott it stude waist in the yeir of the comptaris office, lyke as it standis yit waist and no man will tak it oure his heid, ...	xxx^s
Item, with the yeiris male of the chop pertenyng to Cristell Galbrayth, goldsmyth, ...	xxx^s
Item, with the yeiris male of Androw Heleis stand in the kirk dur, .	xl^s
Item, with the yeiris male of Eduard Ryndis chop, quhilk in lyke maner standis waist, bot suld pay, ...	xxx^s
Item, with the yeiris male of Eduard Bassenden, quhilk suld pay xxx^s, bot it standis waist as is notourlie knawin, . .	xxx^s
Item, with the yeir chopis male of Adam Alane, goldsmyth,	xxx^s
Item, with the yeiris male of Jhonn Mosmanis chop, .	xxx^s
[275] Item, with the yeiris male of Jhonn Gilbert goldsmythis buithe, . .	liij^s iiij^d
Item, with the chop male of David Denneistonis chop, . .	liij^s iiij^d

JOHN PRESTOUN, Dean of Guild, 1566-67.

Soume, hale choppis and standis malis in the said yeir is (*blank*).

Summa of the haill chairge, ane hundreth foure scoir nyne pundis iiij^{s} vj^{d} obolus.

THE COMPTARIS DISCHAIRGE.

Item, in the first, the comptar dischairgis him with the money gevin to the tuelfe ordinar officiaris with the javelour, Androw Lyndsay, gevin to thame for thair burgeschippis in the yeir of the comptaris office, viz., everilk officiar with the javelour iij^{li}; soume, ... xxxix^{li}

Item, the comptar is to be dischairgit with xx^{s} gevin to everilk ane of the foirsaidis ordinar officiaris with the javelour, quhilk is gevin to thame be the gude toun to absteine fra the seking of sylver through the honest mennis houssis in the tyme callit Yule, ... xiij^{li}

Item, the comptar is to be dischairgit with the feis of Patrik Gouvane, belman, Jhonn Symsoun, ringar of the bellis, and Robert Drummond, gild servandis, to everilk ane of the thrie in the yeir viij^{li}, . . xxiiij^{li}

Item, the comptar dischairgis him with the bying of ane roll of walx, to Jhonn Cairnis, redar, the xxv day of October 1566, for reding of the common prayeris in wynter, ... iiij^{s}

Item, the feird day of October 1566, gevin for ane pece of greit trie to be ane bar to the buriall yet, and ane cutting of ane auld aikin burde to put without the said yet, ... iiij^{s} vj^{d}

Item, for xx double garroun nales to William Smyth to set on the said greit bar on the said yet, and to mend it, pryce of the pece iij^{d}; soume, v^{s}

Item, to the said William Smyth for xviij singill garroun nales, . xviij^{d}

Item, to him for ane yrne plait, ... vj^{d}

Item, to Thomas Kennedye, wrycht, for mending of the said yet and on-putting of the barris, ... iij^{s}

Item, the viij day of October 1566, for ane lade of lyme to mend the greit hole in the buriall dyke quhair the folk, young and auld, clam in and furth, ... ij^{s} ij^{d}

Item, for tua laidis of sand to it, ... xij^{d}

Item, to ane maissoun to big up the said hole, and for walter, and his warkman to help him, . . . iij^{s}

JOHN PRESTOUN, Dean of Guild, 1566-67.

[276] Item, the xx day of October 1566, for tua greit thak stanis to mend the chairteris hous with, ... iiij s.
Item, of cairt hyer and bringing of thame furth of Railestoun quarrell, . v s.
Item, for foure laidis of lyme, pryce of the laid ij s. ij d.; soume, . viij s. viij d.
Item, for aucht laidis of sand to it, iiij s.
Item, for walter, ... vj d.
Item, for tua warkmen tua dayis and ane half, ilk man in the day ij s.; soume, x s.
Item, gevin to Jhonn Inglis and Gilbert Cleuth for hewing, tournyng tilling and theking and poynting of the said chairter hous, for thair lauboris, ... xxx s.
Item, the vij day of November 1566, for nailles and mending of the mariage saittis, ... xij d.
Item, the xx day of November 1566, for mending of the saittis and nailles to the saittis about Sanct Mongowis pillaris, . xvj d.
Item, the xxiij day of November 1566, gevin to David Duncane, smyth, for tua greit yrne bandis and tua yrne botis to bind the staill quhair the provost and counsell sittis, quhilk stall was all brokin and lowss, . v s. vj d.
Item, for tua ponds of leid to yet the boittis with, xviij d.
Item, to ane maisson to mak the boit hoillis, . viij d.
Item, to the wrycht for his laubouris, ... ij s.
Item, on Friday the first day of December 1566, efter the greit wynde blew and raife the kirk in syndrie places, gevin for iij c. sklaittis in the leicht, ilk c. xj s.; soume, ... xxxiij s.
Item, for upbringing of thame fra Leyth, ilk hundreth ij s., vj s.
Item, for four laidis of lyme, . viij s. viij d.
Item, for aucht laidis of sand, iiij s.
Item, for watter, ... vj d.
Item, to William Robesoun, sclater, for his lauboris for new theiking and poynting, ... xl s.
Item, the xiiij day of December 1566, for ane uther roll of wax to Jhonn Cairnis, ... iiij s.
Item, the samyn day, gevin to George Jhonnstoun for ane greit wax candill to set befoir my lord the Erle of Bedfurde, Ambassadour of Ingland, beand heir sone in the mornyng at the sermond, iij s.

JOHN PRESTOUN, Dean of Guild. 1566-67.

Item, the xx day of December 1566, gevin to Nicoll Andersoun, maissoun, to hing the yrne elwand in the nether Tolobuith, . xvj^{d}

Item, for ane pund and ane half of leid to hing it with, . . . xiiij^{d}

Item, the xxj day of December 1566, for ane yrne bot with ane yrne cleik and ane stappell to the north west kirk dur, . iij^{s} vj^{d}

Item, for leid to yet the bot with, . . . xij^{d}

[277] Item, to ane maisson for making of the hoill and yetting of it, xvj^{d}

Item, for mending of the lok and key to the samyn kirk dur, . . ij^{s}

Item, the thred day of Januar 1566, for ane new greit lang jammay band to the eist dur of the stall quhair the provest and counsell sittis at the sermonds in the kirk, to David Duncane, smyth, ij^{s} viij^{d}

Item, to ane wrycht to put it on, ... vj^{d}

Item, the sevint day of Januar 1566, for thre lang yrne linkis to the kirk, iij^{s}

Item, the xxiiij day of Januar 1566, for ane ledder to the stepill, . vj^{s}

Item, for candill all the Sonedays in the mornyngs betuix Hallowmess and Candilmes, to the mornyng prayeris, ... xj^{s}

Item, for ule olyve all the haill yeir to the kirk, and delyuerit to Patrik Govane, ... xij^{s}

Item, the first day of Februar 1566, gevin to David Bynnyng, paynter, to paynt upoun the pillar of repentence thir wourdis, This is the place appoyntit for publick repentence, ... v^{s}

Item, that samyn day, to William Smyth for irne and making of xxxviij glaspis to the thre beris quhilk was all brokin, pryce of ilk glasp iiij^{d}, . xij^{s} viij^{d}

Item, for ane hundreth and ane quarter hundreth planchour naillis to him for the mending of the said beris, pryce of the hundreth ij^{s} viij^{d}, . iij^{s} iiij^{d}

Item, for tymmer to be gavillis and barris to thame, . . iiij^{s}

Item, to ane wrycht for mending of the thre beris, . . . viij^{s}

Item, the xxv day of Merche 1567, gevin to Michell, the calsay maker, for the making of tua rudis and thre quarteris of new calsay, begynnand at the Stinkand Style and passand about the Tolbuyth dur and Bestis Wynde heid, pryce of the rude xxxvj^{s}; soume, . . . iiij^{li} xix^{s}

Item, for bering away of the red and stanis, ... iij^{s} iiij^{d}

Item, for bering of the formes furth of the Kirk to the uver Tolbuyth, in agane, at the tua Generall Assembleis of the kirk in wynter and symmer, xvj^{d}

JOHN PRESTOUN, Dean of Guild. 1566-67.

Item, the xxvj day of Merche 1567, for ane trie to be ane mid standart to the greit yet in the kirk yaird, pryce, ... xj^s

Item, gevin to David Duncane for ane greit lok with ane key and ane kepar to the said yet, ... xij^s

Item, for garroun nailes and planchour nailes to the said yet, . . viij^d

Item, to Thomas Kennedy for the mending of the said yet and making and inputting of the standard, ... vj^s

Item, for ane greit band to it, becaus the auld band was stowin away, . v^s

[278] Item, for greit nailles to it, ... vj^d

Item, the xviij day of Aprile 1567, gevin to Sir Thomas Wilkeye for doun taking of the auld cok, ... x^s

Item, the thred day of Maij 1567, gevin to David Duncane, smyth, for ane new lok and ane key to the pulpeit dur, ... v^s

Item, for ane greit hingand lok with twa greit stapellis to the yet of the buriall, pryce of the lok xx^s, and the stappillis iiij^s; soume, . . xxiiij^s

Item, the vj day of Maij 1567, to Jhonn Moresoun, gairdnar to Oure Soverane, for his laubour and stufe furneist in the yaird of the Counsalhous, be ane precept direct to the comptar thairof, . . xl

Item, the xxvij day of Junij 1567, gevin for writting of lvij lettres missives and prenting lx Commissionis at the requeist of the Generall Assemblie of the Kirk, and be ane precept directtet to the comptar thairfoir, ... iij^{li}

Item, the last day of Junij 1567, for ane eln of small braid lynnyng clayth to be for the ministeris handis at the baptesme, . . iiij^s iiij^d

Item, the vj day of July 1567, gevin to Robert Gray for foure faddom of ane cord to the greit bell, pryce of the faddom viij^d; soume, . ij^s viij^d

The expenses made upoun the service of the Communiouns :—

The First Communioun.

Item, the last day of November, quhilk was Setterday, and the evin of the first Communioun, for tua dosane and four torches to serve the four nychtis and in the mornyngis on the Sonedayis, pryce of the dosane xxx^s, ... iij^{li} x^s

Item, to Jhonn Clavie, candilmaker, for ane stane and fyve pundis of candill, pryce of the stane xviij^s viij^d; soume, . . xxiiij^s vj^d

JOHN PRESTOUN, Dean of Guild. 1566-67.

Item, to the foure werkmen to beir the tymmer dailles and setting of the fournes and buirdis bayth the Setterdayis at evin, and bering away of thame agane on the Sonedayis, ... viij^s

Item, for ane hundreth planchour nailles for the travisses, iij^s

Item, for ane quart of aill to thame ilk Setterday at evin, . . xvj^d

Item, to Thomas Kennedy, wrycht, for the making and doun taking of the travisses four tymes, ... x^s

Item, coft fra Issobell Fergesoun, tavernour, for wyne to the Communioun, the first Sonday viij gallonis thre quartis, and the second Sonday nyne gallonnis ane quart, makand, the ij Sondayis, xviij gallonnis, pryce of the pynte xvj^d; soume, ... ix^li xij^s

Item, gevin to William Fiddes, bakister, for foure dosane of Communioun breid the tua Sonedayis, pryce of the dosane xiiij^s, . lvj^s

[279] Soume of the first Communioun is xviij^li iiij^s x^d

The Second Communioun.

Item, the viij day of Apryle 1567, for bering of the fournes fra the Kirk to the Tolbuyth to the Assembly of the Kirk, and inbering of thame to the Kirk, ... viij^d

Item, for ane hundreth planchour nailles, ... iij^s

Item, to the werkmen for bering of the tymmer and bering of the fournes buirdis the tua Sonedayis and Setterdayis, ... viij^s

Item, to Thomas Kennedy, wrycht, for the making and doun taking of the travesses four tymes, . . . x^s

Item, to Jhonn Hamyltoun for ane pounchoun of wyne, . viij^li x^s

Item, for cairt hyre fra Leyth, . . ij^s

Item, for inlaying of it in my cellar, ... iiij^s

Item, for four dosane and ane breid, to William Fiddes, for bayth the Sonedayis, pryce of the dosane xiiij^s; soume, . . . lvij^s ij^d

Item, for ane quart of aile, Setterday at evin, to the werkmen, . xvj^d

Soume of the expenssis of the second Communioun (*blank*).

The Thred Communioun.

Item, the xiij day of July 1567, for ane punchoun of wyne fra James Prestoun, ... viij^li x^s

Summe of the first Comptment
is [illegible]

The Second Comptment

Item ye xxvij day of aprile 1567 for beringe of ye
Comunes fra ye kirk to ye tolbuith to ye assemblie of
ye kirk [illegible] ——— viij d

Item for ane [illegible] ——— iij s

Item to ye werkmen for beringe of ye tymmer [illegible]
[illegible] ——— viij s

Item to Thomas [illegible] for ye [illegible]
[illegible] ——— v s

Item to [illegible] for ane [illegible] ——— viij li x s

Item [illegible] ——— iij s

Item for ye laying of it in ye cellar ——— iiij s

Item for [illegible] to Wm [illegible] for [illegible]
ye [illegible] ——— xl s vj d

Item for [illegible] to
ye werkmen ——— xl s

Summe of ye expensis of ye
second Comptment.

The Third Comptment

Item ye xxv day of July 1567 for ane [illegible]
[illegible] ——— viij li x s

Item for beringe [illegible] ——— iij s

Item [illegible] to Wm [illegible] to ye
[illegible] ——— xl s

Item to ye werkmen for [illegible] of ye tymmer to ye
[illegible] ——— v s

Item to ye [illegible] for making
[illegible] ——— iij s

Item for ane [illegible] to ye
[illegible] ——— iiij s

Item for [illegible] of ye [illegible]
[illegible] ——— xl s

Summe of this third Comptment
is [illegible]

The hale soume [illegible]
[illegible]

The expensis maid upon ye kirk [illegible]
steple

Item ye first day of may 1567 [illegible]
in ye [illegible]
[illegible] of ye [illegible]
[illegible] of ye
[illegible] ——— iij li [illegible]

JOHN PRESTOUN, Dean of Guild. 1566-67.

Item, for bering of it fra Leyth, ... ij^{s}
Item, for four dosane of breid, to William Fiddes, to the Communioun, pryce of the dosane xiiij^{s}; soume, ... lvj^{s}
Item, to the werkmen for bering of the tymmer of the travesses and fourmes and buirdis setting, ... vj^{s}
Item, to the wrycht, Thomas Kennedye, for making of the travesses, x^{s}
Item, for ane hundreth planchour nailles to the travesses, iij^{s}
Item, for wesching of the Communioun naiprie in the yeir, vj^{s}

Soume of this thred Communioun is, xij^{li} xiij^{s}.

The hale soume of all the thre Communionis is xliij^{li} x^{s} iiij^{d}.

The expenses maid upoun the Cok of the Stepill :—

Item, the fyft day of May 1567, coft fra Robert Hog in the Potterraw, and delyuerit to Alexander Hunyman, maker of the said cok, xv punds and 3 quarteris of ane pound of coppar to be the bodye of the cok, pryce of the pund v^{s}; soume, ... iij^{li} xviij^{s} ix^{d}
[280] Item, delyverit to the said Alexander Hunyman to by soudry with, . xx^{s}
Item, mair, the xiiij day of May 1566 [1567], coft fra the foirsaid Robert Hog and delyverit to Alexander Hunyman to be the tale of the cok, vij ponds sax unces of coppar, pryce of the lib v^{s}: soume, . . xxxvj^{s} x^{d}
Item, to him for ane unce of boras to the said Alexander Hunyman, xiiij^{s}
Item, for tua laidis of peitis to him, . . ij^{s} viij^{d}
Item, for tua laidis of charcoillis to the said Alexander, . . xvj^{s}
Item, the xiiij day of Junij 1567, gevin be me at the command of the provest, baillies and counsell, be thair precept directtit to me thairfoir, for the making of the said cok and utheris caussis contenit in the said precept, ... x^{li}
Item, to Sir Thomas Wilkye for his paynis and travell, as is contenit in the said precept, ... xxvj^{s} viij^{d}
Item, to Alexander Hunymanis chylder in drynk sylver, . . ij^{s}

The hale soume of the expenssis of the said cok is xix^{li} xvj^{s} xj^{d}.

Item, mair, the comptar is to be dischairgit with tua markis gevin be him to Robert Drummond for furneissing of candill in wynter to the Sessioun of the Kirk and Generall Assemblie, as the precept directtet thairupoun to the comptar beris; soume, . . . xxvj^{s} viij^{d}

Item, to the pure auld man callit for the souping and halding clene of the passage fra the entres of the Stinkand Style to the entres of the nether Counselhous, ouklie vj^{d}; soume in the half yeir, . . xxvj^{s}

Item, the comptar dischairgis him with his fie in the yeir of his office, vj^{li} xiij^{s} iiij^{d}

Item, the comptar is to be dischairgit with ane fie of ane servand ouersear in the said office in the yeir of the comptaris office, . . iiij^{li}

Item, the comptar is to be dischairgit with xl^{s} gevin be him to George Gourlay, officiar, for the ingathering of the mailles and dewties of the said office in the comptaris yeir thairof, ... xl^{s}

Item, the compter is to be dischairgit with the maill of Robert Murray goldsmythis chop in the yeir of the comptaris office, quhilk chop stude waist in the said yeir, lyke as yit stands waist, and na uther man will take it ouer his heid, ... xxx

Item, the comptar dischairgis him with the yeris male of Eduard Ryndis chop, quhilk in lyke maner standis waist, the said Eduard beand ane young boy unable to occupye it him selfe he can get fra na uther sa mekle he suld pay yeirlie male to the toun for the samyn, . . (*blank*)

Item, the comptar is to be dischairgit with the male of Eduard Bassendenis chop besyde the clarkis chalmer, quhilk in lyke maner standis waist as is notourlie knawin, ... xxx^{s}

[281] Summa of the comptaris dischairge is ane hundreth four scoir sevin pund ten^{s} vij^{d}: sic restat per computantem, xxxiij^{s} xj^{d} obolus

The xxiiij day of Januar the yeir of God J^{m} v^{c} lxvij yeris, the compte of Maister Jhonn Prestoun, Dene of Gild, the second year of his office, begynnand the feird day of October J^{m} v^{c} lxvj, induring quhill October J^{m} v^{c} lxvij, be the auditouris underwrettin, hard, sene, and understand, it is found be thame the comptar restis awin to the gude toun, de claro, the soume of xxx thre^{s} xj^{d} obolus.

[The Account is not signed.]

INDEX.

C

H

N

T

U

V

W

END OF VOL. II. OF THE BURGH ACCOUNTS.

Colston & Coy. Limited, Printers, Edinburgh.

www.ingramcontent.com/pod-product-compliance
Lightning Source LLC
Chambersburg PA
CBHW032109230426
43672CB00009B/1684
* 9 7 8 3 7 4 4 7 1 7 0 1 4 *